Principles of Land Administration at Work

Lawrence Wai Chung Lai
Jason Wai Yin Kwong
Daniel Chi Wing Ho
Editors

Principles of Land Administration at Work

The Hong Kong Practice

palgrave
macmillan

Editors
Lawrence Wai Chung Lai
Department of Real Estate and Construction
The University of Hong Kong
Hong Kong, China

Jason Wai Yin Kwong
Department of Real Estate and Construction
The University of Hong Kong
Hong Kong, China

Daniel Chi Wing Ho
Department of Real Estate and Construction
The University of Hong Kong
Hong Kong, China

ISBN 978-981-95-2971-1 ISBN 978-981-95-2972-8 (eBook)
https://doi.org/10.1007/978-981-95-2972-8

This Palgrave Macmillan imprint is published by the registered company Springer Nature Singapore Pte Ltd.
The registered company address is: 152 Beach Road, #21-01/04 Gateway East, Singapore 189721, Singapore

To all surveyors

Foreword

This edited volume provides an in-depth study of the history of the activities that make up land administration—primarily surveying and land-use planning—in the history of colonial and post-colonial Hong Kong. However, this does not mean that it is only of interest to those specifically concerned with Hong Kong's urban development. *Principles of Land Administration at Work: The Hong Kong Practice* includes contributions by some of the city's leading experts in the field. It elucidates universal principles that the authors apply to a fascinating case study.

Hong Kong is a particularly interesting case because it illustrates the way land administration practices based on a well-established legal framework, English common law, negotiated and ultimately altered the land-use patterns of largely informal rural villages that reflected traditional Chinese customs.

In the early British colonial period of the nineteenth and early twentieth centuries, the authors show the overriding importance of surveyors as *de facto* town planners, instituting a practice best described as "planning by contract." Potential private developers of land would bid for leaseholds, which included various regulations and restrictions on the use of land that would also apply to subsequent transactions, including private transactions leading to fragmentation or pooling of original surveyor-delineated lots. This contractual approach provided a framework for market valuation of alternative bundles of land-use regulations, thus conveying valuable feedback to planners and other land administrators.

However, in the post-1945 period, more comprehensive statutory plans became more important, and contracting became more complex and time-consuming. In other words, Hong Kong adopted a planning regime that moved away from value-enhancing cultivation of innovative land uses towards ever-tighter regulatory constraints. Transaction costs increased, and the playing field became ever more tilted in favour of large property developers that could absorb the mounting costs of regulatory compliance. Hong Kong followed a familiar pattern pioneered in the United Kingdom, albeit as a less extreme version of a global tendency.

One of the many strengths of this edited collection is that it provides a rich description of various stages of land administration in the specific instance of Hong Kong, while never losing track of more universal economic principles that explain the effects of different approaches. Fortunately, the authors adopt economic theories in the tradition of Ronald Coase and other neo-institutional economists, which are better at accounting for the messy frictions of real-world governments and markets than traditional equilibrium models of the urban economy. Such institutional theories elucidate the overall effects of specific laws and regulations as applied to a particular place. The approach adopted in this book is also unlike conventional planning approaches, which tend to gloss over economics in favour of treating planning as an engineering problem.

I consider this volume an essential reading for anyone concerned with urban planning or property development in Hong Kong. Moreover, it offers many valuable insights to researchers and students in surveying, urban planning, institutional economics and Hong Kong history.

Professor of Management at National Sun Yat-sen University, Kaohsiung, Taiwan

May, 2025 David Emanuel Andersson

Preface

Government's administration of its land as private property operates under certain generic principles common to all places. But everywhere, the application of these is contingent upon the place's socio-economic history. This may seem to render education on land administration to be a hopelessly parochial, jurisdiction-specific endeavour.

While this "local practice" characterization may be adequate for those only interested in professional practice in a given place, it is unhealthy for university education, which goes beyond vocational training for specific industries. The United Nations has promoted a universalist understanding of land administration with a host of "principles." However, these principles, such as "gender equality" and "transparency," are general values that require operational principles to implement. It is within this global context that this Hong Kong case study, which illustrates the relevance of several operational principles informed by the works of Mitchell et al. (2019) and Williamson et al. (2010), is offered to university students who aspire to serve society in land administration as policymakers or practitioners, as well as members of the public who want to better understand land administration.

Public administration of government land as leasehold property in Hong Kong is a very complicated and challenging area of knowledge for property users, owners, investors, researchers, and regulators. This book covers fundamental concepts and practices of this area to provide students and the general public with the context and basics to understand other works on Hong Kong, such as those by James Roberts and Roger Nissim. Unlike the book, *Change in Use of Land: A Practical Guide to Development in Hong Kong*, by Lawrence W.C. Lai, Daniel, C.W. Ho, and H.F. Leung, this book does not cover the detailed procedures or law of land administration, which are mainly internal and matters of professional practice. What it covers are basic principles informed by three concepts that help appreciate them.

The first concept is that land as property has always had a locationally unique "lot boundary" recognized *ex post*, if not delineated by the state *ex ante* (before allocation) as a matter of foundational town and country planning. The lot is the basic *unit* of recognition, land ownership, planning, use, and accounting (valuation and taxation), according to common law and other institutional and physical constraints its owner or user must observe.

The second concept is that a "Government Lease" (formerly Crown Lease) is *contractual* with conditions mutually agreed upon *ex ante*, which enter the state and lessee into a binding legal relationship protected by the doctrine of the privity of contract. This is the basis of the idea of "planning (and development) by contract." In land administration, this concerns land contracts as vehicles for the allocation and regulation of property rights and obligations regarding land units (lots). This theoretical point about these contracts, the core of his doctoral thesis, was disseminated by the first editor in the research books and papers he published over the past 30 years first appearing in *Town Planning Review* (1994, 1998) and *Progress in Planning* (1997). The idea is a highly "universal" and "historical" (in the sense of real life) practice in the opening up of the "New World" to common law jurisdictions (say, British US and Australian colonies). That brings to mind various companies that opened up territories for factories and plantations under royal charters (a kind of contract). In these places, land declared to be Crown land was surveyed, laid out as parcels (lots), and sold (or granted) according to specific terms specified by the state. The way of allocation was contractual rather than by command. This can easily be followed by any reader even without a legal history and neo-institutional economics background. Peel Town, Western Australia, and Discovery Bay, Hong Kong, are good examples to demonstrate this form of planning and development. The former failed and the latter succeeded.

The third concept is that the property valuation method is an *institutionalized process* of judgement based on commonly agreed-upon criteria, so as to reduce the transaction costs of resource allocation (exchange through auctioning, tender, negotiation; conflict resolution; and fundraising by, say, IPO) and distribution.

This book is organized into four parts with eighteen chapters based on the contributors' teaching and research experiences for CPDs and university courses and professional practices. Part I deals with the basic principles and concepts of land administration. Chapter 1 presents ten operational land management principles discerned from a reading of the literature. Chapter 2 is a general statement of the genesis and evolution of the "lot." Chapter 3 covers the contractual nature of planning and private property development based on government "lease conditions." Chapter 4 deals with the three main types and sequences used by developers and land users to obtain development approvals.

Chapters 5, 6, 7, 8, 9, 10, 11, 12 and 13 in Part II form the core of the local surveying practice and cover, respectively, Crown/Government Leases, the modification of Government Leases, basic valuation concepts and techniques, government land management of unallocated land, lease enforcement, land resumptions, lot boundary surveys, and aerial photo geo-referencing and interpretation of change in use of land.

Chapters 14 and 15 in Part III cover two recurrent local social issues, the so-called small house (New Territories Exempted House) and conservation of government and private built-heritage.

Part IV is concerned with capturing land values by a parcel of land. Chapter 16 covers the assessment of development potential of land without changing its property boundary. Chapter 17 covers land readjustment, which rearranges the individual property boundaries of a host of lots upon land pooling, as a possible local application. Chapter 18 covers the rating of properties.

The contributors are indebted to architect Wai Ping Cheung and fellow surveyor David King for their comments and advice on, respectively, Chaps. 16 and 18 of this book.

Disclaimer: This book is purely written for teaching, academic inquiry, and professional discussion. It should not be relied on for business, investment decisions, litigation, or statutory review/appeal purposes. There is no claim that the presentation of the lease documents considered exhausts all modes of lease drafting. The authors accept no liability for the statements made in this book. The reader is advised to seek independent legal advice on the statements made in this book if he or she finds some of its points or facts pertinent for investment or legal purposes.

Hong Kong, China
9 December 2025

Lawrence Wai Chung Lai
Jason Wai Yin Kwong
Daniel Chi Wing Ho

References

Coase, Ronald H. 1974. The Lighthouse in Economics. *Journal of Law and Economics* 17: 357–376.

Lai, Lawrence W. C., and Jason W. Y. Kwong. 2015. Hong Kong Land Policy for Bus Depot Allocation: A Valuation Analysis. *Surveying & Built Environment* 23 (1): 24–56.

Lai, Lawrence W. C., and Frank T. Lorne. 2012. Schumpeterian Innovations, the Coase Theorem, and Sustainable Development: A Hong Kong Case study of Bus Innovations. In *The Spatial Market Process*, ed. David Emanuel Andersson, Vol. 16, pp. 141–179. Advances in Austrian Economics. Bingley: Emerald.

Lai, Lawrence W. C., and Frank T. Lorne. 2015. The Fourth Coase Theorem: State Planning Rules and Spontaneity in Action. *Planning Theory* 14 (1): 44–69.

Lai, Lawrence W. C., K. W. Chau, and Polycarp A.C.W. 2012. Scale Economies of the Franchised Buses and Ferries of Hong Kong, 1948 to 1998. Review of Urban and Regional Development Studies 24 (3): 121–140.

Lai, Lawrence W. C., Stephen N. G. Davies, and Polycarp A.C.W. 2011. Government Transport-land Use Planning and Development by Implicit Contract for Franchised Buses and Ferries in Hong Kong: 1933 to 1972. *Planning Practice and Research* 26 (4): 435–464.

Lai, Lawrence W. C., Stephen N. G. Davies, and Frank T. Lorne. 2008. The Political Economy of Coase's Lighthouse in History (Part I): A Review of the Theories and Models of the Provision of a Public Good. *Town Planning Review* 79 (4): 395–425.

Lai, Lawrence W. C., Stephen N. G. Davies, and Frank T. Lorne. 2008. The Political Economy of Coase's Lighthouse in History (Part II): Lighthouse Development along the Coast of China. *Town Planning Review* 79 (5): 555–579.

Lai, Lawrence W. C., K. W. Chau, Jason W. Y. Kwong, Ken S. T. Ching, Polycarp A. C. W. Cheung, and Frank T. Lorne. 2013. Acquisition and Redevelopment of Bus Garages: a Hong Kong Land Policy and Planning Case Study. *Habitat International* 39: 75–84.

Lai, Lawrence W. C., K. T. Liu, Polycarp A. C. W. Cheung, Castor T. C. Wong, and Jason W. Y. Kwong. 2015. Redevelopment of Bus Depots upon Lease Modifications: A Valuation Analysis. *Surveying & Built Environment* 24 (1): 37–40.

Lorne, Frank T., and W. C. Lawrence. 2011. Schumpeterian Innovation for Regulated Natural Monopoly as a Corporate Strategy. *International Journal of Information Systems for Logistics and Management* 7 (1): 1–7.

Acknowledgements

The authors acknowledge the funding support for this note by a Public Policy Research Grant No.HKU7007-PPR-11.

Contents

Notes on Contributors

Polycarp C. W. Cheung Academic qualifications: B.Sc. (Surv) (HKU), M.Phil (HKU). Professional qualifications: M.H.K.I.S., M.R.I.C.S. Publications: has published six referred journal articles.

Ken S. T. Ching Academic qualifications: BEng (Hons) (UNSW); MGIS (HKU); PhD (HKU). Professional qualifications: Authorized Land Surveyor of the HKSAR; RPS(LS); FHKIS; FRICS; MCIArb; MIS; MSSI. Publications: has published over 50 referred journal articles.

Lennon H. T. Choy's Academic qualifications: BSc (HKPolyU); MUrb Des (HKU); PhD (HKU). Professional qualifications: MRICS; FHKIS. Publications: over 50 refereed journal articles and 5 book chapters on real estate and property rights.

Daniel Chi Wing Ho Academic qualifications: B.Sc. (CNAA), MBA (CUHK), Ph.D. (HKU). Professional qualifications: F.R.I.C.S., F.H.K.I.S., Hon.PFM. Present position: Honorary Professor, Department of Real Estate & Construction, University of Hong Kong. Publications: has published 67 refereed academic research papers and 11 books.

Jason Wai Yin Kwong Academic qualifications: B.Sc. (Surv) (HKU), Ph.D. (HKU). Professional qualifications: M.R.I.C.S., F.H.K.I.S., R.P.S. (GP). Present position: Executive Director, Head of Land Consultancy, Valuation and Advisory Services, Colliers Internation (Hong

Kong) Limit; Part-Time Lecturer, Department of Real Estate & Construction, University of Hong Kong. Publications: has published five referred journal articles and one book for town planning (as co-author).

Valerius W. C. Kwong Academic qualifications: B.Sc. (Surv) (HKU), Ph.D. (HKU). Professional qualifications: M.R.I.C.S., M.H.K.I.S., CIREA (APP), CIREA (AGENT). Present position: Senior Associate Director, Cushman & Wakefield. Publications: has published two referred journal articles.

Lawrence Wai Chung Lai Academic qualifications: B.Sc. (HKU), M.T.C.P. (Sydney), M.Soc.Sc. (Econ) (HKU), LL.B (London), Ph.D. (HKU). Professional qualifications: M.A.P.I., F.R.I.C.S., F.H.K.I.S. Present position: Honorary Professor, Ronald Coase Centre for Property Rights Research; Department of Real Estate & Construction, University of Hong Kong. Publications: has published since 1985 a total of 178 refereed academic research papers and 17 books in English on town planning and property rights, heritage conservation, sustainable development and related subjects.

K. T. Liu Academic qualifications: B.Sc. (Econ) External Degree (University of London). Professional qualifications: F.R.I.C.S., F.H.K.I.S. Present position: Managing Director, K.T. Liu Surveyors Ltd.; Part-Time Lecturer, Department of Real Estate & Construction, University of Hong Kong.

Castor T. C. Wong Academic qualifications: B.Sc. (Surv) (HKU), Ph.D. (HKU). Professional qualifications: M.R.I.C.S., M.H.K.I.S., R.P.S. (GP). Present position: Executive Director, Albert So Surveyors Ltd.; Part-Time Lecturer, Department of Real Estate & Construction, University of Hong Kong. Publications: has published three referred journal articles.

List of Figures

List of Tables

PART I

Basic Concepts of Land Administration

CHAPTER 1

Principles of Land Administration

Lawrence Wai Chung Lai

Introduction

Every competent government effectively administers the land within its jurisdiction because all human activities, with few exceptions, occur on or are related to land. More precisely, land excluding inland waters and territorial seas, all human activity in a given territory by definition takes place on land or real property of one kind or another.

Such administration is essential because land-occupying activities entail *location-specific* units of space to be delineated that are assigned to/recognised as for holders, dedicated to specific uses,[1] and protected from undue interference by third parties. This principle of the necessity of unambiguous land administration is an *institutional means*, but is not an end in itself. Rather, it is only the foundation for other intermediary means that help fulfil the second fundamental principle of land administration, which this author holds to be the welfare of the users of land and those affected

[1] Which uses may or may not be the "best" uses to which the land can be dedicated.

L. W. C. Lai (✉)
Department of Real Estate and Construction, The University of Hong Kong, Hong Kong, China
e-mail: wclai@hku.hk

L. W. C. Lai et al. (eds.), *Principles of Land Administration at Work*, https://doi.org/10.1007/978-981-95-2972-8_1

by those uses. Accordingly, all other principles are either an elaboration or intermediation of these two principles.

Unfortunately, such an important government function in developed economies is often seen instrumentally as a mere means to extract fiscal revenue (derived from levies on real estate development, sale, and occupation), or as a matter of public bodies regulating private land uses for broad environmental or other reasons. The users are either ignored, or are treated as just payers into the revenue, or as recipients of economic benefits, rather than as individuals and groups with needs and aspirations. This chapter holds that land administration can be seen as both an *institutional* and *public health and safety* matter with the welfare (basic needs) of landholders and/or land occupiers in mind.

As regards the first principle, land property is a major asset. This point needs no further elaboration. Theoretically, land property is a possession that attracts specific legal treatment and government involvement. For one thing, unlike personal property, the rights and liabilities of land or real property "run with land" to bind all subsequent owners/occupants. Second, real property, properly understood, is unitised land with a unique boundary. The delineation of such boundary in newly developed land has come to rely on planning by the state that is often executed directly via a designated agent. As regards human needs and aspirations, public safety and health are basic for human habitation with dignity, which is a *normative* principle stressed by the United Nations (UN), as the author will demonstrate. Being the foundation and goal of the public administration of land, both principles apply not only to land well secured, but also contested territories.

A quick survey of the literature found little trace of any dedicated general treatment of land administration other than general works supporting the United Nations' Sustainable Development Goals (SDGs) and New Urban Agenda (NUA). A good example is Williamson et al. (2010), who conceived of a land administration system under a "land management paradigm" subjected to a broad "land policy" umbrella. The land parcel (lot or plot described in Chap. 1) is *the fundamental unit of the system* mediated by the land cadastre.

Mitchell et al. (2019) is a good and handy source for learning the UN principles of "responsible land administration," especially those under the SDGs and the NUA, which anchor the obligations of the UN's international human rights framework.

The NUA is guided by the three sustainable development principles: (a) leaving no one behind, (b) ensuring sustainable and inclusive urban economies (including promoting secure land tenures), and (c) ensuring environmental sustainability (UN 2016: 13–14).

NUA Item 13a envisages cities that incorporate the "full realization of the right to adequate housing" (UN 2016: 13). Item 35 promotes the "increased security of tenure for all, recognizing the plurality of tenure types, and to developing fit-for-purpose and age-, gender- and environment-responsive solutions within the continuum of land and property rights, with particular attention to security of land tenure for women as key to their empowerment, including through effective administrative systems" (UN 2016: 21).

Five principles of the Voluntary Guidelines on the Responsible Governance of Tenure (VGGT) of Land, Fisheries, and Forests in the Context of National Food Security (CFS and FAO 2012; see Mitchell et al. (2019)) are presented in Table 1.1. Being very general, they do not pinpoint specific mechanisms of implementation.

The VGGT principles of implementation are summarised in Table 1.2. Again, they are far too general and not operational, being applicable to public administration or even politics writ large. Real respect for human dignity from conception, the rule of law, transparency, and accountability does not exist in many countries—not even in the form of lip service.

The paucity of universal operational analysis of land administration, as a special arm of public administration and based on fundamental principles, may well perpetuate the misunderstanding that "it is all a matter of local practice." Conditioned by a diversity of land administration practices in different common law jurisdictions, this is surely a wrong understanding apart from the fact that many *techniques* are common to all jurisdictions. Examples are valuation/appraisal and land surveying methods.

Researchers have attempted to offer general accounts of land administration. Table 1.3 shows the "ten land administration principles" of Williamson et al. (2010) as an example of a recent endeavour to highlight the nature of land administration. However, these attempts tend to address urgent contemporary issues that are "in fashion" in the academic industry but and do not support their "cutting edge" accounts on solid foundations of what land administration is *generically* about or offer operationally useful directives. This does not improve students' policy understanding and, hence, does not prepare them for professional careers in public administration or private practice.

Table 1.1 Five principles of the Voluntary Guidelines on the Responsible Governance of Tenure of Land, Fisheries, and Forests in the Context of National Food Security

VGGT Principle	*Content*
1. Recognize and respect all legitimate tenure right holders and their rights.	Take reasonable measures to identify, record and respect legitimate tenure right holders and their rights, whether formally recorded or not; to refrain from infringement of tenure rights of others; and to meet the duties associated with tenure rights.
2. Safeguard legitimate tenure rights against threats and infringements.	Protect tenure right holders against the arbitrary loss of their tenure rights, including forced evictions that are inconsistent with their existing obligations under national and international law.
3. Promote and facilitate the enjoyment of legitimate tenure rights.	Take active measures to promote and facilitate the full realization of tenure rights or the making of transactions with the rights, such as ensuring that services are accessible to all.
4. Provide access to justice to deal with infringements of legitimate tenure rights.	Provide effective and accessible means to everyone, through judicial authorities or other approaches, to resolve disputes over tenure rights; and to provide affordable and prompt enforcement of outcomes. States should provide prompt, just compensation where tenure rights are taken for public purposes.
5. Prevent tenure disputes, violent conflicts and corruption.	The state should take active measures to prevent tenure disputes from arising and from escalating into violent conflicts. They should endeavour to prevent corruption in all forms, at all levels, and in all settings.

Source: CFS and FAO (2012), Section 3.1:3–4

This chapter makes an attempt to organise the authors' knowledge of land administration, based on reflections of Hong Kong's case, and in terms of ten principles. Such organisation should be helpful for comparative studies, especially the basic mechanism of Hong Kong predicated on land contracts, which has remained *primeval* even as it matured during the nineteenth century as a British colony when practices of common law jurisdictions began to travel under diverse historical paths. This *primordial nature* of Hong Kong's land administration serves as a useful control for policy comparisons to other local examples.

Four key knowledge areas of land administration covered for an elucidation of principles are concerning:

Table 1.2 VGGT principles of implementation

VGGT principle of implementation	*Content*
1. Human dignity	Recognize the inherent dignity and the equal and inalienable human rights of all individuals.
2. Non-discrimination	No one should be subject to discrimination under law and policies as well as in practice.
3. Equity and justice	Recognizing that equality between individuals may require acknowledging differences between individuals, and taking positive action, including empowerment, in order to promote equitable tenure rights and access to land, fisheries and forests, for all, women and men, youth and vulnerable and traditionally marginalized people, within the national context.
4. Gender equality	Ensure the equal right of women and men to the enjoyment of all human rights, while acknowledging differences between women and men and taking specific measures aimed at accelerating *de facto* equality when necessary. States should ensure that women and girls have equal tenure rights and access to land, fisheries, and forests independent of their civil and marital status.
5. Holistic and sustainable approach	Recognizing that natural resources and their uses are interconnected, and adopting an integrated and sustainable approach to their administration.
6. Consultation and participation	Engage with and seeking the support of those who, having legitimate tenure rights, could be affected by decisions, prior to decisions being taken, and responding to their contributions; taking into consideration existing power imbalances between different parties and ensuring active, free, effective, meaningful and informed participation of individuals and groups in associated decision-making processes.
7. Rule of law	Adopt a rules-based approach through laws that are widely publicized in applicable languages, applicable to all, equally enforced and independently adjudicated, and that are consistent with their existing obligations under national and international law, and with due regard to voluntary commitments under applicable regional and international instruments.
8. Transparency	Clearly defining and widely publicizing policies, laws and procedures in applicable languages, and widely publicizing decisions in applicable languages and in formats accessible to all.
9. Accountability	Holding individuals, public agencies and non-state actors responsible for their actions and decisions according to the principles of the rule of law.
10. Continuous improvement	States should improve mechanisms for monitoring and analysis of tenure governance in order to develop evidence-based programmes and secure on-going improvements. (CFS and FAO 2012: 4–5)

Table 1.3 Ten land administration principles tabulated by Williamson et al. 2010

Aspects of Land Administrative Systems (LAS)	*Principles*
1. LAS	LAS provide the infrastructure for implementation of land polices and land management strategies in support of sustainable development. The infrastructure includes institutional arrangements, legal frameworks, processes, standards, land information, management and dissemination systems, and technologies required to support allocation, land markets, valuation and control of use and development of interests in land.
2. Land Management Paradigm	The land management paradigm provides a conceptual framework for understanding and innovation in land administration systems. The paradigm is the set of principles and practices that define land management as a discipline. The principles and practices relate to the four functions of LAS, namely land tenure, land value, land use and land development, and their interactions. These four functions underpin the operation of efficient land markets and effective land use management. "Land" encompasses natural and built environment including land and water resources.
3. People and Institutions	LAS is about engagement of people within the unique social and institutional fabric of each country. This encompasses good governance, capacity building, institutional development, social interaction and a focus on users, not providers. LAS should be re-engineered to better serve the needs of users, such as citizens, governments and businesses. Engagement with the society, and the ways people think about their land, are core. *This should be achieved through good governance in decision making and implementation. This requires building the necessary capacity in individuals, organisations and wider society to perform functions effectively, efficiently and sustainably.
4. Rights, Restrictions, and Responsibilities	LAS form the basis for conceptualising rights, restrictions and responsibilities (RRR) related to policies, places and people. Rights are normally concerned with ownership and tenure whereas restrictions usually control use and activities on land. Responsibilities relate more to a social, ethical commitment or attitude to environmental sustainability and good husbandry. *RRR must be designed to suit individual needs of each country or jurisdiction, and must be balanced between different levels of government, from local to national.

(*continued*)

Table 1.3 (continued)

Aspects of Land Administrative Systems (LAS)	*Principles*
5. Cadastre	The cadastre is at the core of any LAS providing spatial integrity and unique identification of every land parcel. Cadastres are large scale representations of how the community breaks up its land into useable pieces, usually called parcels. Most cadastres provide security of tenure by recording land rights in a land registry. The spatial integrity within the cadastre is usually provided by a cadastral map that is updated by cadastral surveys. The unique parcel identification provides the link between the cadastral map and the land registry, and serves as the basis of any LAS and the land information it generates, especially when it is digital and geocoded. *The cadastre should ideally include all land in a jurisdiction: public, private, communal, and open space.
6. LAS are Dynamic	LAS dynamism has four dimensions. The first involves changes to reflect the continual evolution of people to land relationships. This evolution can be caused by economic, social and environmental drivers. The second is caused by evolving ICT and globalisation, and their effects on the design and operation of LAS. The third dimension is caused by the dynamic nature of the information within LAS, such as changes in ownership, valuation, land use and the land parcel through subdivision. The fourth dimension involves changes in the use of land information.
7. Processes	LAS include a set of processes that manage change. The key processes concern land transfer, mutation, creation and distribution of interests, valuation and land development. The processes, including their actors and their obligations, explain how LAS operate, as a basis for comparison and improvement. While individual institutions, laws, technologies or separate activities within LAS, such as property in land, a land registry, a specific piece of legislation or a technology for cadastral surveying are important in their own right, *the processes are central to overall understanding of how LAS operate.
8. Technology	Technology offers opportunities for improved efficiency of LAS and spatial enablement of land issues. The potential of technology is far ahead of the capacity of institutions to respond. Technology offers improvements in the collection, storage, management and dissemination of land information. At the same time developments in information and communications technology (ICT) offer the potential for the spatial enablement of land issues by using location or place as the key organiser for human activity.

(*continued*)

Table 1.3 (continued)

Aspects of Land Administrative Systems (LAS)	*Principles*
9. Spatial Data Infrastructure	Efficient and effective LAS that support sustainable development require a spatial data infrastructure (SDI) to operate. The SDI is the enabling platform that links people to information. It supports the integration of natural (primarily topographic) and built (primarily land parcel or cadastral) environmental data as a pre-requisite for sustainable development. The SDI also permits the aggregation of land information from local to national levels.
10. Measure for Success	A successful LAS is measured by its ability to manage and administer land efficiently, effectively and at low cost. *The success of LAS is not determined by complexity of legal frameworks or sophisticated technological solutions. Success lies in adopting appropriate laws, institutions, processes and technologies designed for the specific needs of the country or jurisdiction.

(1) The nature of land as "property": land given a unique boundary and, thus, unitised for private planning, use, and development under an adopted land planning system with specific land tenure.
(2) The ways of exclusive rights allocations and reassignments (property transactions): private acquisitions of possession from government land grants, sales, grandfathering, purchases, and squatting.
(3) Land boundary delineation (via planning and land surveying) and readjustment.
(4) Capturing of values for private fiscal, regulatory, and social purposes.

Part I of this book pertains to Area 1; Parts II and III to Area 2; and Parts III and IV to Areas 3 and 4. The basic principles of land administration are provided below.

Principles of Land Administration

Land administration is part of public administration and, hence, should be a reasonable, certain, transparent, fair, efficient, and accountable <u>public service</u> in support of (a) the land requirements of other government departments; and (b) private and social needs that are land based.

As a special division of public administration, land administration requires not only the application of good modern public management principles based on the assumption of a Weberian (rational) and publicly accountable bureaucracy, but also mastery of special legal and policy knowledge and sensitivity regarding land as property affected by the long-term planning and development of a place. Land policies need to be boundary specific and take into account the interests of different landowners and users.

Certain land administration functions are, by nature, governmental, but most can be supplemented by or relegated to private organisations, which are often ahead of the government bureaucracy in innovative potential. Planning and allocating land, for instance, has a historical origin of strong private involvement and there is no reason that modern practices cannot be delegated to the private sector. However, a central land registry of land boundaries and titles necessitates a government system by default due to the permanence of government and its land data collection authority.

The ten land administration principles presented below are consistent with the aforesaid UN policy-oriented and, hence, prescriptive SDGs and NUA. They are not descriptive for empirical modelling.

Nature of Land as Property

Principle 1: The first principle of land administration is to establish land as numerically manageable property parcels (called lots/plots in most jurisdictions), each with a planimetrically precise boundary as the basic units of land use and development.

In other words, land administration is about the establishment and operation of a *land system* in which rights and interests are allocated and reallocated by market and non-market transactions. Forming the legal basis of a land system, with the lot parcel as its basic unit, is land tenure, which, according to FAO, is the "relationship, whether legally or customarily defined, among people, as individuals or groups, with respect to land … Land tenure is an institution, i.e., rules invented by societies to regulate behaviour. Rules of tenure define how property rights to land are to be allocated within societies. They define how access is granted to rights to use, control, and transfer land, as well as associated responsibilities and restraints. In simple terms, land tenure systems determine who can use what resources for how long, and under what conditions".

As explained in Chap. 2, land possessed and used by the government is not "common," but the exclusive property of the state. That such land may be open to the public at no cost, as in the case of national parks, does not mean that anyone can occupy or use the land at will.

Principle 2: Principle 1 entails a good land (sub)division exercise (usually called town planning), which lays out the land pattern of a place for use and development by individual lot owners. As the layout loses its putty-like nature as a mere plan and becomes extremely rigid upon the assignment of rights, the first planner must adopt a wise layout design.

As explained in Chap. 2, the foundational plan of a place, its first layout, was likely the product of the surveyor. However, over the years, modern town planners imposed statutory town plans on this layout. The relationship between the foundational and latest statutory plans depends on the planning law and land administration policy of the place. In the case of Hong Kong, as covered in Chaps. 2 and 3, both systems continue to jointly affect development rights.

Principle 3: As the value of land is not just a matter of its area, but also its location and configuration, the value of each land parcel, particularly in urban areas, needs individualised assessment with the help of appraisal methods adopted by valuers over a long period of time.

Due to their locational specificities, land parcels cannot be treated as *homogeneous units of goods* such as petroleum, coal, sand, or standardised prefabricated housing units. Valuation, the subject of Chap. 7, is a way to present *verifiable evidence* to reach an opinion on a property unit's worth. While it is true that any person can perform valuation, professional valuation in written statements is essential for auditing and accountability purposes.

Principle 4: Land proprietorship and transaction data should be registered by the government and made publicly available at a low fee to lower transaction costs and allow easy public scrutiny, as property ownership has an important social and economic dimension.

This principle concerns the need for an open and accurate cadastre, a general topic of Chap. 2 and a major focus in Chap. 11, in relation to land boundary information. Current studies are driven by new information technology and what it promises, which is fine. However, the principle remains that technology is a means to something and not an end in itself.

Unofficial cadastres should be allowed to operate because they can cater to special market niches.

It is expected that a modern land administration system is data-driven and will, sooner or later, become fully digital. An interconnected data network should lead to better decision-making by land administrators/ managers so that the public could benefit from improved data quality. However, the most important consideration in technological innovation is social. It should attain appropriate standards within the feasible operational capacities and legislative measures. A good database cannot, in itself, remove uncertainties, so land administrators should not chase the latest in geospatial technologies without considering their costs and benefits. Cadastral surveyors have the vital role of upholding the reliability of cadastres, which is a vital pillar of a healthy land administration system.

Note that the digital revolution has impacted the balance in public data management between privacy protection and public utilisation rights.

Every land administrative system is unique in terms of its social background and level of development. Developing countries are generally constrained by a lack of human capital and technological resources to implement and/or reform their land administration systems in accordance with management ideals. Thus, unofficial cadastres could be very useful to developing countries as "fit-for-purpose" mechanisms. Even in advanced economies, private cadastres or registers are highly useful because the state, by nature, tends to be less innovative and slower in its responses to market needs than the private sector. The history of private charting is a case in point (Davies 2024).

Ways of Exclusive Rights Allocation, Reassignment, and Resumption

Principle 5: The norm of ordinary land allocation for private uses by government should be <u>open-market competition,</u> so the government should not interfere with private land property transactions without genuine and serious public reasons, as other means of competition breed corruption and abuse.

Market allocation avoids the problems of favouritism and arbitrary decisions associated with non-price allocation. An open auction is the ideal way to sell land rights. However, auctions *per se* may not be fair, especially if it is part of a compulsory sale in which collusion is rampant.

Principle 6: Land uses permitted by the government should not be subsequently and unilaterally restricted or revoked by the state even on valid public grounds without due compensation.

There is an inherent danger of land administrators, as holders of public power over an important and valuable public resource, treating themselves as the *alter egos* of the state as the ultimate land controller. Their powers must be specific, open, and carefully constrained by the law, by open and clear policies, precedents, and by free media. Lending any public power to assist developers in land assembly on whatever grounds is suspect even if "due process" is followed, as that is simply rule by law. If the law is wrong, any proper procedure for implementing it cannot make it less wrong.

Principle 7: Squatting and irregular land uses, other than when causing obvious immediate and substantial public harm, should be given sympathetic treatment in land enforcement.

There should be preferential treatment for the poor and needy who occupy public land for shelter, as it is a matter of human rights. This also makes great economic sense because squatters can improve the land they occupy. The granting of a degree of rights to them can stimulate development. The period for the adverse possession of government land can be reduced, while that for private land should be lengthened.

Land Boundary Delineation (via Planning and Land Surveying) and Readjustment

Principle 8: The government should guarantee the accuracy of cadastral boundaries of lot holders.

A point mooted in Chap. 11, this principle is cardinal for the land market to operate efficiently. It is a sign of competent government because it can reduce the costs of litigation among property owners.

Principle 9: Land readjustment is a superior way to handle land pattern restructuring than by compulsory resumption or sale to government or developers.

Land readjustment, the subject of Chap. 17, is not alien to the common law land system. To rely on resumption is an example of bureaucratic apathy and inertia.

Capturing Values for Private Fiscal, Regulatory, and Social Purposes

Principle 10: The purpose of land administration is to promote efficient, equitable, and sustainable land use and development that improves land rather than maximises fiscal revenue.

When a land administration system and land market are healthy, the former can attract healthy land revenue as a consequence, but the aim should not be revenue alone.

Epilogue: Developing Principles of Public Administration

In their practices as civil servants and practitioners, the authors of this book are accustomed to relying on court decisions, policy manuals, instructions, and practice notes, which systematically state the latest procedures and criteria of professional decision-making.

Shaped by this custom, they have attempted to offer the ten most important principles from such practical experience, as well as academic studies, to state their case. They do not claim to have exhausted all principles of land management, but rather hope that it would stimulate further and better research on the general operational principles of land administration that are true of all jurisdictions with land markets based on private property.

Questions for Revision and Discussion

1. Discuss if and to what extent the *laying out of land* for urban development can be privatised.

Laying out land for town development by companies has been a common feature of urban growth. The caveat is that such layout has prior official support or endorsement. The best Hong Kong example is Discovery Bay.

The case of Discovery Bay is an interesting and successful story of planning by contract through an initial Coasian negotiation between two parties with an international political background. "It all began during the 1970s when an overseas Chinese investor purchased a number of agricultural lots under leasehold tenure near Silvermine Bay (Mui Wo) on Lantau

Island and then only connected to the rest of Hong Kong by sea transport. His purpose was to gather adherents of a non-Christian religion to make pilgrimages. This person suffered financial problems and had to surrender his land holdings to the bank of a major Cold War player, USSR, to the great embarrassment of the British Colonial Administration, which did not want to upset China by allowing that player to own a settlement in Hong Kong. Through skillful manoeuvring, the government ensured that the land was sold to a Hong Kong company with the condition that the place would be developed into a residential area. The terms were harsh from the vantage point of a normal developer. According to the Conditions of Exchange (for New Grant No. 6122), the government, as the landlord, did not need to provide any road connection, any infrastructure such as water supply, drainage, sewerage, and so on, or any site formation for essential public transport facilities. The developer, as the lessee, had the obligation to erect, maintain and keep in use on the lot membership club houses and a leisure resort and associated facilities which shall include an hotel or hotels, a dam, a reservoir, salt and fresh water storage and treatment areas, a sewage treatment plant, a refuse disposal point, a cable-car system, a ferry pier and a non-membership golf course (in these Conditions called "the minimum associated facilities"). In addition, he had to build "at his own expense" a fire station and drill yard and a police station according to government standards to be leased at US$ 0.2 per annum each to the government, water supply for fire fighting, and so on. The government did not conduct any administrative layout planning for the area. The developer had to formulate its own master layout plans and "design and disposition" of all buildings for the prior approval by the Secretary for the New Territories (later Lands and Work) and then build the whole settlement from scratch. Therefore, the developer acted as a private new town corporation. While there was no time frame for "the minimum associated facilities," and no hotel or cable car system has been built, the developer did construct a reservoir by damming a valley. It built a golf course. It erected a fire station, a police station, and a sewage treatment plant. And it constructed a pier and established a private high-speed ferry service to make the sale of its first developments viable".

In this case the government did not even layout the settlement, but all development needs the prior approval of government and the first statutory Outline Zoning Plan was imposed on Discovery Bay in 2000 when its development, as a town favoured by expatriates and those who preferred a non-urban style of living, had already matured.

2. Discuss the feasibility of a completely *private cadastre.*

The credibility of a private cadastre is tested by the market. See Bogaerts, Theo, and J. Zevenbergen. "Cadastral systems—alternatives." *Computers, Environment and Urban Systems* 25, nos. 4–5 (2001): 325–337.

3. Identify and discuss the key principles of land administration from ten other books on the subject with respect to property rights.

This is a very challenging exercise. Widen the search to include "land policy."

See Van der Molen, P. & C. Lemmen. "Unconventional approaches to land administration: a point of view of land registrars and land surveyors." In FIG 2005: Secure Land Tenure: New Legal Frameworks and Tools in Asia and the Pacific: proceedings of an expert group meeting held by FIG commission 7, December 8–9, 2005, Bangkok, Thailand.

References

Committee for World Food Security (CFS) and the Food and Agriculture Organization (FAO). 2012 *Voluntary Guidelines on the Responsible Governance of Tenure of Land, Fisheries And Forests in the Context of National Food Security, Food and Agriculture Organization of the United Nations*, Rome, Section 2 (General Matters), pp. 3–10.

Davies, Stephen N. G. 2024. Counter-current: The Move from Private to Public in the Provision of British Charts and Pilots in the China Seas. *Surveying & Built Environment* 33 (2, Sept.): 5–39.

Mitchell, David, Siraj Sait, Jean du Plessis & Agnes Mwasumbi. 2019. "Core Values and Principles of Responsible Land Administration Responsible Land Administration Teaching Essentials," a project initiated and funded by the Global Land Tool Network (GLTN) and UN-Habitat.

United Nations. 2016. *New Urban Agenda.* Habitat III Secretariat.

Williamson, Ian, Stig Enemark, Jude Wallace, and Abbas Rajabifard. 2010. *Land Administration for Sustainable Development.* Redlands, CA: ESRI Press Academic.

CHAPTER 2

The Nature and Life Cycle of a Lot as Part of a Layout

Lawrence Wai Chung Lai

Introduction

The authors begin this book on "land administration" by discussing town planning. This may surprise the reader, but it is really nothing strange. Rather, it is highly relevant.

Historically, the surveyor, as an agent of the state, was the first town and country planner for a typical European colonial settlement, which was called a "plantation" or "colony." Back then, the profession of "town planner," as distinct from the surveyor, did not yet exist. But town planning pre-dated the town planning profession, whose practitioners might have *never* engaged in making survey maps or town plans, as explained below.

One job of the surveyor was to lay out/plat a town or farming area in unoccupied or squatted government land, whether or not there were indigenous occupants who were bought out or driven away, according to some government planning instructions guidelines or even laws such as the US *Land Ordinance*.

L. W. C. Lai (✉)
Department of Real Estate and Construction, The University of Hong Kong, Hong Kong, China
e-mail: wclai@hku.hk

L. W. C. Lai et al. (eds.), *Principles of Land Administration at Work*, https://doi.org/10.1007/978-981-95-2972-8_2

The town layout usually divides land into rectilinear street blocks (which may be grouped into wards), within which allotments (or simply lots) are further delineated. Each lot fronts at least one street. Each lot's width-to-depth ratio varied from place to place.

Most agricultural or farm lots were often "ribbon lots" with their fronts having riparian access. They had small width-to-depth ratios to maximise the number of lot holders who could enjoy river transport.

The government's allotment of land and (allocation of) lots to grantors could be by sale, grandfathering (lottery or queueing), or squatting.

The Question of Town Planning for Home Buyers and Property Investors

What are the main features of town planning in a certain city? A home buyer's interest would lie mainly in civil liberties; the quality and stability of the city's natural, social, and planned environment; along with its accessibility, employment and educational opportunities, and availability of healthcare. An investor would mostly be concerned with the prospects of economic growth and social development. The decisionmaker who understands the economic significance of town and country planning would pay attention to (a) the "planning unit" as a platform for and constraint to growth, as well as (b) the institutional arrangements of forward planning and development control. This chapter introduces the planning unit beginning with the "survey map" of a city.

The Town Plan, Town Map, or Survey Map of a Town

A "town plan," better known as a "town map" or "survey map" of a town "as built," shows the town's *de facto* built-up/land pattern. Any boundary depicted on this map or plan is *bona fide*. For convenience sake, the authors shall use the Hong Kong expression, "survey map," to avoid confusing it with "layout" or "town plan," which refers to a plan designed for a town. Any boundary depicted on this plan with zoning implications or plan is a *fiat* boundary.

From this survey map, one can deduce whether or not there was any town plan that accounted for the town map's features. A town plan likely existed or still exists if the map shows a formal land pattern with straight and/or smooth curvilinear streets.

Any boundary on a town plan should (but not always) tally with that on the survey map, which, in turn, should normally and neatly fit that on a cadastral map (also known as a "lot index plan" in Hong Kong). A lot, as delineated on a cadastral map, is the basic unit of planning.

Apart from being a source of wonder about the urban structure of a town, a town survey or cadastral map can help one decipher its planning, social, and economic history (especially when a series of chronological maps is available), understand its current planning issues, and predict the mode of its future growth.

A study of a survey map of a long-established town is the starting point of a planning study of that town. On this map, a town planner can plot the results of a land use survey, which will reveal the amount and spatial distribution of the town's land uses and use it as the "base plan" for re-planning its road and land uses.

In a common law jurisdiction, re-planning can always be done by state command (i.e., edict) or contract.

The Lot

The lot is the basic unit of land ownership, planning, use, and accounting, according to common law in relation to the rest of the world (Lai 2021, 2023; Lai and Davies 2017, 2022).

The Legal Creation, Description, and Registration of the Lot

A lot in common law is created through a deed (a written document signed, sealed, and delivered) by a grantor (the state) in favour of a grantee (its first owner).

A deed was originally handwritten, then typewritten, and is now computer-generated.

A lot always has, as the principle of it as land property (real estate), a locationally unique boundary that defines its area. This boundary is invisible. To show the world its presence, rights, and obligations, the grantor will use the deed, often accompanied by a lot map as an integral part of it, to describe its geographical location and area, as well as the terms of its use by the grantee. The grantor and, more likely, the grantee, who is the "owner" or occupant of the lot, will use "metes and bounds" (some visible physical signs such as stakes, marker stones, fences, walls, moats, etc.) to demarcate the boundary.

The deed, the property's "birth certificate," is deposited in a government or publicly recognised register, while the lot boundary is recorded on a government lot map. Both the deed and lot map are usually public documents open to public inspection.

In Hong Kong, a Crown Lease as a paper document containing a lot map was granted to a lessee after the lessee fulfils every positive covenant specified in the land grant contract (the "Conditions of Sale/Grant/Exchange/Regrant/Extension"). Such a paper is no longer physically provided, as it has been replaced by a legal fiction under the *Conveyancing and Property Ordinance*, in which a Crown (Government) Lease is considered granted once these positive covenants are fulfilled, as evidenced by a "Certificate of Compliance" (CC) issued by the land authority. Deeds are no longer physically provided—perhaps to save on the resources used to produce them for lots on which numerous property units (especially flats) are built as parts of high-rise developments.

Cadastral System

> The cadastral system defines and records the location and extent of property rights, restrictions and responsibilities. It includes a geometric description of land and real property boundaries linked to other records describing the nature of the interests, the ownership or control of those interests, and often the value of the parcel and its improvements. The cadastral system comprises mechanisms that collectively ensure all land and real property can be easily, uniquely and accurately identified in a common reference system. This includes a digital representation of land parcels (digital cadastre), instruments defining land, information delivery and access systems, a legal framework, survey marks and other physical evidence of property boundaries, registered surveyors, records of surveys such as plans, and standards for definition and surveying of land (Intergovernmental Committee for Surveying and Mapping. (ICSM) 2015: 7)

> The cadastral system, in combination with the land registration system, is a powerful economic lever. It assembles, manages and shares information that defines and reinforces property rights. In turn, these property rights translate into economic development, social stability and physical wellbeing. (ICSM: 9)

> Cadastral surveys are not only concerned with measurements and description which may have to stand the tests of long periods of time; they are

> concerned with the needs of people and the proper administration of land, that fundamental resource without which no one could exist. From a systems point of view, the operation of a cadastral survey has four stages: adjudication, demarcation, survey and recording or description. (Dale 1979: 621)

Enjoyment of a Lot

The enjoyment of a lot is subject to the duties or obligations of its owner, apart from those expressly specified in the deed, to observe the rights of way and easements, refrain from generating nuisances for neighbours, and whatever legislation affects the land interests at the time.

The rights to and obligations of land property are "real interests" that "run with the land," binding not only the current owner, but also all subsequent owners. A lot owner can make covenant with neighbouring owners on land matters regarding, say, nuisances and the protection of views.

Subdividing and Recombining Lots

The common law rights to unconstrained subdivision and residential use (in a process now called "densification") produced poor housing conditions during the Industrial Revolution. Hence, written laws and regulations were justified and enacted to regulate development and use of lots; and to enable compulsory purchase of the state of private land for road widening, open space, and the like.

When development control takes away rights and/or imposes restrictions on private lots obtained from land sales, whether or not compensation is paid, private property rights are attenuated.

In the post-industrial world, governments and/or developers with big financial backing purchase private lots from small individual owners and combine them into large single lots, thereby reversing the subdivision process (land reassembly) and redeveloping these for residential or commercial purposes. The rationale behind this is often contentious, especially when the state forces the sale of private land for profit-making ventures.

A far better method of land assembly is land readjustment, the subject of Chap. 17, by which all private lot owners surrender their present holdings in exchange for shares in future joint redevelopment projects based on more efficient urban layouts proportional to their current ownership shares in the affected area. No owner is displaced and every owner is regranted a property in-*situ* and/or entitled to ownership in the new

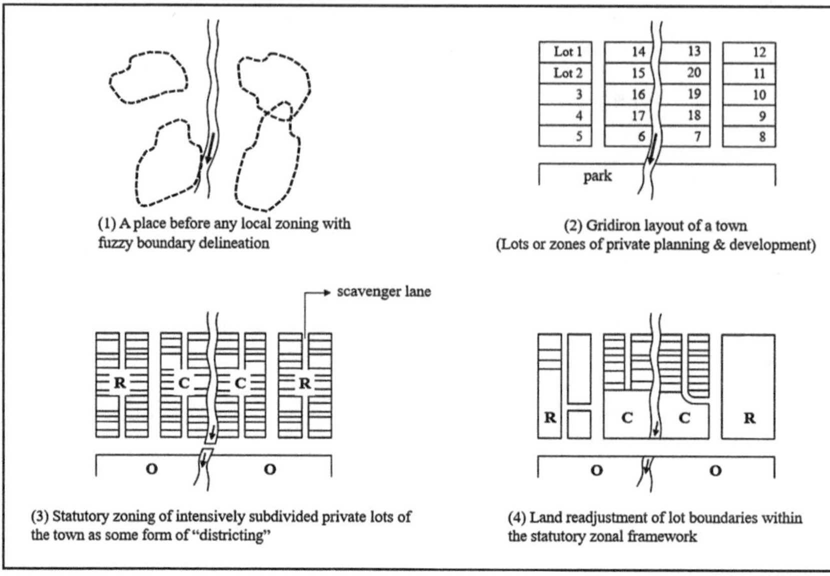

Fig. 2.1 Changes in land zoning for a place. (Drawing by Dr Adam Chun Liang Lin)

development after deducting the portion reserved for the general public's use.

Figure 2.1 presents the four idealised stages in the zoning of land for a place from pre-planning communal society stage to the readjustment of old lots in modern society.

Some Aspects of Private Lots in Hong Kong

Lot Types

A private lot in Hong Kong can have other names:

1. Demarcation District (DD) Lot
2. Farm Lot
3. Garden Lot
4. Inland Lot (IL) (in Hong Kong, Kowloon, New Kowloon, Aberdeen, etc.)

5. Marine Lot (ML)
6. New Grant Lot (NGL)
7. Rural Building Lot (RBL)
8. Survey District (SD) Lot

"Missing Lots"

A new landowner, usually a successor of land who has never occupied the land, may not know where his/her property is located if the lot map is missing from public records. This owner can ask the government to obtain the grant for a new lot in the general locality upon the surrender of the "missing lot."

The title documents of some New Grant Lots (NGLs) in the New Territories were lost during the 1941–1945 Japanese occupation. One may obtain a copy of the *New Grant Register*, which contains some information on these NGLs. However, the *Register* is not an official record held under the *Land Registration Ordinance*. One may also approach the Lands Department's District Lands Office for additional information, if any.[1]

Subdivision of Lots in Hong Kong

Unless restricted by the terms of his/her lease (or any applicable ordinance), a landowner in Hong Kong has the right to subdivide his/her lot. The subdivision is effected by a deed poll.

The Land Registrar can, under the *Land Survey Ordinance*, refuse the registration of a deed poll effecting the division of land if it is not accompanied by a land boundary plan that is duly certified by an Authorised Land Surveyor (ALS). However, a refusal of registration does not invalidate the deed poll as a legal document.

[1] Q10 https://www.landreg.gov.hk/en/faq/faq_search_1.htm

Land Registers and Searches in the Land Registry of Hong Kong

Land Registers

There are two types of land register in Hong Kong's Land Registry: "current" and "full."

The "current" register contains the latest information on a property such as the most recent transaction in its "Owner Particulars" section and only those subsisting (now affecting) incumbrances.

The "full" register contains the historical and current information on a property, such as every transaction that has been made on the property from the date the conditions of sale/grant/exchange/regrant/extension were executed.

Each land register has four sections:

(1) Property particulars
- Lot number and address
- Share of lot
- Lease term (e.g., commencement date)
- Rent per annum

(2) <u>Owner particulars</u>
- Name of owners
  Historical owner(s) (chain of ownership)
  Current owner(s)
- Capacity (if not Sole Owner) Joint Tenants
  Tenants in common
- Administrator Executor
- Date of Instrument (transaction)
- Date of Registration
- Consideration

(3) Incumbrances that affect the property, but may not change its ownership such as:
- A Court Order (e.g. Charging Order, etc.)
- A Mortgage

- An Occupation Permit (OP), Deed of Mutual Covenant (DMC) (for the age and use of the building)
- An Agreement for Sale and Purchase
- A Sub-sale Agreement, Nomination

(4) Deeds pending registration that cover documents already lodged for registration against the property, but whose registrations have not been completed for one reason or another.

Land Searches for Title Documents

Anyone can obtain the land registers and copies of land documents for properties in Hong Kong from the Queensway Customer Centre or the NT Search Offices of the Land Registry.

Anyone can obtain a copy of the land register via IRIS Online Services (http://www.iris.gov.hk) and select "Search Land Register" or at the Queensway or NT Search Offices after paying the prescribed fees.

The Land Registry has stopped accepting applications for any search on properties registered under someone else's name unless that person supplies the applicant with an authorisation document.[2]

This protects the privacy of the person at the expense of government transparency if the person holds an official or public position.

NT land record types kept at the Lands Department and Land Registry are shown in Table 2.1.

Title Documents of Surrendered Lots

The Land Registry no longer keeps the title documents of lots already surrendered to the government after transferring them to the Government Records Office (GRO).

Appendix A shows a guide to searches for Crown/Government Leases in the Land Registry.

[2] Q5 https://www.landreg.gov.hk/en/faq/faq_search_1.htm

Table 2.1 NT land record types kept at the Lands Department and Land Registry (Partly after Tau (2015))

Records found at the Lands Department	*Records found only at the Land Registry*
Aerial photo and orthophoto	Building licence plan
A-book/lot record book	DD/SD Sheet attached to Block Crown (Government) Lease (BCL/BGL)
Blue key/Green key/Black key	Deed of rectification
Boundary stone book	Gazetted resumption plan
Boundary (digitised) of resumption limit, as requested by ALS	Grant plan
Demarcation District control sheet	Indenture (deed)/Schedule of BCL/BGL
Double lot sheet (DD Field Sheet)	LBP for subdivision submitted by ALS
Field area statement	Lease plan (Lot map)
Historical map	SRP for subdivision submitted by ALS
House lot plan	
Quarter sheet/A sheet/B sheet/Cad sheet	
Lot identification plan (Lot index plan)	
Permitted burial ground (PBG)	
Survey map	
Village environs plan	

The Lot in Terms of Property Rights and Access

There are three types of property rights: common, communal, and private. Rights are *de jure* in that they are socially, if not also legally, recognised and honoured as binding on all members of society. When these rights are neglected by their holders or denied by third parties, the law is a means to peacefully resolve any conflict that may arise.

Common property is *de jure* open access and applies to maritime resources outside territorial waters and exclusive economic zones around the world. But it is extremely rare on land. *De facto* open-access land is actually communal or private property without access restrictions. Good examples are country parks under government administration and marine sand vulnerable to theft (Edwards 2015; Lai et al. 2016a).

Communal and private property rights to land are exclusive and based on effective management with reference to boundaries. A stranger who crosses a boundary without permission is trespassing. As an exclusive communal or private property, a lot is not common property. Its holder may, by goodwill, choice, or neglect, open the property to public access (Lai et al. 2022).

Table 2.2 A matrix of property rights and *de facto* access control

De facto access control		*Property rights regime*		
		Non-exclusive	*Exclusive*	
		Common property	*Communal property (exclusive vs. outsiders)*	*Private property (Exclusive against rest of the world)*
No physical entry barrier	Open and unmanaged	1. Ocean outside any maritime zones	2. Abandoned vacant communal land	3. Abandoned vacant property; unpatrolled public property
	Open and managed	4. Ocean under maritime zoning	5. Communal land actively used	6. Property taken care of by volunteers, visitors, squatters
Presence of physical entry barriers	Restricted, but unmanaged	7. Abandoned pirate fortification on land not under any jurisdiction (?)	8. Abandoned vacant communal land	9. Gated facility neglected or abandoned
	Restricted and managed	10. Pirate fortification on land not under any jurisdiction	11. Fenced-off communal land actively used	12. Gated development (with a "property manager")

Table 2.2 is a matrix of *de jure* rights and *de facto* access control.

Private Land Administration

Before 1997, many private lots on Cheung Chau were administered by Wong Wai Tsak Tong (WWTT). This body corporate was first granted land on Cheung Chau by a Block Crown Lease in 1905. Since then, the WWTT was granted additional land parcels on Cheung Chau under New Grants. As such, WWTT was, at one point in time, the registered owner of 90% of the private land on Cheung Chau. This arrangement was extinguished by the *Block Crown Lease (Cheung Chau) Ordinance* in 1995.

Much land in Causeway Bay is still a private zone controlled by the Lee Hysan Company, Ltd (the company). There is a special clause in the first assignment from the company to a buyer, which states that any future development required the company's approval. While this special clause does not appear in second assignment, as part of the first assignment, it binds the second. The issue of restrictive and positive covenants was tested in the Court of Final Appeal, which found in favour of the company [*Sky Heart Limited v. Lee Hysan Company Limited*, Final Appeal No. 9 of 1998 (Civil) on appeal from CACV No.64 OF 1997].

Private Property Rights on Land

Property rights on land have different types, as summarised in Fig. 2.2 (Lai 1997). They pertain to freehold interests, those under tenancy agreements, and licences.

All are exclusive. Freehold interests differ from the others in that they have no pre-specified duration and can be taken back by the state as sovereign.

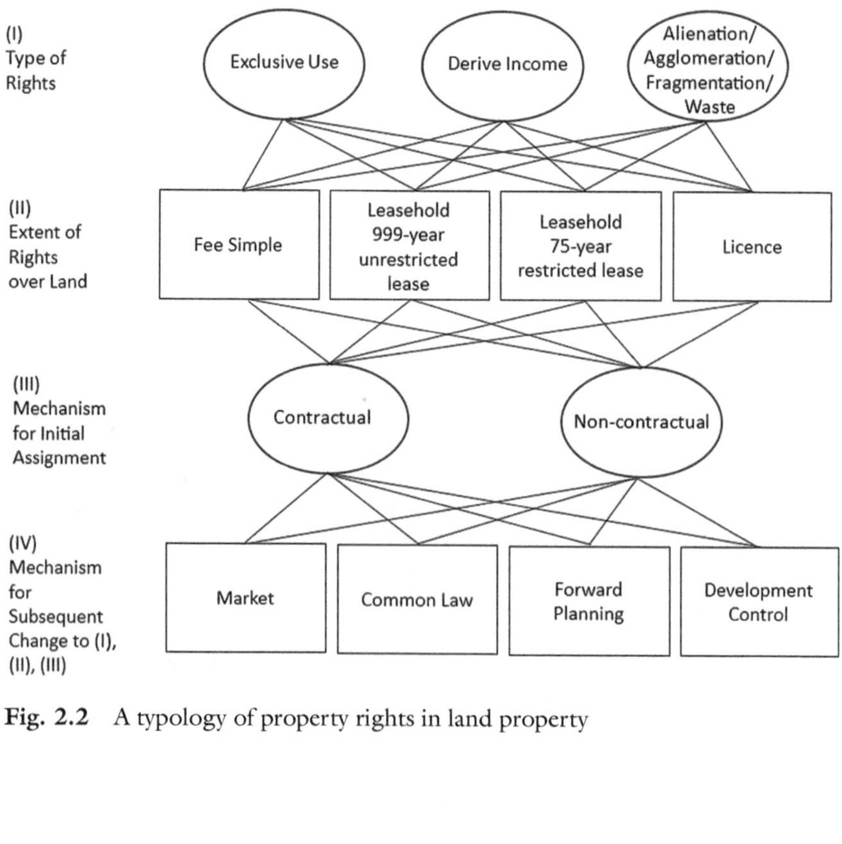

Fig. 2.2 A typology of property rights in land property

All rights are held together with some duties to the grantor, and every lot under each category has a unique boundary.

It is wrong to say that a leasehold is incomplete or only confers the rights of use, but not ownership. Leasehold interest holders enjoy exclusive rights to use, derive income from, and alienate their properties, but all of these rights are limited to specified terms (usually years).

Questions for Revision and Discussion

1. Discuss the scenario in which a society's land users only know the boundaries of their own properties, but have no way to identify those of other users in a land registry.

The transactional costs of development and redevelopment would be higher than in the case of an open land registry.

2. Discuss the differences between a freehold lot and an adjoining 999-year leasehold lot of the same size and shape.

The only significant difference is that a leasehold lot has a definite pre-specified life. See Lai and Kwong (2025).

3. Examine the history of the development of Discovery Bay, Lantau Island, from 1980 to 2000 prior to the Town Planning Board's imposition of the first outline zoning plan (OZP) (Lai et al. 2016b). Discuss the role of the Public Works Department (PWD) and its successor in the planning of this development.

The PWD (later Buildings and Lands/Lands Department) was the *de jure* town planning board for Discovery Bay.

References

Edwards, Bruce. 2015. The Insatiable Demand for Sand. *Finance & Development (IMF)* 52 (4): 46–47.

Dale, P. F. 1979. Photogrammetry and Cadastral Surveys within the commonwealth.*The Photogrammetric Record* 9(53): 621-631.

Intergovernmental Committee for Surveying and Mapping (ICSM). 2015. *Cadastre 2034: Powering Land and Real Property (Cadastral Reform and Innovation for Australia – A National Strategy)*. Australia: Canberra ACT.

Lai, Lawrence W. C. 1997. Property rights justifications for planning and a theory of zoning. Progress in Planning 48, no. 3: 161-246.

Lai, Lawrence W. C. 2021. A Dialogue on Town Planning and Boundary Delineation. *Planning Practice & Research* 36 (5): 483–490.

Lai, Lawrence W. C. 2023. "No property is an island": The Private Lot as the Basic Unit of Land Use Planning & Management of a Wider World. *COSMOS + TAXIS* 11 (1–2): 90–96.

Lai, Lawrence W. C. and Kwong, Jason W. Y. 2025 *Principles of Town Planning Translating Concepts to Applications*. Edward Elgar: Cheltenham.

Lai, Lawrence W. C., and Stephen N. G. Davies. 2017. A Coasian Boundary Inquiry on Zoning and Property Rights: Lot and Zone Boundaries and Transaction Costs. *Progress in Planning* 118 (2017): 1–28.

Lai, Lawrence W. C., and Stephen N. G. Davies. 2022. Is Non-zoning of Land Impossible? Eight Fundamental Propositions of Zoning. *Journal of Environmental Policy & Planning*1–16. https://doi.org/10.1080/1523908X.2022.2098096.

Lai, Lawrence W. C., K. W. Chau, and Frank T. Lorne. 2016a. The Rise and Fall of the Sand Monopoly in Colonial Hong Kong. *Ecological Economics* 128:106–116.

Lai, Lawrence W. C., Stephen N. G. Davies, and F. T. Lorne. 2016b. Creation of Property Rights in Planning by Contract and Edict: Beyond "Coasian bargaining" in Private Planning. *Planning Theory* 15 (4): 418–434.

Lai, Lawrence W. C., Stephen N. G. Davies, Lennon H. T. Choy, and K. W. Chau. 2022. Land Planning, Property Rights & Management of Built Heritage: Some Hong Kong Observations of Colonial Military Buildings. *Land* 11:1516.

Tau, Yu Ming. 2015. *HKIS CPD PowerPoints* (Cadastral Surveying) 8 May.

CHAPTER 3

The Nature of Land Administration in Hong Kong: Planning and Development by Contract

Lawrence Wai Chung Lai

It is a well-known legal fact that Hong Kong's land administration and property law system is predicated on a leasehold land system. How this system works, however, needs explanation in conceptual and practical terms.

The Meaning of Private Development

To understand the nature of this system, the first thing to bear in mind is the meaning of "private development." Private development is not necessarily private in the sense that it is for domestic or commercial use. It can be for a community or institutional use, such as a cemetery, church, temple, or school.

A private development in Hong Kong means a *building(s)* developed by any individual or body other than the government for private or public

L. W. C. Lai (✉)
Department of Real Estate and Construction, The University of Hong Kong, Hong Kong, China
e-mail: wclai@hku.hk

L. W. C. Lai et al. (eds.), *Principles of Land Administration at Work*, https://doi.org/10.1007/978-981-95-2972-8_3

use on land obtained from the government. Normally, building permissions are required to carry out building development or redevelopment on a plot of land, which can be just one "lot" or a group of "lots."

All private developments on any plot of land can only take place in a government-delineated area and in accordance with the terms of "lease conditions" (typically land uses and building forms) drafted by the government. The expression, "lease conditions" (or simply "terms of the land lease" or "the lease"), refers to the terms in a contract for government land sale/grant/exchange/regrant/extension (hence, the "Conditions of Sale/Grant/Exchange/Regrant/Extension") as recited in an ensuing deed called a Crown Lease until 1984 and a Government Lease ever since to remove its colonial connotation.

. A "lot plan" can be found as part of the Conditions or the Lease. This plan delineates the boundary of the property allocated as a leasehold lot. This means the state has complete control over the location and form of private development.

The Town Planning Function of the Leasehold Land System

However, the land system is far more than merely one of tenure or government control. It is also one of administration in a wider sense and town planning in a substantial sense.

To form a more complete understanding of the leasehold and land administration systems in Hong Kong, we need to appreciate that land for private development has mainly been allocated by public auction (i.e., the rights to a plot of land are sold in the open market) and, sometimes, tender.

Since a set of lease conditions with its lot map is a town's *bona fide* site or lot plan and that the rights to carry out this plan are purchased by individuals in a voluntary open market, it is correct to describe the leasehold system as one of planning by contract from the point of view of the government (Table 3.1).

This system is also one of development by contract from the point of view of the purchaser of the property rights, as stated in the terms of the lease, because s/he has an economic incentive to develop the lot as soon as possible to realize his/her property rights.

This book is not an apology for private planning in the absence of any state planning or regulation. This is a statement of the real-world practice

Table 3.1 Planning and contractual elements of a lease in Hong Kong

Planning elements	*Contractual elements*
It is state planning because the state drafts the terms of the land lease and delineates the lot	It is contractual, as the rights to obtain and develop the lot is based on a sale and purchase agreement with the state
It is planning because there is land use, transport, and building control provisions in the land lease	It is a public lot plan purchased by an individual in a sale
It can be a form of comprehensive state planning because there is no limit to the types of land use, transport, or building control clauses	It is a comprehensive public lot plan purchased by an individual in a sale

of more than 160 years of a system of sustainable state planning in which land use and building controls are a matter of mutual consent between the state and individuals.

Planning by Contract vs. Planning by Edict

For a long time, the idea that town planning as a state activity regulating the land market has been associated with planning theorists and practitioners with legislative control of changing the use and development of land by the private sector. Such control is typically exerted by the imposition of a system of town plans produced under state legislation, each covering a large number of individually owned lots and produced under a local or national planning act or ordinance that unilaterally modifies existing private property rights over land.

While such a modification can enlarge the original bundle of rights, in practice it invariably attenuates, compromises, or extinguishes existing rights. This legislative or statutory interference in the rights of property owners and the degree of freedom of developers, or "planning by edict," which regulates private planning of individuals, is often justified on the basis of the public interest concerning the environment, if not also on the grounds of social equity. The social concern with equity is sometimes driven by a certain contempt for the concept of private property. Its proponents can hardly accept the natural law concept of property as an institution for the common good.

The Political Economy of Planning by Contract

The history of town planning in practice in Hong Kong testifies to the fact that state planning can be carried out on a contractual basis. Such "planning by contract" or "planning by (mutual) consent" need not be an alternative to planning by edict.

It is, in fact, a vehicle to accumulate wealth on land by attracting investments and promoting betterment so that subsequent statutory planning has a meaningful role to play. In fact, this form of planning used to generate so much revenue that the colonial government was able to maintain a low tax regime and increase public spending on Hong Kong's physical and social infrastructure that well accommodated sustained growth in its population (at a rate of one million people per decade since the end of the World War II until recent years), whose per capita income has continually increased.

Since the return of Hong Kong from the UK to China, this system of planning in Hong Kong has become subject to the provisions of a written law, the *Basic Law*, that constitutionally guarantee the continuation of a *capitalist* market economy. Interestingly, while China has remained constitutionally socialist, she has adopted the same planning by contract approach to her "land use rights" reform that can hardly be distinguished from the Hong Kong model, save for the form of competition for such rights. A contractual approach to property rights on land and other resources, with a minimum degree of respect for human rights (the right of free exit of human and financial capital), is the foundation of market capitalism, if not also a social contract theory of the state.

Planning by Contract at Work

Ever since 1842, the prime mover of urbanization of Hong Kong has been planning by contract (Lai 2011). The idea of planning by contract is put into practice by the allocation of leasehold land interests, rights, and obligations over land for private purposes from the state to individuals through price competition by auction and tender; and the development of land according to the rights and interests specified in the Conditions of Sale/Grant/Exchange/Regrant/Extension and the Crown (now Government) Lease. Overt market competition, notably by auction, is not only efficient, but transparent. Both are preconditions for sound public finance and a clean government.

The land lease specifies for a well-delineated piece of land the land use and built form permitted by the state for a specified period of time (typically 999 years or 99 years in the oldest leases, 75 years in more recent leases, and 50 years since 1997).

This lease, a public document, is a covenant between the state and a land purchaser (and all subsequent owners) to develop and use the plot of land in accordance with a public plan for a site delineated by the state for sale.

The covenant is an agreement (in the form of a deed) entered into by mutual consent, as evidenced by a simple written contract for the sale and purchase of Crown (Government) land in a government land auction, government land grant, or the surrender of a plot of private land in exchange for a plot *in-situ* or otherwise. That simple written contract is the Conditions of Sale/Grant/Exchange/Regrant/Extension.

The consideration of a lot is reached by market competition. The land purchaser is, at the same time, a development plan purchaser. It is through the cumulative selling of land use and development rights planned at the margin by the state that has, through the years, built up the fiscal reserves of geographically tiny Hong Kong to the amazement of the world.

The outcome of this sale of rights on land has achieved something that goes beyond the imagination of the supporters of Henry George, who proposed a 100% land tax. It is the incremental consequence of the private implementation of these site plans that has shaped the built form of Hong Kong, which is being rapidly replicated in the major cities of China. This kind of planning by consent is also the most open and effective form of planning to the developer and property buyer, as the "conditions" and the lease (or just the Certificates of Compliance) are public documents, forming the "root of title" in property transfers.

This kind of planning by consent is the most efficient in measuring the performance of the state planners as the plan purchasers "vote with their cash" in bidding for the land rights. A planning error made by the planner will be reflected in the returns collected from the land sale. This kind of planning by consent is comprehensive beyond the imagination of many comprehensive planning theorists who advocate planning by edict.

There is no question of "piece meal planning" in this form of state site planning most acceptable to the public because the government would normally sell a site that has been demarcated as a part and parcel of a wider "layout," which internalizes present and foreseen externalities perceived at the time among a large number of individual properties.

Such a layout was initially the product of military engineers and later chartered surveyors. That they were not labelled as "town planners" should not affect our understanding of such layouts as town plans. These layouts have become known as "Layout Plans" (LPs) and "Outline Development Plans" (ODPs). ODPs have been used since the 1970s to convert rural areas into new towns, each of which accommodates a population of over half a million people.

The lots within a layout are subject not only to the lease conditions particular to a lot in its specific location, but also to some blanket administrative measures for a designated district (Special Control Areas) or generally for a group of districts such as a density control zone (Kwong 2020).

There is no question that multiple ownership in high-rise building blocks renders compliance with lease terms difficult because each owner must enter into a multilateral contract, a Deed of Mutual Covenant, which provides for a management company and other elaborated legally enforceable rules governing the use of public and private areas of the properties. In this way, the contractual planning for the use of a site is translated into planning for the use of individual flats and common areas.

There is no question about the ability of an individual lease as a site plan to adapt to modern environmental conditions when there is new market demand for a change in use that is not permitted by the terms of the lease. The reason is that modification of the terms of lease is subject to state approval and the imposition of new environmental protection clauses. Also, such modification is an opportunity for taxing any gain in value as a return for the granting of new terms. The state seldom misses any opportunity to levy such taxation or "modification premium."

In other words, there is no doubt that the system is sustainable given the rule of law.

Complications Under Statutory Town Planning

The role of modern planning legislation in Hong Kong is to introduce an extra state screening procedure that precedes the normal process of lease modification. This procedure is required by statutory plans made under a town planning ordinance.

The first batch of statutory town plans for Hong Kong was first introduced only about 40 years ago (within the ambit of the pre-war *Town Planning Ordinance* of 1939), and such statutory plans do not abolish the contractual control by way of the land leases, but form another layer of land use and building form control. Note that the first statutory zoning exercise for Hong Kong did not come along with the *Town Planning Ordinance* enacted in 1939, but under a series of racially discriminatory laws: the *European District Reservation Ordinance* of 1888, the *Hill District Reservation Ordinance* of 1904, and the *Peak District (Residence) Ordinance* of 1918. Similar zoning was imposed in 1919 on "Cheung Chau Peak" under the *Cheung Chau (Residence) Ordinance*. These zones were removed by the *Peak District (Residence) Repeal Ordinance* and *Cheung Chau (Residence) Repeal Ordinance* of 1946 under the governorship of Sir Mark Young (Lai and Yu 2001; Lai and Kwong 2025).

Usually produced long after a development area, such as a new town, is completed and has become mature and inhabited, these statutory plans tend to reflect on and consolidate the existing land use pattern. They never abolish any existing use. Depending on the type of zone unilaterally imposed, their impact is to impose the need for planning permission for a specified change in use or development before a request for lease modification to allow such change or development may be entertained. This need arises if such change or development falls within a list of specified uses.

The uses in the Notes under Columns 1 and 2 of a statutory plan for each type of statutory zone vary from plan to plan and may change with time. The definitions of each use also change and care must be duly taken to ensure that the time and place in which a definition operates stays updated. Appendix A shows an example of the changes in the definitions of one use.

The government has a statutory duty to decide within a specified period, and the applicant has a statutory right to review any decision and to make a statutory appeal if the decision upon review is unsatisfactory. There is also a host of specified uses that do not require such permission for any type of zone or specified type of zone. Housing development may be permitted in most types of zones, including green belts, and commercial uses are always permitted in many types of zones.

Private requests for changing the zoning of a plot of land in a statutory plan are possible, and unlike applications made in accordance with the plan, the law does not provide a time limit for entertaining such requests. This system of statutory planning allows a high degree of public or third-party participation in planning, as there is a statutory right of any person, whether having proprietary interest or not, to raise an objection to a draft plan or an application for planning permission.

The Future of Planning by Contract

The contractual nature of planning in Hong Kong has been threatened by legislative activism, which extends the power of statutory plans to regulate temporary uses; narrows the meaning of existing uses; broadens the scope and extent of third-party participation to decisions about planning permissions; and increases the transaction costs of making planning applications. Indeed, the production rate of statutory plans has exceeded that of administrative town plans (Kwong et al. 2021).

Such activism has been propelled by those who have no reasoned sensitivity to the fact that statutory plans have often unilaterally infringed upon the set of common law rights conferred by way of planning by contract without due compensation. Arguably, such infringement is a violation of the spirit and provisions of constitutional capitalism in Hong Kong (Lai 2014).

The above observation should not divert attention away from the fundamental argument of this chapter. The idea of planning by contract as comprehensive public planning by mutual consent that generates huge fiscal revenue should provide some clues for those who wonder about the rapid accumulation of wealth and the emergence of market capitalism in a resource-poor enclave. The heavy involvement of the state in planning by contract testifies to the potency of the idea of properly constrained spontaneity in balancing public and private interests. The state of affairs is also a curious achievement of a kind of "market socialism" by consent between the state and individuals, and between individuals and individuals.

The past economic and environmental success of the land leasing system in Hong Kong is one in which "standard contracts" of planned land rights (i.e., leases drafted by the state) held out for sale are the key. This approach may not be adequate, as it only invites "take it or leave it" decisions based on profit calculation. But equally, the real challenge to the legislator is not a race to impose more restrictions by way of unilaterally imposed town plans that erode property rights, as this strategy does not embody the idea of dialogue that is central to the idea of sustainable development. A meaningful dialogue can hardly be carried out in a setting of commands. A major dimension of this challenge is how this kind of fruitful dialogue can be institutionalized. This should be the subject of another work.

One should note that at all time, there has been no lack of non-governmental charity in Hong Kong, which has been ranked again as the freest economy by the Heritage Foundation until 2019. The amount of cash donation raised by Hong Kong citizens and NGOs for aiding the victims of December 26 tsunami is just one indication that Hong Kong's capitalism, based on a system of planning by contract, does have a human face.

Boundaries Matter

Having explained the particular features of the Hong Kong leasehold system as a planning and development engine, the authors proceed to its actual configuration and operation. Before doing so, they need to understand how Hong Kong's past treaties still affect land administration in the city in terms of rating, land policy.

Figure 3.1 shows the Hong Kong-Mainland Chinese "border" and internal "boundaries" of Hong Kong as a colony and then a special administrative region of the People's Republic of China.

Areas I, II, and III were created, respectively, by the Treaty of Nanking (1842), Convention of Peking (1860), and Convention for the Extension of Hong Kong Territory (1898). Area IV is still called the New Territories. Before 1997, this area was divided into several parts: the Chinese exclave of Kowloon (Walled) City, which resulted from the 1898 treaty; New Kowloon from December 1900 by ordinance, Cheung Chau (under Wong Wai Tsak Tong); and the Border Close Area (which includes the Sha Tau Kok Border Close Area) from the 1950s.

Under the *Sino-British Agreement* and the *Basic Law*, an additional 3% rate was payable for private land (immovable) property in (a) Area III after 30 June 1997 and (b) any land parcel for which a lease was executed after the Agreement.

The small-house policy, the subject of Chap. 14, applies only to Area III outside of New Kowloon and Cheung Chau.

Land under "Block Crown (Government) Leases" (BCL) can be found in Areas I and III.

Unlike their Japanese counterparts in Taiwan, the British colonial administration in Hong Kong did not perform any systematic land readjustment or re-lay the occupied lands for the NT villages except for those in New Kowloon.

Those who think that Hong Kong's old boundaries are "outdated" and hence irrelevant should perhaps ask why there still exists a heavy cross-harbour tariff for the Mass Transit Railway.

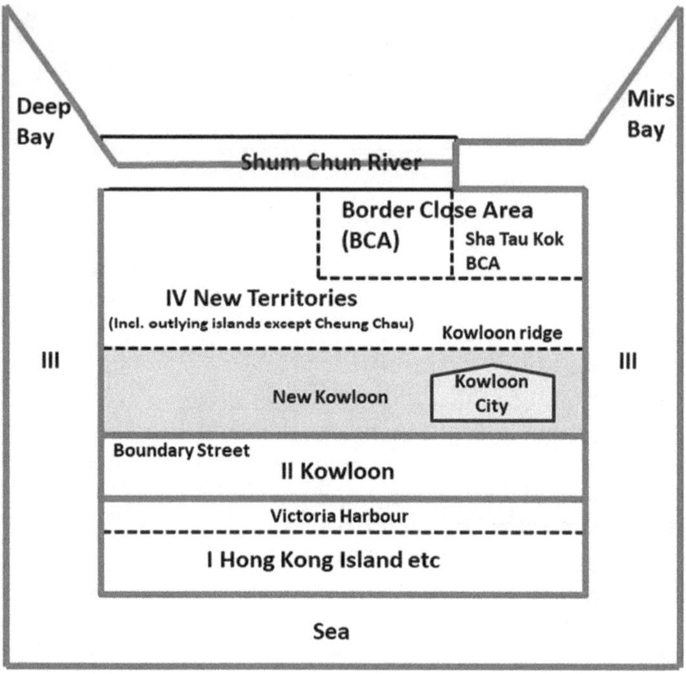

Fig. 3.1 The border and internal boundaries of Hong Kong

Questions for Revision and Discussion

1. Discuss if planning by edict enables better development in the absence of a Government Lease.

The answer is no. Without property rights, no private development is possible in Hong Kong. See Lai, Lawrence W.C. "The leasehold system as a means of planning by contract: the case of Hong Kong." *Town Planning Review* 69, no.3 (1998): 249–275.

2. Browse the pre-war photos of urban Hong Kong on both sides of Victoria Harbour. Prior to the inception of the *Town Planning Ordinance* of 1939, how was urban Hong Kong planned?

It was generally planned for private development with the government laying out the land and allocating leasehold interests by auction or tender, subject to ordinances governing land use and building development. See Lai, Lawrence W.C. & Daniel Chi-wing Ho. *Planning Buildings for a High-rise Environment in Hong Kong: a Review of Building Appeal Decisions.* Hong Kong: Hong Kong University Press, 2000. For specific zones on the Peak and Cheung Chau, see Lai, Lawrence W.C. & Valerius W.C. Kwong. "Racial segregation by legislative zoning and company law: An empirical Hong Kong study." *Environment and Planning B: Planning and Design* 39, no.3 (2012): 416–438.

3. Compare the governance of planning for the land owned by the Shek O Development Company (Lai and Kwong 2012) and Discovery Bay prior to 2000 (Lai et al. 2016).

Residence in the former is only permissible by shareholders of a company with approval by its board of directors.

References

Kwong, Jason W. Y. 2020. Historical Research on Density Zoning: A Development Control Policy Through Administrative Means. *Surveying & Built Environment* 29 (1): 26–38.

Kwong, Jason W. Y., W. C. Lawrence, K. W. Chau Lai, and Vincent N. H. Chan. 2021. A Race Between Urban Growth and Regulation: An Empirical Case Study on the Layout Plan. *Land Use Policy* 101:105184.

Lai, Lawrence W. C. 2011. *The Ideas of Ronald H. Coase: Market Failure and Planning by Contract for Sustainable Development*, Routledge Studies in the History of Economics. 1st ed. Oxon: Abingdon.

Lai, Lawrence W. C. 2014. Planning by Contract: Two Dialogues. Chapter 7 in *Cities and Private Planning: Property Rights, Entrepreneurship and Transaction Costs*, eds. David Andersson and Stefano Moroni, pp. 135–152. Cheltenham: Edward Elgar.

Lai, Lawrence W. C., and Kwong, Jason W. Y. 2025. *Principles of Town Planning Translating Concepts to Applications. Edward* Edward Elgar: Cheltenham.

Lai, Lawrence W. C., and Valerius W. C. Kwong. 2012. Racial Segregation by Legislative Zoning and Company Law: An Empirical Hong Kong Study. *Environment and Planning B: Planning and Design* 39 (3): 416–438.

Lai, Lawrence W. C., and Marco K. W. Yu. 2001. The Rise and Fall of Discriminatory Zoning in Hong Kong. *Environment and Planning B: Planning and Design* 28 (2): 295–314.

Lai, Lawrence W. C., Stephen N. G. Davies, and F. T. Lorne. 2016. Creation of Property Rights in Planning by Contract and Edict: Beyond 'Coasian Bargaining' in Private Planning. *Planning Theory* 15 (4): 418–434.

CHAPTER 4

The Three Types and Sequences of Obtaining Development Approvals

Lawrence Wai Chung Lai

The system of planning and development by contract described as an ideal type in Chap. 2 has, in practice, been transformed into a complicated development approval web for regulating private developments, which naturally favours large developers due to the resources available to them and readiness to hire experts and lobbyists.

Three Powerful Approval and Enforcement Bodies

This approval web has three distinct sectors concerned with Land, Planning, and Building approvals and overseen by three governmental bodies: the Lands Department, Town Planning Board, and Building Authority (BA), respectively.

Approval by the Lands Department is typically required if a Government Lease so prescribes or if the lease needs to be modified. If no prior approval is obtained in these instances, the title of the property becomes defective

L. W. C. Lai (✉)
Department of Real Estate and Construction, The University of Hong Kong, Hong Kong, China
e-mail: wclai@hku.hk

L. W. C. Lai et al. (eds.), *Principles of Land Administration at Work*, https://doi.org/10.1007/978-981-95-2972-8_4

and the government may charge a fine and/or re-enter the land ("re-entry" of land), after which the owner will lose it.

Approval by the Building Authority is always required unless the development is exempted under the *Buildings Ordinance* (BO). If such approval is not obtained, the building is an "unauthorised building work" and cannot be rectified retrospectively. This may trigger re-entry by the Lands Department, as the land lease specifies, or entail sanctions under the *Buildings Ordinance*. Only an "Authorised Person" (AP) under the *Buildings Ordinance* may apply for building permission.

Approval by the Town Planning Board, if the use or development so requires it, is through a valid statutory plan. To obtain such approval one needs go through complicated procedures, which are covered by the book, *Change in Use of Land* (Lai et al. 2017). If such approval is not obtained, the Building Authority shall refuse to grant building permission under s.16 (1) (g) of the *Buildings Ordinance*.

Overlapping Jurisdictions of the Three Authorities

The three aforementioned bodies have overlapping jurisdictions (Lai et al. 2017: p.???).

The Correct Sequence of Obtaining Development Permissions

To understand the logic behind the practice of developers in getting approvals, there is a need to understand the priorities of each element within the three possible pairs of combinations.

Regarding approvals by the Land and Building authorities, the former be obtained first, as any private development that contravenes a lease condition is defective in title and the owner may even lose his title to the land. (**Rule 1: a lease modification should be obtained before getting building permission**.)

Regarding approvals by the Land and Planning authorities, the latter should be obtained first, as the Lands Department usually declines to entertain lease modifications that contravene a statutory town plan and it is risky to pay a modification premium, as the Town Planning Board may not approve the proposed development. (**Rule 2: planning permission shall be obtained before paying a lease modification premium**.)

Regarding approvals by the Building and Planning authorities, the latter should be obtained first, or else the Building Authority cannot approve a building plan to contravene the *Town Planning Ordinance*. (**Rule 3: planning permission shall be obtained before seeking building permission**.)

To a developer, the happiest (but extremely rare) scenario is when none of the three approvals is required, while the "worst" (and increasingly common) case is when all three approvals are required.

In the light of the above analysis, if one ignores the happiest scenario, there are five scenarios for successfully obtaining a development approval:

Scenario 1: Lease Modification Only. This only happens when there is no redevelopment, but a change in the use of an existing building without any need for building permission.
Scenario 2: Planning Permission followed by Lease Modification. Again, this only happens when there is no redevelopment, but a change in the use of an existing building without any need for building permission.
Scenario 3: Lease Modification followed by Building Permission.
Scenario 4: Planning Permission followed by Building Permission.
Scenario 5: Planning Permission followed by Lease Modification followed by Building Permission.

Figure 4.1 is a highly simplified chart that shows the decisions and steps for bringing a proposed building development to the stage in which it seeks building permission. Some steps within the three boxes (for seeking planning permissions, rezoning approvals, and lease modifications) marked by dotted lines can be indefinite loops subject to the resource availability of the applicants, who can make multiple planning applications (Lai et al. 2016).

The *Buildings Ordinance* requires the BA to refuse any proposal for building permission if it contravenes town plans, but has no provision for refusing on the grounds of ownership or contravention of a Government Lease . However, since 2010, the BA started to reject GBPs on the grounds of ownership, and this practice was later supported by the 2015 Court of

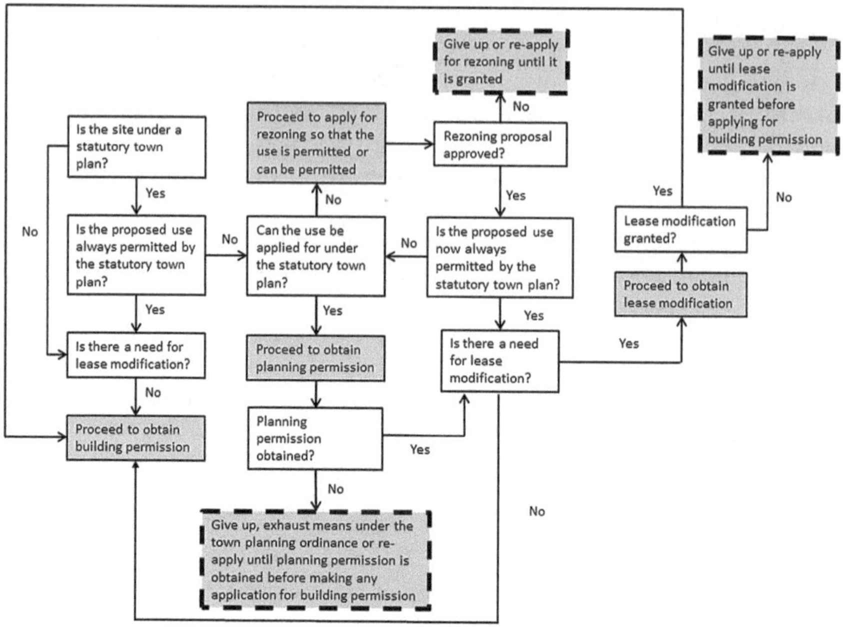

Fig. 4.1 Simplified procedures for obtaining building permission for a proposal to develop a new building for a certain "use" (approval for the general building plans (GBPs))

Final Appeal ruling in *The Real Estate Developers Association of Hong Kong (REDA) vs. Building Authority* case.

The current practice regarding lease matters and building approvals is summarised below:

(1) If a developer cannot demonstrate ownership of a building site, especially in cases that require "land exchanges," the BA may reject its general building plans based on the 2015 Court of Final Appeal ruling on *The Real Estate Developers Association of Hong Kong vs. Building Authority* case.

(2) If land ownership can be demonstrated, but the proposed use is not in compliance with the Government Lease and no objection is received from the Lands Department upon the inter-departmental

circulation of the GBPs before the expiry of the two-month statutory approval period for GBPs, the BA will normally approve them. (Note that the Lands Department will not consider these GBPs as the support for lease modifications or the basis for assessing the premia payable for a modification.)

(3) However, if the BA considers a contravention of the lease as fundamental, it will, under the legal advice regarding the development of *Grand Promenade*, perform its role not only as the BO's administrator, but also as a government officer to safeguard the government's interest. In other words, the BA must reject the plan.

As for what is tantamount to a fundamental contravention is hard to predict, contractually speaking, any departure from the user and/or building restrictions stipulated in a lease would violate that lease.

Informed by current practices, the authors present a very prudent approach in Fig. 4.1 regarding the securing of lease modifications, which is treated as an ownership matter, before applying for building plan approval.

Judicial Reviews of Decisions Regarding Development Applications

Both the Building Authority and Town Planning Board make decisions under ordinances and are judicially reviewable after all statutory provisions for reviews and/or appeals are exhausted.

Decisions by the Lands Department are, generally speaking, not judicially reviewable, as it is hard to establish that they have sufficient public element for review.

The Privy Council case of *Hang Wah Chong Investment Co, Ltd. v Attorney-General [1981] HKLR 336* showed that when the government, as the owner or lessor of government land, decides whether to grant, modify, or terminate a lease or licence, the decision is often taken in the domain of private law and, as such, is not amenable to judicial review.

In 2024 came a Court of Appeal case with the same issue: *Sime Darby Motor Services Limited v Director of Lands [2024] HKCA 207*. The Court held that the Director of Lands' decision to not grant an *in-situ* land exchange for five land lots in Fanling, as they ought to be preserved for indigenous villagers' small-house development, was a decision made squarely within the contractual context of the government acting as private landlord and was, hence, not amenable to judicial review.

Questions for Revision and Discussion

1. The three development approval authorities grew out of the "de-federalization" of the gigantic Public Works Department in 1982. Discuss if combining the three separate approval bodies into one department had fastened and streamlined development planning and control.

   There is no *a priori* reason why a combination is objectionable.

2. "Most Outline Development Plans and Layout Plans are outdated and, hence, are of no relevance for development control." Discuss in terms of the property valuation for the IPO of a company with property land holdings.

   The value of land assets acquired a long time ago may depend on the rights assigned by departmental plans at the time of purchase.

3. Discuss the value effects of the lifespan of a planning permission (Lai et al. 2008).

   The longer it is, the more valuable it would be.

List of Court Cases

Hang Wah Chong Investment Co, Ltd. v Attorney-General [1981] HKLR 336.
The Real Estate Developers Association of Hong Kong vs. Building Authority. Hong Kong Court of Final Appeal No.19 of 2015.
Sime Darby Motor Services Limited v Director of Lands [2024] HKCA 207.

References

Lai, Lawrence W. C., S. K. Wong, Eric C. K. Ho, and K. W. Chau. 2008. Time Is of the Essence? An Empirical Application of the Corollary of the Coase Theorem. *Review of Urban & Regional Development Studies* 20 (1): 34–51.

Lai, Lawrence W. C., Daniel C. W. Ho, Kwong Wing Chau, and Mark H. Chua. 2016. Repeated Planning Applications by Developers Under Statutory Zoning: A Hong Kong Case Study of Delays and Design Improvements in Private Residential Development. *Land Use Policy* 57:709–718.

Lai, Lawrence W. C., Daniel C. W. Ho, and H. F. Leung. 2017. *Change in Use of Land: A Practical Guide to Development in Hong Kong*. 3rd ed. Hong Kong: Hong Kong University Press.

PART II

Basic Areas of Land Administration Knowledge

CHAPTER 5

The Crown/Government Lease and Lease Drafting

K. T. Liu, Valerius W. C. Kwong, and Lawrence Wai Chung Lai

Introduction

The Crown/Government Lease can be seen as the "birth certificate" of a piece of private land. Together with the Conditions of Sale/Grant/Exchange/Regrant/Extension, the lease (or Certificate of Compliance) is the "root of title" of the lot and units developed thereon.

The Leasehold Land System Adopted During British Rule

Hong Kong Island and Kowloon Peninsula (including Stonecutter Island) were ceded to Great Britain in 1842 and 1860, respectively, under two international treaties.

K. T. Liu (✉) • V. W. C. Kwong • L. W. C. Lai
Department of Real Estate and Construction, The University of Hong Kong, Hong Kong, China
e-mail: wclai@hku.hk

L. W. C. Lai et al. (eds.), *Principles of Land Administration at Work*, https://doi.org/10.1007/978-981-95-2972-8_5

It was the Hong Kong government's policy to sell land for a fixed term (time period), only subject to the payment of a standard Crown rent and premium. As a result, all land in Hong Kong legally belonged to the Crown. Interests in land were all granted as leasehold interest except for the Cathedral of the Church of England on Garden Road, which was granted as a freehold estate.

The only true legal difference between leasehold and freehold interests was that for the latter, there was no pre-specified term. Both could be taken back by the Crown by law if there were a need.

An owner or a holder of leasehold land interests enjoyed the land subject to specified term (duration) and conditions contained in the Crown Lease or Crown Grant document, subject to laws enacted as ordinances and regulations from time to time. The terms of the leasehold land lots varied and were a subject for concern of the Colonial Office, which did not favour long-term leases. In any event, some land lots were granted terms of 999 years, and these were once called "virtually perpetual leases." However, most had terms of 75 years plus another 75 years.

Some settled or resettled villages on Hong Kong Island were granted collective leases called "Block Crown Leases" (BCLs). Such leases were, however, far more common in the New Territories, which Britain obtained in 1898, as mentioned below.

The transaction of land/property in Hong Kong and Kowloon was dealt with by lawyers without interference from the government, but there was a need to register transactions with the Land Office (Land Registry).

Britain obtained the New Territories (NT) from China on a 99-year lease that began on 1 July 1898 under an international agreement, which required Britain to respect Chinese customary laws. Settled NT Land was surveyed and divided into Demarcation Districts (DD). For each DD, a DD sheet with numbered lot holdings was drawn after the land was surveyed and a Block Crown Lease (BCL) produced. The BCL records formed a schedule of the name(s) of the owner(s) within an area and the existing land use of each numbered lot within the DD.

The BCL and subsequent land grants in the NT were typically for a term of "75 years plus 24" years, or "99 years from 1 July 1898," but, in any case, "less the last 3 days."

Land transactions in NT were allowed to take place in the District Office. However, this system eventually merged with the same system for Hong Kong and Kowloon from the 1980s.

From 1984, all references to "Crown" in the land documents became "Government" whether or not the transaction occurred before 1984.

What happened under the colonial land system, as outlined above until 30 June 1997, has been allowed to continue after 1 July 1997 and land interests obtained since that date have remained legally valid and binding, as stated by the *Basic Law*.

The Leasehold Land System After 30 June 1997 Under Chinese Sovereignty

Under the *Basic Law*, all land belongs to the state, and the HKSAR government, is authorised to manage and lease such land.

The *Basic Law* holds as valid and binding all Government Leases that were granted by the colonial government before 1 July 1997 anywhere in Hong Kong. The *Basic Law* also expressly protects the rights of "indigenous villagers" in the New Territories.

Owners of interests granted under leases for the New Territories at any time, those leased anywhere in Hong Kong during the period 27 May 1985 to 30 June 1997 (all with terms not expiring after 30 June 2047), and leases anywhere in Hong Kong granted after 30 June 1997 are all subject to the payment of government rent equivalent to 3% of the rateable value of the property. Owners of interests granted in Hong Kong and Kowloon granted before 27 May 1985 are not liable for such rent.

The Current Land Allocation Policy of Government

It is the government's policy to grant leasehold interests for specific types of development for fixed terms by:

(a) Public auction—sale of land interests to the highest bidder in an open auction
(b) Public tender
(c) Private treaty—sale of land to specific individuals or bodies at market or concessionary prices in special circumstances, sometimes requiring the permission of the Executive Council

Aspects of the Land Grant Documents

The land grant documents are a set of documents with interests obtained contractually and "running with the land" between the government (grantor/landlord/lessor) and the grantee/lessee. They include:

(1) Conditions of sale/conditions of regrant/conditions of exchange/conditions of extension
(2) Crown/Government Lease; Block Government Lease and New Grants (the former are found mainly and the latter solely in the New Territories)
(3) Tenancy agreements

A land grant document always shows:

(1) A unique lot number
  (a) Names of parties to the grant: the government, the grantor as lessor and the grantee as lessee
  (b) A written description of the lot with dimensions
  (c) A site plan of the lot/lot map

A land grant document usually contains the following terms and conditions:

(1) Term/Tenure: renewable/non-renewable—such as 999 years, 75 years, 99 years (non-renewable), 75 years plus 75 years, 99 years plus 99 years (renewable)
(2) Crown (Government) rent payable
(3) Site area–with a written description and a site plan
(4) Building covenants—the obligation to complete a building of a specified worth or of a certain gross floor area (GFA) within a specified period of time
(5) Development clause–restrictions on such matters:
  (a) Type of buildings, e.g. "a European-type house," "one detached residence (or dwelling)," "one semi-detached European-style residence (or dwelling)"
  (b) Building height in terms of storeys, feet (metres), e.g. "a building not exceeding 35 feet (10.668 metres) in height"
  (c) Site coverage, plot ratio, gross floor area (GFA)

(6) User restriction/clause, such as for:
  (a) Residential use
  (b) European-type house
  (c) Commercial/residential use
  (d) Private residential purposes
  (e) Non-industrial use
  (f) Industrial use
  (g) Industrial/office use
  (h) Commercial use
  (i) Government reservations, such as:
    i. Right of way
    ii. Easement
  (j) Resumption clause–the government reserves the right to resume the land for public use subject to a three-month notice and the payment of fair compensation
  (k) Non-offensive ("obnoxious") trade clause
  (l) "Rate and Range" clause
  (m) "Design Disposition and Height" (DDH) clause

For newer Conditions of Sale/Grant/Exchange/Regrant/Extension and Conditions of Modification, the following clauses are usually incorporated:

(1) Premium
(2) A detailed definition and description of the "user" (land use)
(3) Compliance with the *Buildings Ordinance*, *Town Planning Ordinance* and other ordinances
(4) A landscaping clause
(5) Restrictions on alienation before compliance clause/consent for pre-sale
(6) Restrictions against partitioning clause
(7) Provision of sales office and show flats clause
(8) Standard recreational facilities clause
(9) Deed of Mutual Covenant (DMC) incorporating management agreement clause

"Unrestricted Leases"

For valuation purposes, the less restrictive are the lease conditions, *ceteris paribus*, the higher is the value of the lot. Many old urban leases under 999-year terms are supposedly "unrestricted," but are actually mostly subjected to a non-offensive ("obnoxious") trade clause that lists a host of old trades such as tavern, oilman, lard boiling, etc.

The Lands Department tends to have a wide modern reinterpretation of this clause to deem a petrol-filling station an oilman.

One developer owns land on Hong Kong Island under a completely unrestricted lease and, hence, there is no need to modify its lease.

Typical Colours on Lease Plans

The colour code may differ from lease to lease. For details, refer to the conditions or clauses of each lease. Figure 5.1 shows the typical colour codes on lease plans in modern leases.

Only areas under coloured pink are "private lot" areas. Non-pink areas are government land.

Rural Lots in the New Territories

For dealing with land matters in the New Territories, the first step is to ascertain two main pieces of information: (1) lot number and (2) type of land grant.

(1) Lot No.: e.g. Lot No.123 in Demarcation District 12 (DD12 Lot123)
(2) Types of government grant:
   (a) Block Government Leases (Block Crown/Government Lease)
   (b) New Grants

Lots Under Block Crown/Government Leases (BCL/BGL)

Lots under Block Crown/Government Leases (BCLs/BGLs) are grouped by "Demarcation District" (DD) and planimetrically recorded on survey maps called DD sheets. They are often called "Old Schedule Lots" or DD Lots."

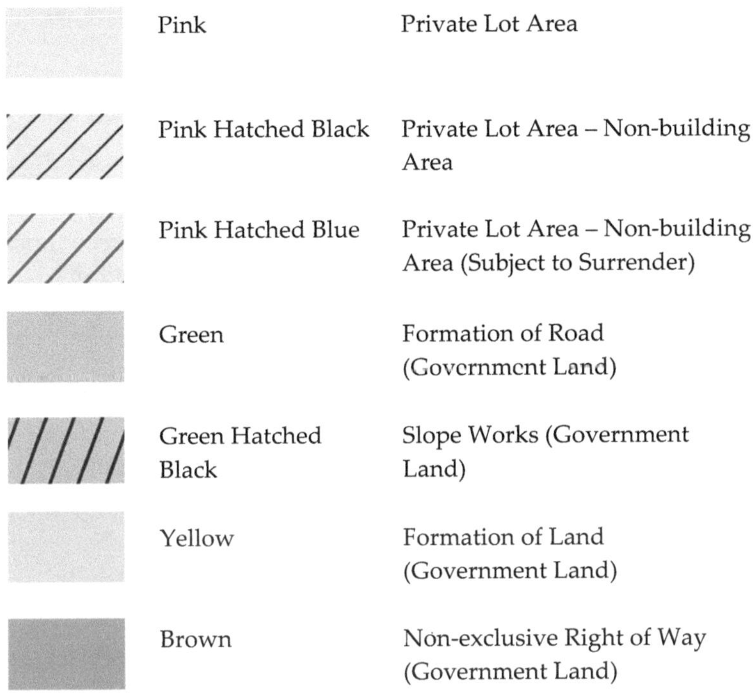

Fig. 5.1 Typical colours on lease plans

Unlike urban lots, which are generally rectilinear in shape and on levelled sites, DD lots are normally irregularly shaped and sized and often situated on unlevel ground. They are remnants of traditional Chinese farmland parcels that were recorded on the registers of San On County during Imperial Chinese times.

The contents of a BGL include:

(1) A copy of a standard lease–one is not allowed to build on agricultural land
(2) A schedule recording the land ownership in 1905
(3) A DD sheet showing the boundaries of individual lots with their own unique lot numbers, along with roads, paths and watercourses
(4) A "schedule of Crown lessees" showing:

(a) Lease term: 75 years from 1898, but statutorily renewed for another 24 years and extended thereafter to 30 June 2047
(b) Lot numbers, as indicated on the DD Sheet
(c) Area of each lot: in terms of "X" acres with the smallest unit being 0.01 acre, which does not necessarily equal 435.6 sf. onsite
(d) A brief description of the land use (User), such as "Dry Cultivation," "Padi" (rice), "Waste," "Latrine," "House" or "Building"
(e) Names of the owner(s), both human persons and communal/ancestral body ("T'so"/"Tong") in Chinese and English
(f) Crown rent (now called government rent) in terms of "X" per cent (replaced by 3% of the rateable value of the property after 1 July 1997)

The lots contained in the schedule are commonly called "Old Schedule Lots."

Lots Under New Grants

Lots granted by the colonial government after the granting of the BCL are commonly called "New Grant Lots."

Like urban lots, these lots are generally rectilinear in shape and on levelled sites. They may or may not be part of a layout.

The contents of a New Grant document could be very simple and lengthy and will always contain the following elements: Certificate of Compliance

(1) Lease term: normally 75 plus 24 years from 1 July 1898 or 99 years from 1 July 1898 minus the last three days (as further extended to 30 June 2047 subject to the payment of government rent equivalent to 3% of the rateable value of the property)
(2) Government rent
(3) Premium
(4) Lot area
(5) User restrictions
(6) Development restrictions
(7) Location plan (not necessarily available in the old New Grants)

Gazette notices (GN) were issued from time to time for the blanket control of New Grants Lots (NGLs).

Short-Term Tenancy

See Chap. 8.

Lease Drafting

Throughout time, lease conditions have become increasingly elaborate, but there is no standard rubric for lease drafting. The bureaucratic tendency to "play safe" entails that with time, a grantor adds more covenants to the lease conditions, especially when the economy grows so fast that it appears it would never come down.

However, one must never presume that the way of drafting is stable even in the "short run." The best advice to follow is to examine a lease lot by lot, especially those allocated along the same street at about the same time. The 95 ways of drafting users' restrictions for rural building lots (RBLs) found in the Land Registry, as shown in Table 5.1 and based on the work of Kwong (2008), along with the 26 ways of doing so for industrial leases, as shown in Chap. 9, remind readers that great care must be taken to interpret the leases for a particular locale.

To control NT "New Grant Lots," the colonial government issued via gazette government notifications (GNs) some standard General Conditions and Special Conditions of Sale with the most famous being GN 364 (1934). These GNs still apply. As the selection of any or all of these for each new grant lot is entirely up to the government, one must not presume that all conditions apply to a lot.

Questions for Revision and Discussion

1. Discuss the differences between Government Leases in Hong Kong's urban areas and Block Crown/Government Leases in the New Territories.

With a few exceptions, each lot on Hong Kong Island, in Kowloon, and New Kowloon has a lease plan and conditions.

Crown/Government Leases in urban areas are typically granted for specific plots of land and are often subject to covenants tailor-made for each of them. Block Crown/Government Leases (BGLs) in the New Territories were issued for a total of 477 land parcels or "blocks" (Demarcation Districts, or DD) with lots devoted to agricultural, residential or other specific purposes at the time they were surveyed.

Table 5.1 Summary of main categories of user/building restriction clauses of 312 land lots on The Peak and owned by the Shek O Development Corporation

Category	*Key requirements of user/building restrictive clauses*	*Year (no. of samples)*
I	Promotion of charitable design	[1883] (1 sample)
II	No. of house/block/building(s) + Special approval for design of exterior elevation, the disposition or building height + Height restrictions	[1888–1954] (2 samples)
III	Special approval for design of exterior elevation, the disposition or building height	[1889–1951] (2 samples)
IV	Non-offensive trade	[1901–1971] (69 samples)
V	Garden purpose + No erection of building/flat(s)	[1901–1954] (12 samples)
VI	Non-offensive trade + No. of house/block/building(s) + ***European style house*** + Special approval for design of exterior elevation, the disposition or building height + Height restrictions	[1920–1972] (23 samples)
VII	Non-offensive trade + No. of house/block/building(s) + Special approval for design of exterior elevation, the disposition or building height + Height restrictions	[1920–1939] (8 samples)
VIII	No. of house/block/building(s) + ***European style house*** + Special approval for design of exterior elevation, the disposition or building height	[1920–1961] (6 samples)
IX	Non-offensive trade + No. of house/block/building(s)	[1922–1925] (3 samples)
X	Non-offensive trade + No. of house/block/building(s) + Height restrictions	[1922–1924] (5 samples)
XI	Non-offensive trade + Hospital purpose	[1926–1964 (2 samples)]
XII	Non-offensive trade + No. of house/block/building(s) + Height restrictions + ***European style house*** + Special approval for design of exterior elevation, the disposition or building height + ***Application for the consent of Governor for residence***	[1928] (1 sample)
XIII	Non-offensive trade + No. of house/block/building(s) + ***European style house*** + Special approval for design of exterior elevation, the disposition or building height	[1930–1976] (7 samples)
XIV	Non-offensive trade + No erection of building/flat(s)	[1932–1954] (3 samples)

(*continued*)

Table 5.1 (continued)

Category	*Key requirements of user/building restrictive clauses*	*Year (no. of samples)*
XV	Non-offensive trade + ***European style house*** + ***Restriction against assigning any right or benefit under the demise without the consent of the Governor-in-Council having first been obtained*** + Special approval for design of exterior elevation, the disposition or building + Domestic building purpose + No hotel, boarding house, shop or business premises erected	[1934–1941] (12 samples)
XVI	Non-offensive trade + ***European style house*** + ***Restriction against assigning any right or benefit under the demise without the consent of the Governor-in-Council having first been obtained*** + Special approval for design of exterior elevation, the disposition or building height + No hotel, boarding house, shop or business premises erected + Domestic building purpose (or golf club house purpose)	[1934] (1 sample)
XVII	***Restriction against assigning any right or benefit under the demise without the consent of the Governor-in-Council having first been obtained*** + Garden purpose + No erection of building/flat(s)	[1934–1987] (7 samples)
XVIII	***Restriction against assigning any right or benefit under the demise without the consent of the Governor-in-Council having first been obtained*** + Garden purpose + No erection of building/flat(s) + Conversion into RBL(s)	[1934] (2 samples)
XIX	Conversion into RBL(s) + ***European-type house*** (for conversion lot only) + ***Restriction against assigning any right or benefit under the demise without the consent of the Governor-in-Council having first been obtained*** + Domestic building purpose + No hotel, boarding house, shop or business premises erected	[1934] (1 sample)
XX	No. of house/block/building(s) + ***European style house*** + Special approval for design of exterior elevation, the disposition or building height + Height restrictions	[1935] (1 sample)
XXI	No. of house/block/building(s) + ***European style house*** + Special approval for design of exterior elevation, the disposition or building height + Height restrictions	[1935] (1 sample)
XXII	Non-offensive trade + Special approval for design of exterior elevation, the disposition or building height + Height restrictions	[1939–1954] (2 samples)
XXIII	Non-offensive trade + Special approval for design of exterior elevation, the disposition or building height	[1948–1970] (49 samples)

(*continued*)

Table 5.1 (continued)

Category	*Key requirements of user/building restrictive clauses*	*Year (no. of samples)*
XXIV	Private residential purpose + No. of house/block/ building(s) + No. of storey(s) + Height restrictions + Special approval for design of exterior elevation, the disposition or building height + No partitioning + Site coverage	[1948] (1 sample)
XXV	Non-offensive trade + No. of house/block/building(s) + Special approval for design of exterior elevation, the disposition or building height	[1949–1970] (2 samples)
XXVI	DMC (Deed of Mutual Covenant)	[1951] (1 samples)
XXVII	Non-offensive trade + No. of house/block/building(s) + ***European style house*** + ***Restriction against assigning any right or benefit under the demise without the consent of the Governor-in-Council having first been obtained***	[1952–1955] (2 samples)
XXVIII	***European style house*** + Special approval for design of exterior elevation, the disposition or building height + Private residential purpose	[1952] (1 sample)
XXIX	Non-industrial purpose + No factory building(s) + Special approval for design of exterior elevation, the disposition or building height	[1952] (1 sample)
XXX	No. of house/block/building(s) + ***European style house*** + ***Restriction against assigning any right or benefit under the demise without the consent of the Governor-in-Council having first been obtained*** + Special approval for design of exterior elevation, the disposition or building	[1953] (1 sample)
XXXI	Non-offensive trade + No. of house/block/building(s) + ***European style house*** + Special approval for design of exterior elevation, the disposition or building height + Further residential restriction for and during the period of 20 years from and after the date of commencement	[1954–1955] (2 samples)
XXXII	Non-offensive trade + No. of storey(s) + Special approval for design of exterior elevation, the disposition or building height + Private residential purpose	[1955–1965] (3 samples)
XXXIII	Non-offensive trade + Special approval for design of exterior elevation, the disposition or building height + Private residential purpose	[1956–1971] (2 samples)
XXXIV	No. of storey(s) + ***European style house*** + Special approval for design of exterior elevation, the disposition or building height + Height restrictions	[1956] (1 sample)

(*continued*)

Table 5.1 (continued)

Category	*Key requirements of user/building restrictive clauses*	*Year (no. of samples)*
XXXV	Non-offensive trade + No. of house/block/building(s) + No. of storey(s) + Special approval for design of exterior elevation, the disposition or building height + Private residential purpose + No erection of building/flat(s)	[1960] (1 sample)
XXXVI	Special approval for design of exterior elevation, the disposition or building height + Private residential purpose + Height restrictions + Site coverage + No partitioning	[1960] (1 sample)
XXXVII	Special approval for design of exterior elevation, the disposition or building height + Private residential purpose + Site coverage + No partitioning + Car park purpose + Non-building area	[1960] (1 sample)
XXXVIII	***European style house*** + Special approval for design of exterior elevation, the disposition or building + Domestic building purpose + ***Restriction against assigning any right or benefit under the demise without the consent of the Governor-in-Council having first been obtained*** + No hotel, boarding house, shop or business premises erected + Non-building area	[1961] (1 sample)
XXXIX	***European style house*** + ***Restriction against assigning any right or benefit under the demise without the consent of the Governor-in-Council having first been obtained*** + Special approval for design of exterior elevation, the disposition or building + Domestic building purpose + No hotel, boarding house, shop or business premises erected	[1962] (1 sample)
XL	No. of house/block/building(s) + No. of storey(s) + Special approval for design of exterior elevation, the disposition or building height + Site coverage + Car park purpose + Private residential purpose + Height restrictions + Non-building area	[1963] (2 samples)
XLI	No. of house/block/building(s) + No. of storey(s) + Special approval for design of exterior elevation, the disposition or building height + Site coverage + Private residential purpose + Non-building area	[1963] (1 sample)
XLII	No. of storey(s) + Special approval for design of exterior elevation, the disposition or building height + Site coverage + Private residential purpose + No partitioning	[1963–1972] (3 samples)
XLIII	No. of storey(s) + Private residential purpose + Site coverage	[1963] (1 sample)
XLIV	No. of storey(s) + Site coverage + Private residential purpose + Non-building area + No partitioning	[1963] (1 sample)

(*continued*)

Table 5.1 (continued)

Category	*Key requirements of user/building restrictive clauses*	*Year (no. of samples)*
XLV	Non-offensive trade + No. of house/block/building(s) + Special approval for design of exterior elevation, the disposition or building + Private residential purpose + No erection of building/flat(s) + Car park purpose	[1964] (1 sample)
XLVI	No. of house/block/building(s) + Special approval for design of exterior elevation, the disposition or building height + Site coverage + Car park purpose + Private residential purpose + Height restrictions + Non-building area	[1964] (1 sample)
XLVII	Special approval for design of exterior elevation, the disposition or building height + Site coverage + No partitioning + Private residential purpose	[1964] (1 sample)
XLVIII	Non-offensive trade + Garden purpose + Garage purpose	[1965] (1 sample)
XLIX	Non-offensive trade + No. of house/block/building(s) + No. of storey(s) + ***European style house***	[1965] (1 sample)
L	Non-offensive trade + No. of house/block/building(s) + No. of storey(s) + Private residential purpose + Car park purpose + Special approval for design of exterior elevation, the disposition or building height + No erection of building/flat(s)	[1965] (1 sample)
LI	Non-offensive trade + No. of house/block/building(s) + No. of storey(s) + ***European style house*** + Special approval for design of exterior elevation, the disposition or building height	[1966] (1 sample)
LII	Non-offensive trade + No. of house/block/building(s) + No. of storey(s) + ***European style house*** + Special approval for design of exterior elevation, the disposition or building height + Private residential purpose + Site coverage + Car park purpose + No partitioning	[1967] (1 sample)
LIII	Non-offensive trade + Special approval for design of exterior elevation, the disposition or building height + DMC	[1967] (1 sample)
LIV	Non-offensive trade + No. of house/block/building(s) + ***European style house*** + Special approval for design of exterior elevation, the disposition or building height + Private residential purpose	[1969] (1 sample)
LV	Non-offensive trade + No. of house/block/building(s) + Special approval for design disposition or building height + Height restrictions + Electrical substation purpose	[1969] (1 sample)

(*continued*)

Table 5.1 (continued)

Category	*Key requirements of user/building restrictive clauses*	*Year (no. of samples)*
LVI	Non-offensive trade + No. of storey(s) + Special approval for design of exterior elevation, the disposition or building height + Non-building area + Workshop purpose + Private residential purpose	[1969] (1 sample)
LVII	Non-offensive trade + Private residential purpose + ***European style house*** + Special approval for design of exterior elevation, the disposition or building height	[1969] (1 sample)
LVIII	No. of storey(s) + Special approval for design of exterior elevation, the disposition or building height + Private residential purpose + Maximum GFA and site coverage + No partitioning + Car park purpose	[1969–1976] (2 samples)
LIX	Special approval for design of exterior elevation, the disposition or building height + Private residential purpose + Site coverage + No partitioning + Car park purpose + Height restrictions + Non-building area	[1969–1972] (3 samples)
LX	Air-conditioning purpose	[1970] (1 sample)
LXI	Non-offensive trade + DMC + Private residential purpose + Special approval for design of exterior elevation, the disposition or building height	[1970] (1 sample)
LXII	No. of house/block/building(s) + Private residential purpose + Site coverage	[1971] (1 sample)
LXIII	Special approval for design of exterior elevation, the disposition or building height + School purpose + Treating all national groups alike + Non-building area + Height restrictions	[1971–1976] (2 samples)
LXIV	No. of storey(s) + Special approval for design of exterior elevation, the disposition or building height + Private residential purpose + Site coverage + No partitioning + Non-building area + Watchmen's or caretakers' office/ accommodation	[1972] (1 sample)
LXV	Non-offensive trade + ***Restriction against assigning any right or benefit under the demise without the consent of the Governor-in-Council having first been obtained*** + No hotel, boarding house, shop or business premises erected + Special approval for design of exterior elevation, the disposition or building + Height restrictions	[1972] (1 sample)
LXVI	Non-offensive trade + Private residential purpose	[1972] (1 sample)

(*continued*)

Table 5.1 (continued)

Category	*Key requirements of user/building restrictive clauses*	*Year (no. of samples)*
LXVII	No. of storey(s) + Special approval for design of exterior elevation, the disposition or building height + Private residential purpose + Maximum GFA and site coverage + No partitioning + Car park purpose + Height restrictions + Non-building area + Clothes drying purpose	[1972] (1 sample)
LXVIII	No. of storey(s) + Special approval for design of exterior elevation, the disposition or building height + Private residential purpose + Maximum GFA and site coverage + No partitioning + Car park purpose + Non-building area	[1972] (1 sample)
LXIX	Non-offensive trade + Industrial purpose + No factory building(s) + Toilet and lavatory accommodation	[1973] (1 sample)
LXX	Non-offensive trade + Special approval for design of exterior elevation, the disposition or building height + Industrial purpose + No factory building(s) + Toilet and lavatory accommodation	[1973] (1 sample)
LXXI	Special approval for design of exterior elevation, the disposition or building height + Maximum GFA and site coverage + No partitioning + Car park purpose	[1974] (1 sample)
LXXII	Special approval for design of exterior elevation, the disposition or building height + Private residential purpose + Car park purpose + DMC	[1977] (1 sample)
LXXIII	No. of storey(s) + Special approval for design of exterior elevation, the disposition or building height + Private residential purpose + Maximum GFA and site coverage + No partitioning + Car park purpose + Storage/temporary structure purpose + Non-building area + Watchmen's or caretakers' office/accommodation + Swimming pool purpose	[1979] (1 sample)
LXXIV	No. of house/block/building(s) + Special approval for design of exterior elevation, the disposition or building height + Private residential purpose + Maximum GFA + No partitioning + Car park purpose + Swimming pool purpose + Garden purpose + Non-building area	[1980] (1 sample)
LXXV	No. of storey(s) + Special approval for design of exterior elevation, the disposition or building height + Private residential purpose + Maximum GFA and site coverage + No partitioning + Car park purpose + Height restrictions + Storage/temporary structure purpose + Recreational facilities purpose + Watchmen's or caretakers' office/ accommodation + Non-building area + DMC + Government accommodation	[1982] (1 sample)

(*continued*)

Table 5.1 (continued)

Category	*Key requirements of user/building restrictive clauses*	*Year (no. of samples)*
LXXVI	Special approval for design of exterior elevation, the disposition or building height + Private residential purpose + Maximum GFA and site coverage + No partitioning + Car park purpose + Height restrictions + Storage/temporary structure purpose + Recreational facilities purpose + Watchmen's or caretakers' office/accommodation + Non-building area + DMC + Government accommodation	[1982] (1 sample)
LXXVII	No. of house/block/building(s) + Special approval for design of exterior elevation, the disposition or building height + Car park purpose + Storage/temporary structure purpose + Watchmen's or caretakers' office/accommodation + school purpose + Treating all national groups alike + Non-building area	[1983] (1 sample)
LXXVIII	Petrol filling station purpose + No. of storey(s) + Special approval for design of exterior elevation, the disposition or building height + No partitioning + Watchmen's or caretakers' office/accommodation	[1987] (1 sample)
LXXIX	Petrol filling station purpose + No. of storey(s) + Special approval for design of exterior elevation, the disposition or building height + Watchmen's or caretakers' office/accommodation	[1987] (1 sample)
LXXX	Special approval for design of exterior elevation, the disposition or building height + Private residential purpose + Maximum GFA and site coverage + No partitioning + Car park purpose + DMC + Recreational facilities purpose + Watchmen's or caretakers' office/accommodation + Non-building area + Height restrictions	[1987] (1 sample)
LXXXI	Non-industrial (excluding godown) purpose + Recreational facilitates purpose + Non-building area	[1990] (1 sample)
LXXXII	Radio communication station purpose	[1991] (1 sample)
LXXXIII	Telecommunication station purpose	[1991] (1 sample)
LXXXIV	No. of storey(s) + Special approval for design of exterior elevation, the disposition or building height + Private residential purpose + Maximum GFA and site coverage + No partitioning + Car park purpose + DMC + Recreational facilities purpose + Watchmen's or caretakers' office/accommodation + Non-building area	[1991–2000] (3 samples)

(*continued*)

Table 5.1 (continued)

Category	*Key requirements of user/building restrictive clauses*	*Year (no. of samples)*
LXXXV	Special approval for design of exterior elevation, the disposition or building height + School purpose + No partitioning + Car park purpose + Watchmen's or caretakers' office/accommodation + Height restrictions	[1991] (1 sample)
LXXXVI	No. of house/block/building(s)+ No. of storey(s) + Special approval for design of exterior elevation, the disposition or building height + Private residential purpose + Maximum GFA and site coverage + No partitioning + Car park purpose + Recreational facilities purpose + Watchmen's or caretakers' office/accommodation + Non-building area	[1992] (1 sample)
LXXXVII	Special approval for design of exterior elevation, the disposition or building height + No residential, industrial, godown or petrol filling station purpose(s) + Maximum GFA + Height restrictions + Toilet and lavatory accommodation + Peak Tramway purpose	[1994] (1 sample)
LXXXVIII	No. of storey(s) + Special approval for design of exterior elevation, the disposition or building height + Private residential purpose (excluding service apartment) + Maximum GFA and site coverage + No partitioning + Car park purpose + DMC	[1995–1997] (2 samples)
LXXXIX	Private residential purpose + Site coverage + Car park purpose + Non-building area	[1996] (1 sample)
XC	No. of storey(s) + Special approval for design of exterior elevation, the disposition or building height + Private residential purpose + Car park purpose + Maximum GFA and site coverage + No partitioning	[1997] (1 sample)
XCI	Special approval for design of exterior elevation, the disposition or building height + Private residential purpose (excluding service apartment) + Maximum GFA and site coverage + No partitioning + Car park purpose + Recreational facilities purpose + Watchmen's or caretakers' office/accommodation + Non-building area + DMC	[1999] (1 sample)
XCII	Special approval for design of exterior elevation, the disposition or building height + Private residential purpose (excluding service apartment) + Maximum GFA and site coverage + No partitioning + Car park purpose + Recreational facilities purpose + Watchmen's or caretakers' office/accommodation + DMC	[1999] (1 sample)

(*continued*)

Table 5.1 (continued)

Category	*Key requirements of user/building restrictive clauses*	*Year (no. of samples)*
XCIII	No. of storey(s) + Special approval for design of exterior elevation, the disposition or building height + Private residential purpose + Maximum GFA and site coverage + No partitioning + Car park purpose + Recreational facilities purpose + Watchmen's or caretakers' office/ accommodation + DMC	[2002] (1 sample)
XCIV	***Restriction against assigning any right or benefit under the demise without the consent of the Director having first been obtained*** + Garden purpose + No erection of building/flat(s) + No partitioning	[2004] (1 sample)
XCV	Unclassified Group (The Crown/Government Lease and Conditions were inspected but essential data is either missing or incomplete)	[1881–1901] (5 samples)

The lease plans (DD sheets), as part of the BGLs, are either 1:3,960-scale (16" to one mile) or 1:1,980-scale (32" to one mile), while lease plans for Crown Leases (whether town or farm lots) may assume various scales or units. The land parcels, as shown on the DD sheets, were only graphically depicted with no dimension, while fixed dimensions and areas (whether they were accurate or not is another matter) are shown on the lease plans of non-BGLs.

According to the *Melhado* decision, matters under the column, "Description of Lot," in the BGL are only "descriptive" of the plot's use at the time of the NT land survey and do not "restrict" land use. This means, subject to the applicable ordinance, open storage is permitted on any leased land.

Government Leases on the planned (urbanised) areas of Hong Kong Island, Kowloon, New Kowloon and the New Territories (especially arras designated "new towns") may have different lease terms (varying from 10 to 999 years), while BGLs in the New Territories all have a 75-year lease terms commencing from 1 January 1898 and are renewable for 24 years. A term is deemed to have been renewed under and by virtue of the *New Territories (Renewable Government Leases) Ordinance* (Cap.152) and was extended until 30 June 2047 under Section 6 of the *New Territories Leases (Extension) Ordinance* (Cap.150).

Government Leases in urban areas: After the enactment of the *Conveyancing and Property Ordinance (Chapter 219)*, no paper lease has been issued. A land grant document and Certificate of Compliance are "the root titles" of the land.

2. Discuss the strengths and weaknesses of unrestricted leases.

An unrestricted lease allows the lessee to make changes in land use, subject to statutory planning, without the need to modify the terms of the lease or pay any premium.

Reference

Kwong, Valerius W. C. 2008. *Voluntary and Imposed Racial Segregation Zoning: A Coasian-Olson Hong Kong Comparative Empirical Analysis*. PhD Thesis, Department of Real Estate & Construction, University of Hong Kong.

CHAPTER 6

Modifications of Crown/Government Leases

Jason Wai Yin Kwong

Introduction

Any lease condition and boundary stipulated in a Crown/Government Lease arises from a contract of sale between the state and a non-government party and can be modified by mutual consent and deed.

"Lease modification" is a local jargon which refers to any variation of (a) existing covenants or conditions of a Crown (Government) Lease or any land grant document; and/or (b) the boundary of a lot.

The modification is a matter of mutual agreement between the Government (i.e., the Lands Department) as the lessor and the applicant as the lessee.

Neither the government's decision to permit modification nor the amount of premium it assesses is reviewable by the court. This is based on the fact that members of the public other than the Lessee are strangers (third parties) to the agreement and no judicial review application is valid unless the lease conditions *expressly provide for some kind of public participation or compliance with certain ordinances.*

J. W. Y. Kwong (✉)
Department of Real Estate and Construction, The University of Hong Kong, Hong Kong, China

L. W. C. Lai et al. (eds.), *Principles of Land Administration at Work*, https://doi.org/10.1007/978-981-95-2972-8_6

The Applicant for a Lease Modification

As a land lease is a contract/covenant between the government and lessee (i.e., the landowner; the registered owner), only a lessee can submit a lease modification or any land transaction application to the Lands Department. The Lands Department will verify the applicant's status by checking title records under the Land Registry, while the lessee could appoint an agent (i.e., a land consultant and generally a general practice surveyor) to submit a lease modification on his/her behalf to the Lands Department via a written authorisation letter.

In case the concerned lot(s)/property is under transaction, a prospective buyer who signs a registered agreement for sale and purchase could also submit a lease modification application with the written consent of the registered owner.

The tenant or occupant of a property is not eligible to submit a land application.

Short-Term and Long-Term Lease Modifications

In general, lease modification applications can be divided into two types, short term and long term. The former refers mainly to waivers, short-term waivers, and temporary waivers, while the latter includes modification letters, no-objection letters, land exchanges, and lease extensions.

The differences among four types of short-term or long-term modifications by way of temporary/special waivers or no-objection/modification letters are summarised in Table 6.1.

Short-Term and Temporary Waiver Applications

Short-term waivers generally refer to the exemptions from certain lease conditions such as those that disallow temporary structures to be erected on agricultural lots under Block Crown Leases. Temporary waivers refer to waivers for uses within buildings such as those allowing a retail use within ground floor workshops or a canteen use in industrial lots.

Both short-term and temporary waivers have time limits. Generally, the Lands Department allows an initial fixed term of one to three years and then quarterly/yearly if it is renewed.

Table 6.1 Comparison of four types of short-term or long-term modifications

	Temporary Waiver	*Special Waiver*	*No-Objection Letter*	*Modification Letter*
Description	"Temporary" relaxation	"Long-Term" modification		
Premises	One unit or part of a building	Entire existing industrial building	One unit or part of a building	Whole lot
Term (duration)	Temporary in nature	Lifetime of a building		Permanent in nature
Fee payable	Waiver fee (if any) + administrative Fee	No waiver fee but administrative fee	Land premium + an administrative fee	
Fee/Premium amount	Standard rate/increase in market rental value of the premises arising from the change	N/A	Enhancement in value of the unit or part of the building	Enhancement in land value
Payment terms	Quarterly and reviewed tri-annually or one-off payment	N/A	One-off payment of the premium at the outset	

It should be noted that a temporary waiver is a personal interest, which does not "run with land". If the land or unit witnesses a change in ownership, a new waiver application for it is required.

A waiver fee will be charged for granting waiver approvals to reflect the rental value differences between the "before" and "after" value of the scenarios pertaining to the waiver application. The waiver fee is reviewed triennially.

Lease Modifications *Versus* Land Exchanges

A land exchange is one way to modify a lease. In a land exchange, a surrender and re-grant of the land concerned is executed. The old lot is surrendered to the government, which will grant a new lot with a new term of 50 years and a new lot number.

The Lands Department prefers a land exchange over a lease modification in case of three situations:

(1) A readjustment to lot boundaries or an amalgamation of lots.
(2) An imposition of complex development lease conditions.
(3) A complex title or legal conveyancing problem.

The differences between a lease modification and land exchange are summarised in Table 6.2.

Table 6.2 Differences between lease modifications and land exchanges

	Upon lease modification	*Upon land exchange*
Original lot area/ boundary	No change	Changed • Amalgamation of lots • Inclusion of Gov. land • Minor adjustments to a lot boundary—say, to follow a zoning boundary
Old lease terms	No change	New term of 50 years
Land rent	Nil unless land is in the New Territories or was purchased after the Sino-British Joint Declaration	Definitely payable
Original lot number	No change	New Lot No.

As the term of any new lot after a land exchange is only 50 years, the owner of an old lease with a longer term (say, 150 or 999 years) in an urban area should avoid modifying the land by land exchange. Aside from a shortened lease term, the government would also demand a higher quarterly rent (at 3% of rateable value) after the land exchange, even if there was no need to pay before the exchange.

On the other hand, as the lease terms of most land parcels in the New Territories will expire in 2047 (less than 23 years away, as of this writing), some owners there would prefer a *land exchange* to gain longer-term leases, even if their lot boundaries don't change.

A land premium will be charged for a lease modification or a land exchange application to reflect the land value differences between the "before" and "after" scenarios of the applications.

In the past, the modification of a Government Lease could be executed by a "deed of variation" instead of lease modification letter.

No-Objection Letters: For a Building's Lifetime

The modification of lease conditions by a "no-objection letter" is used when a lot has been subdivided into equally undivided shares with exclusive rights to the use and occupation of various units and if a modification is made in respect of one unit only (Audit Report 2020).

A no-objection letter could allow a change of use for a portion of a building (by way of undivided shares) for the building's lifetime. Upon the building's redevelopment, the original terms of the land lease will revert to its original form. Generally, the owner of a unit could opt between a temporary waiver and a no-objection letter as per his/her own business consideration. The age of the building and a redevelopment plan are major considerations for choosing a no-objection letter, as a substantial premium would still be required for a building-specific change of use.

Extension Letters (for Lot Areas)

Apart from a land exchange, an extension letter is another way to permit an expanded lot boundary. If the lease area is extended, the lot number of the concerned lot would include the term, "& Extension" or "& Ext".

Unlike a land exchange, an extension letter does not change the nature and restriction on the original lot, but would include additional restrictions on the additional land. In Hong Kong, a common example of an extension is for a garden in an RBL on Hong Kong Island.

Consent/Approval Letter: Not a Modification

There is a restriction in which the Lands Department would not entertain any lease modification within five years of the date of the grant if a site is sold via auction or tender. This is to ensure the tender/auction's fairness. However, a consent/approval letter would still be allowed within the first five years of a tender/auction site, which would not be considered a lease modification.

In modern leases, "flexibility clauses" may be included with certain conditions. For example, "*or such other points as may be approved by the Director*" would be incorporated into the vehicular access conditions. In this case, obtaining further approval from the Lands Department under the original conditions would not be regarded as a lease modification.

A premium would still be charged for a consent/approval letter if there is a premium implication (i.e., increase in value).

Lease Modification Application Procedure

It should be noted that there is no statutory time frame for processing a land application. The Lands Department generally follows its performance pledge for the application, but it is not bound by it. Rather, it would need at least one year to obtain the in-principle approval of the application. Premium negotiation depends on the decision of the Lands Department, applicant, and the prevailing market sentiment.

The procedure is similar for all land applications (Fig. 6.1):

- First, the Lands Department will verify the application and demand an initial administrative fee from the applicant. This takes around one month.
- Second, the Lands Department will circulate the application's details to various developments for comments including technical considerations of traffic, drainage, sewerage, and water supply. Prior experience suggests that traffic issues often take longer to resolve. The circulation process is the longest procedure (usually four to eight months), as it depends on comments from various departments.

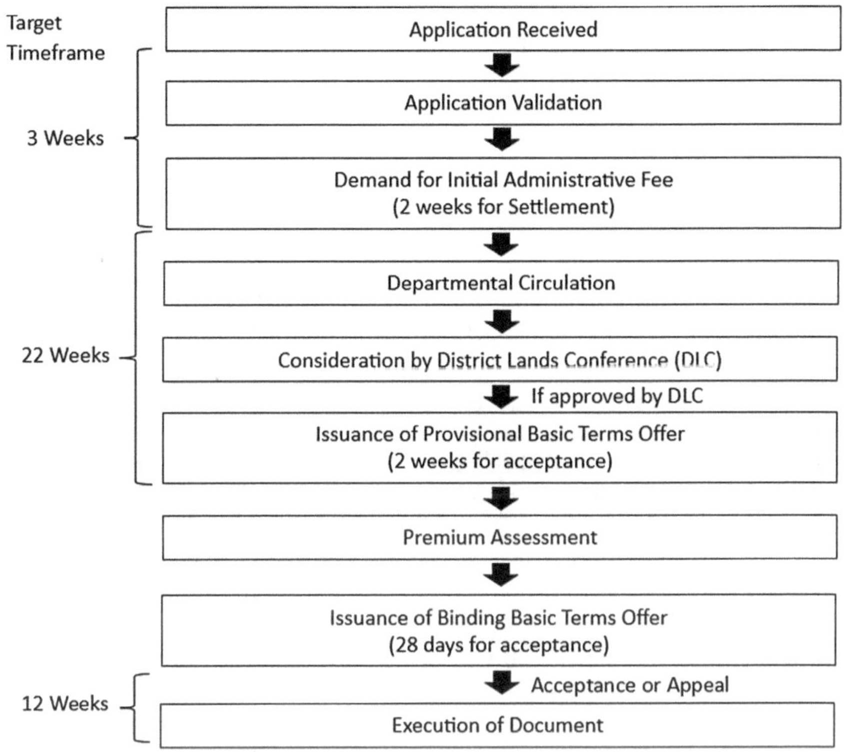

Fig. 6.1 Procedures for lease modification

- Third, the case will be submitted to the District Lands Conference (DLC) for approval. The DLC is chaired by a Lands Department assistant director and attended by representatives of other departments. Upon an application's approval, a Provisional Basic Terms Offer (PBTO) without premium will be issued to the applicant, who has two weeks to accept or reject it.
- Fourth, the premium is assessed. Once the premium offer is ready, a Binding Basic Terms Offer (BBTO) will be issued for the applicant to accept or appeal within 28 days. Each appeal usually takes around six to nine months.
- Finally, if the applicant accepts the premium offer, s/he and the Lands Department will execute the land application document within three months.

The whole process of a lease modification could be around 1.5 years to even much longer time to 10 years, depending on the premium negotiation process.

Each round of premium appeal would take from six to nine months in a normal appeal process. A fast-track appeal, which takes from one to two months, could be requested on the second or third appeal, subject to certain criteria for submitting new justifications.

Method of Premium Assessment

The government fixes the "modification premium" based on the market level on *the assessment date.*

The premium is assessed by the so-called Before Value and After Value methods (i.e., by comparing the difference between the two values of land: that under the control of the Crown Lease *before* lease modification and that under the new provisions of the Crown Lease after modification).

The Lands Department typically employs the residual valuation method to assess the land values for premium.

It should be noted that the "Before Value" and "After Value" are based on land value. An existing building's value (i.e., Existing Use Value or EUV) is disregarded in the "Before Value" situation. However, the demolition cost and period may be allowed in both the "Before Value" and "After Value" situations to reflect the physical existence of the existing building on the land parcel.

Example

Premium payable

After Value−Before Value
=$56,630,000−$9,450,000
=$47,180,000

Latest profit element within the residual valuation:

Residential	20%
Commercial	25%
Industrial	30%

Major conflicts with the premium assessment between the Lands Department and applicants (mainly private developers):

- Design of the schemes under residual valuation for both the Before and After Scenarios
- View of Gross Development Values (GDV) in After Scenario and Before Value (including Hope Value)
- Construction Cost and Marketing Cost

Traditional Premium Assessment and Standard Rates Premium

In view of the slow process of premium negotiation, in 2021, the Lands Department introduced a pilot scheme to charge premiums at standard rates. The scheme is also used to modify leases for industrial buildings completed before 1987, so as to promote the revitalisation of industrial buildings.

Then, the standard rates premium was extended for use in land exchange applications for development in New Development Areas and certain agricultural lands in the New Territories.

In promoting a pilot scheme for a standard rates premium, the government emphasised[1] that the pilot scheme would not provide landowners premium concessions, but would enhance the certainty of land premia being paid to expedite the lease modification process.

However, there is one uncertain factor in the formulation of standard rate premia for industrial buildings: the achievable GFA for the valuation of the "before scenario". Under the policy, the achievable GFA of the "before scenario" could be the existing GFA of the existing industrial building or a hypothetical development scheme allowed under an existing lease. As some existing buildings may not utilise the maximum GFA, this kind of application may fall under the category of the hypothetical scheme. In this case, the Lands Department would determine the final achievable GFA, and its decision is final and binding to the applicant.

[1] https://www.devb.gov.hk/en/publications_and_press_releases/press/index_id_10841.html.

Table 6.3 Key deciding factors of standard rates

	Standard rates	*Conventional assessment*
Key deciding factors	• Early completion of the application (certainty over timing) • NOT tailor-made • NOT attractive for sites with substantial site constraints • Risk of the "before GFA" (in industrial building cases) • NOT attractive during market downturns	• More suitable for sites with substantial site constraints and require a traditional case-by-case assessment approach • Able to negotiate and appeal • Deferral of premium payment

The considerations of adopting standard rates are provided in the Table 6.3 below.

Others Points to Note for Lease Modifications

- **No tailor-made application:** in a normal lease modification, the modified use and maximum development intensity must follow the optimal use under town planning in order to properly use land resources.
- **Technical Modification:** in special cases of minor modifications, no premium may be charged.
- **Empirical Premium:** refers to the premium charged when the enhancement of the land value after modification is not easy to measure by valuation.

  Extension of Building Covenants: a percentage of the clear site value on the building covenant's expiration date is levied.

  1st year 2%
  2nd year 4%
  3rd year 8%
  4th year 14%
  5th year 22%
  6th year 32%

A Lease Modification Decision Is Not Amenable to Judicial Review

Neither the government's decision to permit modification nor the amount of premium it assesses is amenable to judicial review. The leading cases, as mentioned in Chap. 4, are the Privy Council advice in respect of *Hang Wah Chong Investment Co, Ltd. v Attorney-General [1981] HKLR 336* and the Court of Appeal case *Sime Darby Motor Services Limited v Director of Lands [2024] HKCA 207.*

Problems with Lease Modification

The lease modification process is often long, while the market changes very quickly. In a rising market, the premium paid is usually lower than when a new use or redevelopment commences, as desired by the property owner. The reverse is true during a market downturn. Standard rates would help resolve such a problem.

Interpretation of Government Lease Restrictions

The following interpretations are generally acceptable to the government:

(1) "House": a high-rise, flatted development is accepted under the Lands Department's Land Administration Office Practice Note No.3/2000 (except in Green Belt Zones per *Wah Yick*). But, after the Court of Final Appeal's judgement in *Fully Profit (Asia), Ltd. v The Secretary for Justice for and on behalf of the Director of Lads (FACV No.17 of 2012)*, the definition of a house was changed. The meaning of the word, "house," must be taken to mean the type and characteristics of the house existing on the lot concerned at the time the Government Lease was signed. The new practice note, No.3/2000A, was published in 2014.
(2) "A building not exceeding four storeys high": a carport may be treated as one storey.
(3) "A building not exceeding 35 feet (10.668 metres) in height": parapet walls, stairheads, and other roof structures may be allowed in addition to the 35-foot ceiling.
(4) "A European house": the development of high-rise, flatted developments, shops, offices, or even cinemas is generally allowed.

(5) "One detached or semi-detached residence (or dwelling) of European-type": may be confined to one building containing not more than one residence.
(6) "Detached or semi-detached residences (or dwellings)": a block of flats may be accepted.
(7) "Residential use": any kind of residential use is allowed.
(8) "Commercial use": any kind of commercial use is allowed.
(9) "Commercial/Residential use": either commercial, residential, or a mixture of both is allowed.
(10) "Industrial use": any kind of industrial use is allowed, save for offensive trades, unless explicitly allowed.
(11) "Non-industrial use": any kind of use not classified as industrial is allowed.
(12) "Private residential use": a guest house, hotel, or serviced apartment is not allowed.

Questions for Revision and Discussion

1. Lease modification, if required, is the most difficult stage in development. Discuss.

The greatest difficulty of lease modification is uncertainty over both processing time and cost.

Uncertainty over Timing

Unlike planning and building approval processes, a lease modification is not regulated by any ordinance that prescribes a time limit. Thus, there is no statutory time frame for a lease modification process. Although LandsD has a performance pledge, the actual processing time of a lease modification highly depends on the comments and requirements of other departments during the departmental circulation process for a modification application.

In general, it takes at least one year to obtain a "Provisional Basic Terms Offer" prior to a premium assessment.

Uncertainty over Cost

Apart from certain technical modifications, a land premium is charged for effecting a lease modification. The premium amount is normally a huge lump sum if the development's scale is large (depending on the items of the modified lease). Payment of the premium is a major concern for a developer in the processing of a private development.

The time for negotiating a land premium is also less than certain and has exceeded five years in some cases.

2. Discuss if the public should be granted the right to participate in the granting of a modification of user restrictions (other than the premium payable).

Presently, the public can participate in the processing of lease matters including lease modifications indirectly through the following arrangements.

During the lease modification process, comments from the District Office are sought and the District Office solicits local comments when it considers them necessary.

Most private lands in Hong Kong are covered by statutory town plans, which are subject to the public participation process in planning and planning applications.

Within this context, there are two considerations for this question.

On one hand, as a land lease is a private contract between the government and lessee (i.e., the landowner), the public should not be directly involved in the granting of a lease modification as a matter of the privity of contract.

On the other hand, a lot is part of a government plan and, hence, has a public dimension regarding a change in its use, density, or boundary. The public should have a reasonable say in the negotiation even when the TPB is not involved.

A better idea is that LandsD should bear responsibility for representing the public as the landlord in good balancing manner.

3. Should all urban lease terms be standardised like G.N.364?

Every plot of land is unique. A standardised lease may save time and administrative costs and can avoid the problems of complete discretion at the cost of inflexibility. The best approach would be a mixture of standardised and tailor-made terms.

References

Lands Department's Practice Notes.
Lands Department Website: https://www.landsd.gov.hk/en/index.html

CHAPTER 7

Valuation Concepts and Techniques Outlined

K. T. Liu

> Anybody can make a valuation of land, for a valuation is nothing other than the opinion of the valuer of the worth of the land. (Roberts 1975: 1)

Valuation is the formation of an opinion on the worth of something by a person. Any person can value something. The professional valuation of property requires a valuer to weigh each relevant valuation factor that affects the value carefully. The valuer "interprets the market," but not to "create the market," with a view to arriving at the "market value." It must be a comparison exercise based on *true transactions* ("comparables"). It is, by nature, not a precise science, but an art. Above all, the purpose of valuation is to provide a basis for negotiation and/or a reference for a decision on a property.

Definition of Market Value

Professional valuers in Hong Kong accept the concept of the market value of a property as *the estimated amount for which a property should exchange on the date of valuation between a willing buyer and a willing seller in an*

K. T. Liu (✉)
Department of Real Estate and Construction, The University of Hong Kong, Hong Kong, China

L. W. C. Lai et al. (eds.), *Principles of Land Administration at Work*, https://doi.org/10.1007/978-981-95-2972-8_7

arm's-length transaction after proper marketing, wherein the parties had each acted knowledgeably, prudently, and without compulsion.

Arm's-length transactions exclude transactions between related entities such as parents and children or companies and their subsidiaries.

Seven Methods of Valuation

(1) Adjustment of Direct Comparables

This is typically used to value property units and sites of similar sizes and involves a comparison of the property to be valued with a similar property that was recently transacted.

(2) Residual Valuation

This is typically used to value sites and involves deducting the cost of development and the developer's risk from the estimated proceeds of the sales of the development.

(3) Discounted Cash Flow

This method finds out the present value (PV) of the stream of income and expenditures.

(4) Capitalization of Rental Income

This is typically used to value properties with existing tenancies.

(5) Profit Method

This makes use of the profit and loss account to estimate what level of rent can be realized from the profit.

(6) Contractor's Method

This values a property by adding the site value, the construction cost, and the profit element together.

(7) Developer's Rule of Thumb

The developer's method is simple. The aim is to become the highest bidder, but to arrive at a value that is just above the next highest bid so as to allow an estimated profit. This valuation is based on its commercial ability to understand and exploit the rights granted or the exemptions allowed during the development approval process so as to achieve a greater permissible gross floor area (GFA) than that of a rival.

Basic Steps in Getting Information for Valuation

(1) Ascertain the location, address, and boundary of the lot(s) involved.
(2) Make a "land search" for and obtain titles and all relevant land documents, including all cadastral records.
(3) Visit and inspect the site.
(4) Search for and evaluate comparables.
(5) Obtain and study the land grant document, including the deed of mutual covenant (DMC).
(6) Obtain and study any applicable statutory town plan (e.g. an outline zoning plan [OZP]).
(7) Obtain and study any applicable administrative town plan (e.g. an Outline Development Plan [ODP]).
(8) Study the applicable *Buildings (Planning) Regulation*.
(9) Analyse the market situation.
(10) Analyse the property concerned, including its Gross Site Area redevelopment potential.
(11) Apply the law and seek legal and other expert opinions when necessary.

Adjustment of Direct Comparables (Method 1)

This compares the property to be valued with the most direct comparables by making the necessary adjustments in respect of the factors that affect the value. Some important factors are:

(1) Term or tenure of a Government Lease
(2) Date of transaction
(3) Basis of the floor area calculation

(4) Size
(5) Finishes and fittings
(6) Internal layout
(7) Orientation (i.e. aspect)
(8) Age of the building
(9) Location (environment)

Regarding factor (1), surveyors in Hong Kong treat a property with a remaining term of 40–50 years not much differently from another with as many as 888 remaining years, although they would assess a property whose lease expires within 10 years with great caution.

The basis of the floor area calculation has become a great concern in recent years for property units. The "Saleable Area" (SA), which refers to the internal area of a unit inclusive of party walls, but excluding common areas, is only required to be disclosed by the developer for development governed by the "Consent Scheme," which was imposed by the Lands Department and/or by the Law Society. Now the *Residential Properties (First-Hand Sales) Ordinance,* which came into effect on 29 April 2013, requires mandatory use of saleable area in marketing residential units.

Yet most first-time buyers in the past become aware of the true SA only when they sign the Sale and Purchase Agreement, as developers typically market property units in terms of their GFA. This is not an issue when a person buys a property already built first hand or second hand, as he or she can form an opinion on the worth of the property by getting a feel for the internal size of the unit. This becomes a concern when the efficiency ratio between the SA and GFA is lowered for pre-sale in new building units constructed after 1997 due to developers taking advantage of exemptions for GFA calculation under the *Buildings Ordinance.*

Example: Comparable transaction $5000 per square feet (saleable)

Adjustment			
	Timing	−5.0%	
	Size	−5.0%	
	Orientation	+2.5%	
	Finishes	+2.5%	5%
		$4,750 per square feet	
	Size	1,000 square feet (saleable)	
	Value of property	$4,750,000	

Please note that there are two methods of arriving the total adjustment percentage: "addition and subtraction" and "multiplication". The above example used "addition and subtraction" method to arrive the total adjustment percentage, which is usually adopted in general valuation. On the other hand, the Lands Tribunal in Hong Kong has adopted "multiplication" rather than "addition and subtraction" to arrive at the total adjustments. If "multiplication" method is adopted [i.e. ((1-5%) x (1-5%) x (1+2.5%) x (1+2.5%)-1)], the total adjustment would be 5.2% (instead of 5%).

Adjustment of Direct Comparables (Method 2)

This method can also be used for the valuation of a site provided that the comparable sites are very similar, as in the case of rural and small houses. Some important factors are:

(1) Terms of a Government Lease
(2) Date of transaction
(3) Size of the site
(4) Development restrictions
(5) Location (environment)
(6) Class of the site under the Building (Planning) Regulations
(7) Commercial or residential value

Example:

Comparable transaction: $10,000 per square feet (site)			
Adjustment			
Timing		−5.0%	
Size		−5.0%	
Orientation		+2.5%	−7.5%
		$9,250 per square feet	
	Size	1,000 square feet	
	Value of property	$9,250,000	

The site valuation can be made by comparing the "Accommodation Value" (A.V.) with another site transaction.

$$= \text{A.V.} = \frac{\text{Site Value}}{\text{Total gross area to be built on the site}}$$

Residual Valuation

This method is standard for site valuation, involving a consideration of the optimum development potential of the site based on (1) the Government Lease and statutory planning and (2) the market situation and stamp duty.

The first step is to find out the kind of development that will be built and its GFA based on the achievable Plot Ratio.

- Estimate the proceeds of the sale.
- Estimate the construction cost.
- Estimate the development period.
- Deduct the construction costs and developer's profit (risk element) from the proceeds of the sale.
- Find out the present value of the property.

$$\text{Present Value} = \frac{1}{A}$$

Where $A = (1 + i)^n$
Where i= interest
n= length of the period

e.g.

Proceeds

20,000 of @$5,000.00	$100,000,000		
P.V. 1yr @10%	0.9090		$90,900,000

Cost

Construction 20,000 square feet @$1,000.00		$20,000,000	
Professional fees say 5%		$1,000,000	
		$21,000,000	
Developer's Profit 15%	$3,150,000		
			$24,150,000
P.V. ½ yr. @$10%		0.95	$22,942,500

Land & Profit	$67,957,500
Less developer's profit 20%	÷ 1.2
Land Value	$56,631,250
Say	HK$56,630,000

Note: There are too many variables in a residual valuation, and a slight change to any or all variables would cause a big change in the resultant land value

Contractor's Method

This values special properties without useful comparables, such as historical buildings.The formula is: Site value (alternative revenue) + Construction Cost of the building (discounting for age and obsolescence when necessary) + Profit element = Value of the Property.

Profit Method

This is an accounting-method—the value is dependent on the earning capacity of the property. This is typically used to value properties without useful comparables, as in the case of hotels, public housing, theatres, and cinemas.

The formula is:
Gross earning or receipts
Less Working Expenses
Interest on Capital
Remuneration for tenant's risk

= Rent X Y.P. = Value

Developer's Rule of Thumb

The developer assumes a price X to be paid to buy a site
Add construction costs.
Add interest.
Add profits.
All the above are to get a sum, Y. This begs the question, "In three years' time, can I sell Y?" If yes, then bid on the land for X.

Purposes of Valuation

Valuation is significant for:

(1) Sale and purchase of property
(2) Mortgage
(3) Stamp duty
(4) Estate duty
(5) Premium in modification/land exchange
(6) Compensation in resumption
(7) Rent assessment
(8) Rating appeal
(9) Litigation
(10) Company prospectus
(11) Undivided shares and management shares

Valuation for Sale/Purchase Purposes

The aim is to find the best price to obtain from the other party.

Valuation for Mortgage Purposes

Typically, a conservative approach should be taken to exclude any speculative element, so the value attributable to illegal structures must be excluded.

Valuation for Insurance Purposes

Reinstatement costs plus the loss of rental, etc., depending on the policy, are great additional concerns.

Premium for the Modification of a Government Lease

The modification premium payable represents the enhancement in the land value due to modification. The assessment of a premium is made by the Lands Department using the so-called Before and After Value method, which determines the difference between two values of a plot of land (land only, while ignoring any building value or the "clear site value"). One value is the land value under the control of the Crown Lease before modification; the other value is the land value under the new provisions of the Crown Lease after modification.

Modification of a lease can also be made by the method of Land Exchange (especially for the development of a group of old schedule agricultural lots in the NT).

Compensation Under the Lands Resumption Ordinance

The *Lands Resumption Ordinance* contains the basis of compensation for compulsory acquisitions by the government.

The value of the Land resumed is statutorily defined as *the amount for which a plot of land, if sold by a willing seller in the open market, may be able to realize,* but it may ignore the following:

(a) The fact that the resumption is compulsory
(b) Any adverse statutory planning control
(c) Benefits not in accordance with the terms of the Crown Lease

No compensation shall be given in respect of the expectancy or probability of the grant or renewal or its continuance by the Crown or by any person of any licence, permission, lease, or permit whatsoever.

Valuation for Stamp Duty Purposes

Market value as of the date of the transaction (the first contract).

Valuation for Estate Duty Purposes

The focus is the market value on the date of death.

Valuation for Undivided Shares/Management Shares

Undivided shares-	floor area basis/or market value basis
Management shares-	mainly on a floor area basis

Valuation for Company Prospectus for Stock Listing

Valuers owe a duty to the public.

Valuation for Litigation Purposes

Valuers owe a duty to the court, especially when serving as expert witnesses.

Questions for Revision and Discussion

1. "Valuation is at the lower end of the surveyor's profession." Discuss.

"In the Smith v Bush case, Lord Griffiths' view that it is unreasonable for a building society surveyor to use a disclaimer on the grounds that valuation 'is work at the lower end of the surveyor's field of professional expertise' and should not be taken too seriously by surveyors. This simply means, if it is consistent with the economic interpretation of law, that it is to the surveyor's comparative advantage to take care of value, in an almost tailor-made valuation report." See Lai, Lawrence W. C. & Ben T. Yu, The Power of Supply and Demand: Thinking Tools and Case Studies for Students and Professionals. Hong Kong: Hong Kong University Press, 2003, p. 276.

2. Can valuation be done by a commonly accepted computer programme?

Co-pilot gave an answer on 15 December 2024: "Absolutely, valuation can be performed by a computer program! In fact, there are several software tools and algorithms specifically designed to carry out valuations. These programs can evaluate the worth of assets, businesses, real estate, and other entities based on a variety of factors. They typically use statistical models, financial data, and market analysis to generate valuations.

Some common types of valuation software include:

1. Real Estate Valuation Software: These programs analyze market data, property characteristics, and economic factors to estimate the value of real estate properties. Examples include Zillow, Redfin, and HouseCanary.

2. Business Valuation Software: Tools like BizEquity and Equidam help in determining the value of businesses by analysing financial statements, market conditions, and industry trends.
3. Financial Valuation Models: Programs like Bloomberg Terminal and Thomson Reuters Eikon offer extensive data and financial modeling tools for valuing stocks, bonds, and other financial instruments.

These tools can be highly efficient and accurate, but it's important to remember that they work best when complemented by human judgment and expertise. Automated valuation models can provide a solid baseline, but complex or unique assets might require additional insights from professionals."

Note the caveat for software, "they work best when complemented by human judgment and expertise ... complex or unique assets might require additional insights from professionals."

3. Discuss why government town planners do not generally consider the value effects of their plans.

Partly due to a lack of skills, but mainly due to a negative attitude towards redevelopment.

Reference

Roberts, Philip James. 1975. *Valuation of Development Land in Hong Kong*. Hong Kong: Hong Kong University Press.

CHAPTER 8

Government Management of Unallocated Land

Jason Wai Yin Kwong

All lands in Hong Kong belong to the state. The Lands Department allocates lands as leasehold interests to individuals or government users. It manages and controls all lands not leased nor allocated to government bodies as "Unallocated Government Lands". It also allocates "short-term tenancies" (STT) to individuals for temporary uses.

Government Land Control

By 2019, Lands Department[1] managed a total of 1606 unleased government sites with a total site area of 391 hectares. Such unallocated/unleased sites exclude roads, railways or country parks.

[1] https://www.legco.gov.hk/research-publications/english/2021issh06-vacant-government-land-20201117-e.pdf; https://www.info.gov.hk/gia/general/202002/26/P2020022600497.htm

J. W. Y. Kwong (✉)
Department of Real Estate and Construction, The University of Hong Kong, Hong Kong, China

L. W. C. Lai et al. (eds.), *Principles of Land Administration at Work*, https://doi.org/10.1007/978-981-95-2972-8_8

Under the *Land (Miscellaneous Provisions) Ordinance* (Chapter 28), Lands Department could take enforcement action against a person for unlawful occupation of such unallocated/unleased government land. As distinct from land lease enforcement according to lease conditions, it is statutory offence for any person for the occupation of government land without permission and fails to cease occupation upon receipt of a notice under the Ordinance. The government may prosecute and demand fine from such a land occupier. If the occupier has erected a structure on the occupied land, the offence is more serious and fine is higher.

In September 2023, landslides occurred on government slopes in Red Hill (Fig. 8.1) after a heavy rain. The landslides exposed unauthorised building works (UBWs) and signs of unlawful occupation of government land connected with four private houses. The Buildings Department and Lands Department carried out a joint enforcement operation which resulted in removal orders and notices, requiring cessation of occupation of government land to the relevant owners.

Fig. 8.1 Red Hill

Short-Term Tenancies

Apart from long-term alienation of land (notably the grant of private lots), the Lands Department may grant short-term tenancies (STTs) of well-delineated sites to private tenants for temporary uses of unleased and unallocated government land. The STT is usually granted to land not yet scheduled for sale or government development.

The site involved has no lot number, but an STT number. The tenancy agreement is not registered with the Lands Registry and, thus, is not available to the public. Limited information on STTs could be found on the Lands Department website, GeoInfo Map.

STTs could be granted by means of open tender or direct grant. The STTs would normally be granted for a fixed term of one year to five years and thereafter quarterly, half-yearly or yearly. STTs are subject to payment of rental. Similar to waiver, the STT rentals could be reviewed triennially. In the Policy Address 2025, the government proposed longer terms STTs. The government suggested employing flexible land-grant arrangements, encouraging enterprises to set up businesses and invest in the Northern Metropolis of Hong Kong. Sites granted as tenancy instead of land lease may have a term exceeding seven years (up to 21 years by renewal arrangement) to provide greater flexibility.

The common terms and conditions of an STT are:

(1) Term (time period)
(2) Rent
(3) User restrictions
(4) Permitted structures
(5) Non-alienation

One of the common STT use is temporary open car parks (Fig. 8.2). In the NT, some STTs are directly granted for the use of government land around certain private lots.

As STTs are for temporary uses only, Lands Department could terminate the STTs in short notice. If the land is decided for a long-term use, LandsD would take back the land. As this is not a resumption of a private lot, no compensation would be paid by the government.

Some STTs could be used *de facto* for a longer term. Bus depots with substantial structures have been granted as STTs (Fig. 8.3).

Fig. 8.2 A closed car park site under STT in 2023 at Sai Yee Street, Mong Kok (this site was included in the land sale programme as a commercial tender site)

Government Land Allocations

Government developments, say, police stations, schools, parks, pumping stations, occupy government lands. Lands Department grants the relevant government department by way of "Government Land Allocation" (GLA). Each GLA has a number and a set of "engineering conditions" to control the use of the land. Such documents are internal documents within the government and not in the public domain. However, the location and number of GLA could be found on lot index plans.

GLAs could be on a permanent or temporary basis. For some road works, temporary GLAs are made.

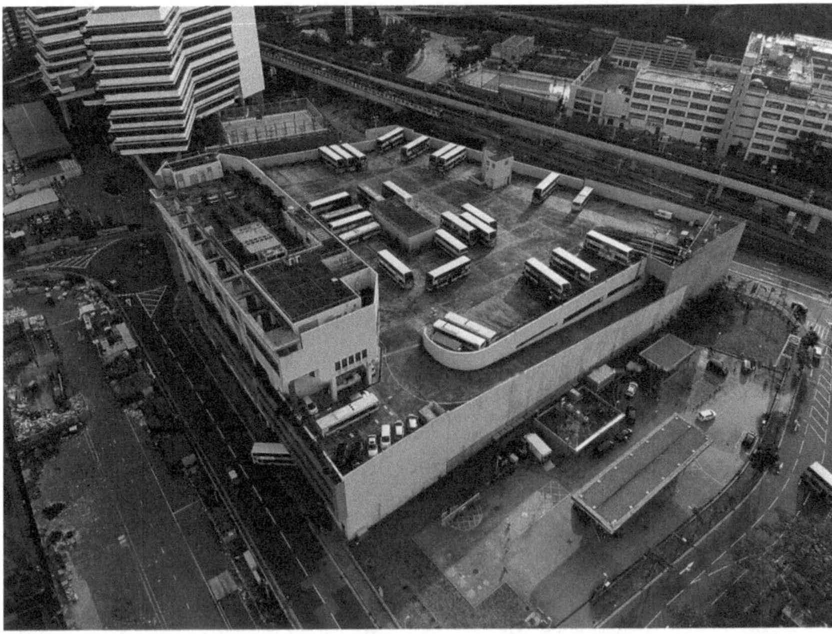

Fig. 8.3 CityBus depot at Chaiwan

Squatter Control

Squatter structures mean structures erected on government land without permission or private land (notably private agricultural lots) contrary to lease conditions.

In 1982, government conducted a squatter survey to record all squatter structures at the time. The survey covered the location, dimensions, building materials and use of each squatter structure.

The government's position is that any surveyed squatter structure on government land is tolerated to remain on a temporary basis. Any extension, new erection, addition, change of use or alteration with materials that does not conform to the survey record would not be allowed. Repair or rebuilding of the squatter structures may be allowed with permission on application to the Lands Department subject to the nature and location of the squatter structure.

Questions for Revision and Discussion

1. Explain the change in policy towards the granting of government land licences.

A government land licence (GLL) was a land instrument issued by the government to mainly regulate unauthorised structures erected on government land in Hong Kong's rural areas before 1997. As public housing supply improved, squatters were no longer tolerated as a matter of policy.

Although no more new GLLs have been issued, many squatter structures are still held under them.

2. Explain the importance of an STT.

STTs are granted to tenants to occupy and use unleased and unallocated government land temporarily. For instance, STT carparks in Hong Kong are important for resolving parking space shortages in different areas. The government can terminate an STT shortly after granting it if it needs the land for something else.

An STT could optimise the use of land resources and allow for flexibility in long-term planning.

STT rentals are a source of public revenue.

3. Explain why open-access government land (e.g. country parks) is not common property.

It is the government's exclusive property open to the public and usually at no entry cost.

References

Lands Department Website: https://www.landsd.gov.hk/en/index.html
GeoInfo Map Website: https://www.map.gov.hk/gm/map/

CHAPTER 9

Enforcement Against Breaches of Crown (Government) Leases

Lawrence Wai Chung Lai and Jason Wai Yin Kwong

When a lessee or tenant breaches a covenant—say, the "user clause"—of a Crown (Government) Lease, the Lands Department can take action against the owner or tenant by demanding prompt rectification, charging a fine or, in default, taking a "re-entry" action.

The owner or tenant can challenge the allegation by appealing to the Director of Lands or seek legal recourse if no such breach has been committed.

At stake is the interpretation of the terms of the lease, which vary from lot to lot. Leases for lots on the same street block granted at more or less the same time could be drafted differently. This chapter uses a few real-life examples of alleged breaches of industrial leases, involving office and private residential uses to illustrate some key factors of lease interpretations.

L. W. C. Lai (✉) • J. W. Y. Kwong
Department of Real Estate and Construction, The University of Hong Kong, Hong Kong, China
e-mail: wclai@hku.hk

L. W. C. Lai et al. (eds.), *Principles of Land Administration at Work*, https://doi.org/10.1007/978-981-95-2972-8_9

BACKGROUND

In accordance with Annex III of the *Joint Declaration of the Government of the United Kingdom of Great Britain and Northern Ireland and the Government of the People's Republic of China on the Question of Hong Kong* (the *Sino-British Joint Declaration*) and the *Basic Law of the Hong Kong Special Administrative Region of the People's Republic of China* (the *Basic law*), Hong Kong's land system has remained a leasehold system since 1 July 1997.

Under this leasehold system, private "landowners," who are actually lessees, hold lands from the government (previously the Crown) for definite periods of time. Land uses ("user") and building forms or their restrictions are specified in the relevant lease documents, namely the "conditions of sale," "conditions of exchange" or the Crown (now "Government") Leases, for such lands (Nissim 1997).

As such documents specify the land use (often expressed in land documents as "user"), building restrictions or even post-development property management responsibilities which are accepted voluntarily by the lessees, Lai has described the leasehold system as a system of "planning by contract" (Lai 1998).

While the effectiveness of leasehold land tenure as a "forward planning" and "development control" system is debatable (Yeh 1994, Lai 1998), there is no doubt that the lease document is a key component of the land use regulatory mechanism of Hong Kong.

The Lands Department is responsible for, among many other duties, the allocation, execution and enforcement of leases and the negotiation of the terms and premium for the leases. Lease conditions, being contractual, are subject to legislative restrictions.

The major restrictions are those imposed by the *Buildings Ordinance* and the *Town Planning Ordinance*. Such legislative restrictions are often imposed unilaterally as post-contractual variation of the conditions specified in the lease documents. The statutory town plans, notably the outline zoning plans (OZPs), prepared under s.3(1) of the *Town Planning Ordinance*, are particularly important. Most urban lands allocated by government have become subject also to OZPs, which may take away some of the property rights specified or implied in the lease documents.

When a lessee is in breach of the conditions of the lease, the Lands Department is entitled to re-enter the land by exercising either the contractual right specified in the lease document by civil action or the exercise of its statutory powers conferred by relevant ordinances.

Before such drastic contractual or statutory rights are exercised, the Lands Department will normally issue a warning letter to the lessee, stating (a) the nature of the alleged breach, (b) the time before which the breach must be rectified and (c) the need for the lessee to pay a fine called "forbearance fee." A debit note demanding payment of forbearance fees to government will follow shortly.

Breaches of the "User Clause" in Industrial Leases

A very common kind of breach is the violation of the user clause of the Crown (Government) Lease by the occupiers of a unit or units in a flatted factory building. The Lands Department has found that many such factory units have been used for "office" or other purposes.

From the government's point of view, this amounts to a breach of the terms of the lease in so far as the office use exceeds a percentage of "usable floor space" specified in an internal set of guidelines, the *Lands Administrative Office Instructions* (LIs). This set of guidelines is a restricted government document, not available to the public. In the relevant warning letter, Lands Department often advises the lessee to "rectify" the breach by making a town planning application under s.16 the *Town Planning Ordinance* within the context of the relevant OZP for the industrial district. Where a planning approval is granted by the Town Planning Board, the lessee needs to follow matter up with the Lands Department by a payment of premium for either a permanent lease "modification" or a temporary "waiver" of the lease conditions governing the user.

In Column 2 of the *Notes* to a typical OZP for an industrial zone, "office other than ancillary office" is a use that requires planning permission under s. 16 of the said Ordinance. However, "existing" uses, namely those uses which existed prior to the publication in the gazette of an OZP, and uses under Column 1 of the Notes, need no permission and are tolerated by the OZP. According to the *Town Planning Board Guidelines* for industrial zones, definitions of "industrial" and various categories of "ancillary office" are given. "Ancillary office" uses exceeding a certain percentage, which was once 30% (Town Planning Board 1990) but now 50% (Town Planning Board Town 1997), shall require planning permission.

While the *Notes* form a part of the OZP as a product of legislation, the said Guidelines are administrative circulars, which are meant to help interpret the provisions of the OZP. Unlike the LIs, such guidelines are available to the public. As far as the provision of ancillary office in industrial buildings is concerned, the definitions of and percentages of land tolerated for various types of industrial and ancillary office uses specified in the relevant LIs are identical to those in the *Town Planning Board Guidelines.*

As the subject under discussion is lease enforcement, one must, therefore, focus first of all on the wordings of the lease.

Lai (2000a) surveyed 50 lease documents obtained from the Land Registry for industrial lots in a district in West Kowloon and identified 26 main categories of wordings in respect of user and/or building restriction clauses. These lease documents are those for a sample of land lots drawn from all existing or previous industrial districts in Hong Kong Island, Kowloon and the New Territories of Hong Kong. The sample contains examples from industrial areas developed during the Victorian period; inter world wars; early post-World War II years as well as in recent years. They cover locations in the old urban core of Hong Kong Island and Kowloon, New Kowloon; satellite towns; modern new towns and industrial estates. Industrial estates are managed by various Industrial Estate Corporations.

Categories of User Restrictions

The general ways of drafting of each of the 26 categories of restrictions are summarised below (with the years of the "signed date" of the lease for first and last sample in square brackets):

Category I: old non-offensive trade clause (typically found in the so-called "999-year unrestricted use") [1864–1968 (6 samples)]
Category II: general industrial purposes + non-domestic building(s) clauses [1910–1910 (2 samples)]
Category III: "similar lots" clause [1924 (1 sample)]
Category IV: specific manufacturing purposes + non-domestic building(s) + old non-offence trade clauses [1935 (1 sample)]
Category V: special manufacturing purposes + non-domestic building(s) clauses [1940–1940 (2 samples)]
Category VI: used for a factory and no domestic building(s) clause [1948 (1 sample)]
Category VII: specific manufacturing purposes + old non-offensive trade clauses [1956 (1 sample)]

Category VIII: general industrial purposes + non-domestic building(s) + old non-offensive trade clauses [1958 (1 sample)]
Category IX: identical volume building + "similar lots" clauses [1959 (1 sample]
Category X: general industrial/godown(s) purposes + factory building(s) clauses [1961–1985 (16 samples)]
Category XI: non-offensive industrial purposes + factory building(s) clauses [1962 (1 sample)]
Category XII: identical volume/building clause [1963 (1 sample)]
Category XIII: special manufacturing purposes and purposes of factory clauses + old non-offensive trade clause [1966–1966 (2 samples)]
Category XIV: specific industrial purposes and factory building(s) and **ancillary offices** + old non-offensive trade clauses [1967 (1 sample)]
Category XV: factory building and **ancillary offices** and general industrial purposes + old non-offensive trade clauses [1968 (1 sample)]
Category XVI: buildings for commercial and **ancillary offices** and factory/factories and ancillary offices + non-offensive trade purposes + industrial user expressed to include go-down, **office** and **research** facilities required to support the principal industrial undertaking clauses [1977 (1 sample)]
Category XVII: buildings for general industrial purposes and non-offensive trade purposes clauses [1980 (1 sample)]
Category XVIII: one building comprising godown(s) and ancillary offices + building for godown purpose clauses [1981 (1 sample)]
Category XIX: building(s) for general industrial purposes + non-offensive trade purposes + factory building (s) clauses [1981 (1 sample)]
Category XX: general industrial purposes + non-offensive trade purposes + factory building (s) clauses [1983 (1 sample)]
Category XXI: general industrial purposes + factory building(s) clauses [1986 (1 sample)]
Category XXII: one godown building and **ancillary offices** clause [1991 (1 sample)]
Category XXIII: general industrial/godown purposes + expressed provisions for ancillary offices and research facilities for industrial user + factory or factories building(s) + expressed provisions for only 30% usable floor area of each factory or godown for **ancillary office** clauses [1994–1997 (2 samples)]
Category XXIV: industrial/godown purposes + bank etc. + public lorry park + expressed provision for "**offices directly related to an industrial/godown operation**" + non-offensive trade clause + planning permission for a "composite Industrial Office Building" (1998 (1 sample)]
Category XXV: industrial/godown purposes + expressed provision for "**offices directly related to an industrial/godown operation**" + non-offensive trade clause + planning permission for a "composite Office

Building" + right to "submit a s.16 application under the revised Guidelines" for Application for Composite Industrial-Office (I-O) Buildings in "Industrial" zone (TPB PG-No.4A) (1998 (1 sample)]
Category XXVI: industrial or godown + "office ancillary and directly related to an industrial or godown operation" or banks ... at the lowest three floors + **"offices ancillary and directly related to an industrial or godown operation"** + planning permission for an "Industrial-Office building" with ancillary car park, bank, restaurant, retail shop, fast food shop and showroom at specific floors (including basement) [1998 (1 sample)]

"Ancillary office" is expressed in these categories: XIV, XV, XVI, XXII, XXIII, XXIV, XXIV, XXV and XXVI.

Practice of Lands Department

Other than for premises controlled by Category I (i.e., "unrestricted lease") restrictions, Lands Department often instigates lease enforcement procedures for premises governed by most categories of lease documents, notably Categories VI and X. These procedures are triggered when its staff discover in their routine inspection that office activities occupy floor space in a premise to an extent that such activities occupy a total area more than the ceiling of 30% usable floor space specified in the LIs within "one unit." That unit is created by strata-titling. It may have a small "gross area" or "saleable area" of 1000 square feet (93 square metres), being one of the ten equal-size units on a floor with a gross area of 10,000 square feet (930 square metres). As mentioned previously, Lands Department will in this situation issue (a) a warning letter requiring rectification (i.e., discontinuation of the office uses) and suggesting the avenue of "regularising" the breach by obtaining a planning approval; and (b) a debit note for forbearance fees payable. It should be noted that the planning approval is "advised" to be sought under s.16 of the *Town Planning Ordinance* in accordance with the relevant *Town Planning Board Guidelines* (1990, 1997).

Only such premises controlled by a lease document under category XXIII, which provides expressly a contractual restriction of the land-take of ancillary offices to a pre-specified percentage of floor space, may attract lease enforcement under two situations. These situations are (a) the office use is not ancillary to any real principal or parent industrial or manufacturing activities; and/or (b) such ancillary office use does exceed the expressed

30% ceiling specified in the lease documents. Other than category XXIII, it is submitted that the approach adopted by Lands Department is not reasonable, other than in a situation where the office uses in question, such as a bank or a surveyor firm, are autarchic and not ancillary to any real industrial or manufacturing uses.

The reasons are that (a) for genuine ancillary office uses, they are indeed permitted under by the terms of the lease; (b) the provisions or ceilings in the LIs, as internal administrative documents of government, are not law or contractual terms, and hence incapable of narrowing or superseding user restrictions already contained in the lease documents; and (c) the Town Planning Board Guidelines as administrative circulars may help interpret but not restrict, enlarge, add, subtract, remove or alter the items under either column of uses (Column 1 or 2) in the Notes to the OZP. An application for "ancillary office use" under the Guidelines is arguably ultra vires, as that use cannot be found under either column of uses for industrial zones.

This analysis confines itself to the first reason, which is developed on the basis of the decisions of the court in two leading Hong Kong cases in the arena of lease enforcement, which were consistent with the English case of *Simmonds Aerocessories (Western) Limited v. Pontypridd Area Assessment Committee and Another* [1944] (the *Simmonds Case*). These cases are briefly described below.

One of the leading Hong Kong cases is *Mexx Consolidated (Far East) v. Attorney General* (High Court Miscellaneous Proceedings No.2421 of 1986) HKLR 1210–1220 (The *Mexx Case*). It involves the interpretation of a user covenant in the deed of variation for a site in Kowloon (Kowloon Inland Lot No.6053). It restricted the use of the premises involved to industrial and godown purposes. The plaintiff set up and operated 11 different departments in the suit premises, which were responsible for the <u>design</u>, <u>research</u> and <u>testing of samples</u> and also the making of patterns for the manufacturing of clothing. The Crown demanded a forbearance fee for an alleged breach of covenant: the real nature of the activities was commercial and not industrial and that the primary use of the premises was a research and design office and that the limited manufacturing and packing activities were subsidiary to that primary use. Deciding in favour of the plaintiff, Judge Cruden held that a broad approach to interpret industrial activities is necessary. "<u>All of the plaintiff's activities within the suit premises must be considered as a whole</u>. Where it is technically possible to break down those activities into separate elements, it is still their cumulative effect and not their individual characteristics, which is more important. When this broader approach is adopted, it is clear that the research, design and testing functions are merely successive stages in one continuous industrial process, resulting in the creation of manufactured garments" (Underline authors').

In short, it was held in the *Mexx Case* that:

1. The primary user of the premises must be industrial before compliance with the user covenant can be achieved and the cumulative effect of all the plaintiff's activities on the premises must be taken into account.
2. The primary use of the majority of the plaintiff's departments was industrial and the remaining departments necessarily and reasonably incidental to the major departments.

The other key Hong Kong case is *Cavendish Property Development, Ltd. v. Attorney General* [1987] (the "*Cavendish Case*"). The case involves the interpretation of the "type of building to be erected" per Special condition (9)(a) and the "user" per Special condition (8)(a) of an Aberdeen lot. **It was held that "industrial purposes" involves a manufacturing process.** The main test for considering whether the building was an industrial building was whether there was any process carried on therein for or incidental to the making of any article or part of an article. It was ruled that the test in the *Mexx Case*, referred to above, applied. If the same test in *Cavendish* is to apply to interpret the nature of premises as to whether it is "a building" or "factory," it is argued that it should be regarded as "industrial" where the premises are used for the carrying out of industrial processes. This is still the case where such processes are aided by computers or other office equipment, for or incidental to the making of manufacturing or industrial products. Examples that the author has come across include air-conditioners, watches and jewellery.

In the *Simmonds Case*, the issue was whether a canteen serving a factory is industrial or not. It was ruled that it is because the canteen is primarily occupied and used for the purpose of a factory or workshop. In the light of this case, offices within a factory serving an industrial undertaking within the factory should also be regarded as industrial, if not "ancillary office."

In pp.341–353, Malcolm Merry's *Hong Kong Tenancy Law* (3rd edition) (Merry 1997), an example of a lease clause for a factory is given:

> Clause 2(g) of the example reads: "Not to use or permit or suffer to be used the Premises or any part thereof for any purposes other than that of a factory only and not to use or permit … parking cars."

Merry has the opinion that this clause will "restrict the floors to factory use only. The essence of factory use is manufacturing, although any type of industrial use is probably allowed by the covenant. A limited amount of office or other commercial use may be consistent with the covenant." Note that Merry has the opinion that "*office or other commercial use*" may be consistent with a lease term that expressly restricts uses to "factory uses." Obviously, Merry's opinion is consistent with any of the three cases cited above.

Problems of the Lease Enforcement Practice of Lands Department Regarding Ancillary Office Uses in Industrial Premises

While there is no doubt that the leasehold land system is an effective land-use control system, there are apparently, from the author's practice, four problems which the government needs to pay attention and address satisfactorily before her lease enforcement actions could be clearly justified. These problems are summarised and discussed below.

Contract Construction: Interpretation of Lease Terms

There is an asymmetry in power between government and the lessee in that the former decides what is and what is not permissible under the lease. It is argued that government should not have taken lease enforcement measures against the industrial and ancillary office uses in those premises which, on the basis of a proper construction of the relevant lease conditions in the light of expert opinion as found in the literature, leading court cases and a careful interpretation of the industrial lease is drafted as surveyed, are in fact "industrial" and "ancillary offices," unless (a) the lease terms expressly restrict the percentages of the latter; AND (b) the use of the premises really exceeds those percentages. In case of ambiguity of lease terms, the benefit of doubt should be given to the lessee under the doctrine of *contra proferentem* for contract construction, given the greater power of the government over the lessee.

Reasonable Use of Industrial Premises by Ancillary Offices
Government lease enforcement actions often follow a restrictive approach. They may sometimes ignore the intention of legislature as expressed in statutory town plans. It is argued that no enforcement action shall be taken or continued, even where the lease contains expressed or implied terms that do not permit ancillary offices, if the actual area of ancillary office use is below the limits imposed by the Town Planning Board Guidelines. These guidelines help interpret the statutory town plans.

Lease Enforcement Surveys
Government lease enforcement surveys actions may sometimes appear to have departed from the approach in the *Mexx Case*. It is argued that these surveys shall be conducted in the light of the "broader approach" recommended by Judge Cruden in the *Mexx Case*. This approach suggests that enforcement inspections shall go beyond an "eye-ball judgement" of the "office appearance" of the premises inspected. It shall instead find out whether individual units surveyed, in fact, belong to one single user. If that is the case, then the survey shall take into account the "cumulative effect" of factory units as well as the industrial organisation and functional relationships of these units and the rest of the industrial establishment before the conclusion that the lease has been breached is made.

Private Residential Uses in Industrial Premises

In most modern industrial leases, residential uses are not allowed. This means that the lot cannot be used as a hotel, "residential care home for elderly" (RCHE) or a residential institution. If a flat is used as an "overnight accommodation" for others (say, a bed and breakfast), it would have breached the restriction against "private residential" use.

The term, "service apartment," has appeared in some older Government Leases (see Table 5.1). A "service apartment" can be divided into two types: a hotel and a private residence. The former must follow the restrictions under the *Hotel and Guesthouse Accommodation Ordinance* (Cap.349) with a hotel licence, which prohibits a kitchen from being included with the room. For a "service apartment" under a private residential lease, its rental period could not be shorter than 28 days, as defined under the *Hotel and Guesthouse Accommodation (Exclusion) Order*. Otherwise, it would be a hotel. The unit could be rented out like other normal residences and is allowed a kitchen.

Questions for Revision and Discussion

1. The Town Planning Board has "definitions of terms" used in the statutory town plans. Discuss if it is desirable for the Lands Department to have official definitions of user clauses.

It would be immensely useful by reducing market uncertainty.

2. Study the court decisions that involved *contra proferentem* in their lease interpretations and explain the importance of this rule.

This rule of interpretation favours the party that has to accept the terms of a contract drafted by the other party.

3. Compare and contrast lease and planning enforcement.

Lease enforcement is a matter of contract enforcement. Actions taken by LandsD in the capacity of a private owner normally do not involve prosecution by LandsD. However, as modern leases have reference to specific ordinances with statutory sanctions, a lessee risks being prosecuted for breaching its respective lease terms and preventing the government's re-entry to the land.

Cases Cited

Basic Law of the Hong Kong Special Administrative Region of the People's Republic of China (The Basic Law).

Building (Planning) Regulations, Chapter 123, Laws of Hong Kong.

Joint Declaration of the Government of the United Kingdom of Great Britain and Northern Ireland and the Government of the People's Republic of China on the Question of Hong Kong (the *Sino-British Joint Declaration*).

Factories and Industrial Uses in Factories and Industrial Undertakings Ordinance, Chapter 59, Laws of Hong Kong.

Town Planning Ordinance, Chapter 131, Laws of Hong Kong.

References

Lai, Lawrence W. C. 1998. The Leasehold System as a Means of Planning by Contract: The Case of Hong Kong. *Town Planning Review* 69 (3): 249–275.

Lai, Lawrence W. C. 2000a. Enforcement against breaches of crown leases in Hong Kong industrial premises. *Property Management 18* (1): 63–73.

Merry, M. 1997. *Tenancy Law in Hong Kong*. 3rd ed. Hong Kong: Butterworths.
Nissim, Roger. 1997. *Land Administration and Practice in Hong Kong*. Hong Kong: Hong Kong University Press.
Town Planning Board. 1990. *Town Planning Board Guidelines for Application for Office Use in Industrial Buildings within Industrial Zone under Section 16 of the Town Planning Ordinance*. TPB PG-No.6 of December 1990.
Town Planning Board. 1997. *Town Planning Board Guidelines for Application for Office and Showroom Uses in Industrial Building within Industrial Zone under Section 16 of the Town Planning Ordinance*. TPB PG-NO.1A of September 1997.
Town Planning Ordinance. Chapter 131, Laws of Hong Kong.
Yeh, A. K. O. 1994. Land Leasing and Urban Planning: Lessons from Hong Kong. *Regional Development Dialogue* 15:3–21.

Law Cases

English Cases

Simmonds Aerocessories (Western) Limited v. Pontypridd Area Assessment Committee and Another [1944] 1 KB: 231.

Hong Kong Cases

Cavendish Property Development Ltd. v. Attorney General (High Court Miscellaneous proceedings No.762 of 1987) CPR 212–220.
Mexx Consolidated (Far East) v. A.G. (High Court Miscellaneous Proceedings No.2421 of 1986) [1987] HKLR 1210–1220.

CHAPTER 10

Land Resumption Practice

K. T. Liu, Ken S. T. Ching, Lawrence Wai Chung Lai, Castor T. C. Wong, and Jason Wai Yin Kwong

Land resumption means that the government takes back the interests of lessees or owners of units of interest in a building before their leases naturally expire.

An example is a lot under a 999-year lease executed during the nineteenth century that was taken back in 1965 to develop a small public garden.

Authority for Resumption

The main source of authority for resumption can be statutory, as sometimes reinforced by contract:

1. The *Lands Resumption Ordinance* (Cap.124 Laws of Hong Kong)
   The resumption is for "public purposes" and must be approved by the Chief Executive in Council.

K. T. Liu (✉) • K. S. T. Ching • L. W. C. Lai • C. T. C. Wong •
J. W. Y. Kwong
Department of Real Estate and Construction, The University of Hong Kong, Hong Kong, China
e-mail: kenching@connect.hku.hk; wclai@hku.hk

L. W. C. Lai et al. (eds.), *Principles of Land Administration at Work*, https://doi.org/10.1007/978-981-95-2972-8_10

2. The Land Resumption Clause, if any, in the Government Lease

The key features of resumption under (1) or (2) above are:

(1) Three calendar months' notice
(2) Full and fair compensation
(3) Serving of notice by:
    - delivery
    - posting on site

The *reversion* to the government occurs after one month or after a longer period, say three months from the posting of the resumption notice.

The District Lands Office (DLO) offers to purchase land from the owner. If the owner refuses, he can go to the Lands Tribunal. Meanwhile, the government pays him an interim payment, which equals 60% of the offer.

Expert Evidence Before the Lands Tribunal

The expert evidence shall cover the following:

1. Plan and valuation
2. Statement of particulars and computation in support of such valuation
3. Statement of any costs of the particulars that are proposed as evidence

Principles of Valuation

To compare the property to be valued with the most direct comparables by making the necessary adjustments in respect of the factors that affect the assessed value.

Some important factors for adjusting the value are:

1. Tenure of Government Leases
2. Date of transaction
3. Basis of the floor area calculation
4. Size of the property
5. Finishes and fittings
6. Internal layout

7. Orientation
8. Age of the property/building
9. Location (environment)

Example

Comparable transaction	$5,000 per square feet (saleable)	
Adjustment:		
Timing	–5.0%	
Size	–5.0%	
Orientation	+2.5%	
Finishes	+2.5%	–5%
		$4,750 per square feet
Size		1,000 square feet (saleable)
Value of the property		$4,750,000

Valuation

Proceeds

20,000 of @$5,000.00	$100,000,000	
P.V. 1yr @10%	0.9090	$90,900,000

Cost

Construction 20,000 square feet @$1,000.00		$20,000,000	
Professional fees, say 5%		$1,000,000	
		$21,000,000	
Developer profit 15%		$3,150,000	
		$24,150,000	
P.V. 1/2 yr. @$10%	0.95	$22,942,500	
Land and profit		$67,957,500	
Less developer◎ profit 20%			÷1.2
Land value			$56,631,250
Say		56,630,000	

Note: There are too many variables in a residual valuation, so a slight change to any or all variables would cause a big change in the resultant land value.

Determination of the Lands Tribunal

The Lands Tribunal makes determination of the following:

1. Value as of the date of reversion to government
2. Value of the land and building

3. Value of the easement or other right
4. Amount of loss due to severance
5. Value of the business loss due to its removal
6. Removal expenses
7. Professional fees

Rules for Determining Compensation

1. No allowance is made for resumption, which is compulsory.
2. No account is taken into of adverse land-use zoning.
3. Statutory town plans are ignored: Section 12(aa) of the *Lands Resumption Ordinance* excludes admission of any town plans under the *Town Planning Ordinance* (Cap 131) for the determination of compensation: "no account shall be taken of the fact that the land lies within or is affected by any area, zone or district reserved or set apart for the purposes specified in section 4(1)(a), (c), (d), (e), (f), (g), (h) or (i) of Cap.131." However, in this part of the world, town plans have been produced not just under Cap.131. See Lai et al. (2018).
4. The value of those uses that are not in accordance with the terms of the Government Lease is ignored.
5. No compensation shall be given in respect of any expectancy of a probability of the grant or renewal or continuance, by the government or any person of any license, permission, lease, or permit whatsoever (unless enforceable as of right).
6. The value of the land resumed shall be taken as the amount at which the land, if sold by *a willing seller* in the open market, is expected to fetch. (This is more generous than the previous rule, which was based on the amount for which it was sold by a willing buyer to a willing seller.)

Resumption Under Other Ordinances

1. *Mass Transit Railway Land Resumption (and Related Provisions) Ordinance*
2. *Roads (works, use, and compensation) Ordinance*

3. *Foreshore and Sea-Bed (Reclamation) Ordinance*
4. The Urban Renewal Authority (URA) can apply to the government to employ the *Lands Resumption Ordinance* to assume the outstanding land-holdings if a majority of the property shares within a development scheme have been purchased.
5. *Land (Compulsory Sale for Redevelopment) Ordinance*
   A developer that has obtained at least 80% of the property shares of a lot can apply to the Lands Tribunal for an order to sell the lot compulsorily in a public auction.
   The proceeds of a sale are to be distributed according to the existing use value of the individual units, while ignoring any redevelopment potential (i.e., "merger value").

Principles of Resumption

Some basic resumption principles in Hong Kong are:

1. The identity and extent of each lot affected by resumption should be ascertained.
2. The land to be resumed should be of **minimum necessity**.
3. Resumption proposals for small areas should be avoided unless there is strong justification for them.
4. Due consideration should be given to the land acquisition perspective for the partial resumption of a lot: any residual portion that is rendered incapable of a reasonable, beneficial use should NOT be included within the boundaries of a resumption. In general, any area smaller than 0.01 acre (435.6 square ft.) should be regarded as incapable of reasonable beneficial use.
5. Land should not be resumed for only temporary purposes, which should be provided for by means of creating temporary easements for the affected owners.
6. The typical plans required to implement land resumption and clearance are:
   (a) Draft land resumption plans
   (b) Final resumption plans
   (c) Clearance plans
   (d) Plans for "Temporary Occupational Areas" (TOAs)

Questions for Revision and Discussion

1. Discuss the relevance of town planning to land resumption.

Statutory plans cannot be relied on for compensation claims in Hong Kong.

2. Discuss the difference between "public purpose" and "public use."

The former is far wider in scope.

3. Discuss the meaning of "urban decay."

"Urban decay" is actually a social and economic, rather than a purely physical, concept. Its signs are depopulation, loss of businesses, high crime, unemployment, and vacancy rates at the same time, an urban phenomenon that is atypical of Hong Kong. See Lai, Lawrence W.C., K.W. Chau & Polycarp Alvin C.W. Cheung. "Urban renewal and redevelopment: Social justice and property rights with reference to Hong Kong's constitutional capitalism." Cities 74 (2018): 240–248.

Reference

Lai, Lawrence W. C., K. W. Chau, C. W. Polycarp Alvin, and Cheung. 2018. Urban Renewal and Redevelopment: Social Justice and Property Rights with Reference to Hong Kong's Constitutional Capitalism. *Cities* 74:240–248.

CHAPTER 11

Cadastral Boundary Surveys

Ken S. T. Ching

This chapter explains some features and problems in boundary determinations by land surveyors for private property holdings in Hong Kong's general boundary system due to the government's reluctance to guarantee the accuracy of lot maps registered by land surveyors. The tendency of property owners to litigate and the desirability of reforms to establish a fixed boundary system are discussed.

Basic Concepts

A piece of land, as property allocated to a government department or a lessee, must have a locationally unique and planimetrically accurately recorded *fiat* boundary. There must be no discontinuity along this boundary.

A land surveyor normally refers his land boundary survey work as one that "redefines" the boundary of a land parcel but does not "define" the parcel's boundary unless it is newly granted. This is because the boundaries of the land were established when the parcel was first granted. Any

K. S. T. Ching (✉)
Real Estate and Construction, The University of Hong Kong,
Hong Kong SAR, China
e-mail: kenching@connect.hku.hk

L. W. C. Lai et al. (eds.), *Principles of Land Administration at Work*, https://doi.org/10.1007/978-981-95-2972-8_11

subsequent action that relates to locating the boundary is a "redefinition" or "re-establishment" of that boundary.

The court will endeavour to interpret the boundary description, both textual and graphical, on the original grant to reconstruct the intentions of the parties for the land parcel's boundary.

In Hong Kong, the land boundary survey expert is an Authorised Land Surveyor as registered under the *Land Survey Ordinance* (Cap.473, *Laws of Hong Kong*).

Defining One's Property Boundary Would Affect Neighbour's Boundaries

Lai (2023), quoting Acton (1988), pointed out that "no property is an Island." He explained that "a lot cannot be an isolated entity but is an integral part of a wider human shore, coordinated or un-coordinated." This statement sheds light on a root problem of property boundary surveys conducted by land surveyors.

Unlike other professionals such as doctors, dentists, accountants, engineers, architects, or non-land surveyors (e.g., quantity and building surveyors), whose professional advice directly and uniquely concerns only their client(s), land surveyors' advice in respect of their clients' property boundaries has direct impacts on all adjoining and/or neighbouring property holdings. This characteristic alone separates land boundary surveying from the other professional services that deal with land.

The reason is simple. Once a land surveyor redefines a client's boundary (according to available boundary evidences), this boundary segment, which is a single line, should also become the same boundary segment for any adjoining owner(s). A land surveyor acting for a lot owner should take heed of the adjacent owner's interest. Yet, in reality, this is a difficult undertaking. The surveyor's findings are prone to be challenged in court by another party who sees that its interests have been jeopardised.

Based on their experiences, the authors have strong reservations about the current Hong Kong land surveying practices in property boundary (re)definition.

As Lai (2023) pointed out, a lot owner could enjoy the rights within the framework subject to common law restrictions on the enjoyment of land property. But these rights are never unlimited or unconstrained. Lai pointed out that the holder of a private land parcel, which is a natural unit

(Lai & Davies 2020) or basic unit (Lai & Davies 2023) of private planning, has obligations as well as rights. Property boundaries should be not only part of the right to exclude, but also part of the right to include.

Consider the authors' analysis (Ching & Yuen 2024) of Observation Post Red Hill situated within RBL777. Even though it is hardly disputable that the OP fell within the boundary of a private land property, it could have been conserved if the developer had perceived it as a valuable public good and historical asset and allowed the relevant experts to conduct necessary conservation or rehabilitation actions for it, before or instead of expunging it as construction waste.

The Hong Kong Context

All land holdings (as lots) in Hong Kong, except the freehold lot granted to the Church of England and occupied by St John's Cathedral along Garden Road, are held as leasehold interests. The registration of a lease and/or any conveyancing document in Hong Kong is a means to record the land rights and obligations of a certain land parcel, but not its unique boundary (which must be a closed loop, not in plurals) vis-à-vis the rest of the world.

As an essential part of land rights, a lot boundary is described by the boundary clause in a land grant agreement (and repeated in a Government Lease) and depicted in a Lot Plan as a titled land grant document. This plan is the legal boundary backdrop for a particular land parcel.

Surprisingly, under the Hong Kong Land Registration System, land conveyancing documents are only prioritised according to their dates of registration without any guarantee of title or land boundary by the government. Accordingly, the Lot Plan referred to in a conveyancing document has no statutory significance in terms of boundary certitude and the involved parties have to determine by agreement the effect of the Lot Plan.[1] When a lot owner appoints a land surveyor to redefine the lot boundary of the owned property in relation to those of an adjoining lot, it is necessary for the surveyor to construe all land grant documents, so as to discover the original intentions of the parties at stake.

The final construction of the original conveyance rests with the court. Accordingly, any cadastral surveyor must ask oneself two fundamental questions before conducting a land boundary survey for a property owner:

[1] The "general" or "approximate" boundary concept.

(1) How would the court interpret the land grant documents?
(2) How would the court adjudicate a boundary dispute?

To address these two questions, the surveyor should appreciate that boundary (re)definition, re-establishment or retracement (Hallman 1978) is a balancing exercise that is based on the best available evidence and must not materially deviate from the intention of the original grant.

In Hong Kong, such a land boundary has to be re-established on the ground as a refined line worked out by an Authorised Land Surveyor (ALS) or a Registered Professional Surveyor (Land Surveying) (RPS (LS)).

Regrettably, the boundary re-establishment process has never gained any legal status. So, in the absence of a legal recognition of a defined boundary, a land surveyor who is hired by a landowner has to bear the full responsibility for any consequence of a boundary that the surveyor helps re-establish.

At present, when a land surveyor is appointed by a client to conduct a land boundary survey, the surveyor would consider all best available boundary evidences and then draw a conclusion by producing a Survey Record Plan (SRP) and a Land Boundary Plan (LBP). Subject to the consent of the client, the SRP and LBP will be deposited to the relevant District Survey Office (DSO) for record and sharing purposes.[2]

Land surveyors in private practice initially welcomed the sharing concept because it appeared to provide a common platform for other surveyors to consult and discover if adjoining lots had been surveyed before deciding if they could adopt the redefined boundary segments to avoid boundary conflicts between neighbouring lot owners.

Should a surveyor refuse to adopt the boundaries previously redefined, that surveyor should provide better evidence to dispute those boundaries,

[2] This is an administrative mechanism for facilitating the sharing of land boundary records. The government always reiterates, by way of standard letter replies to the land surveyors concerned, that it bears no responsibility to verify or approve the data and information shown in the plans and survey reports. The accuracy of these plans and reports is the sole responsibility of the surveyors. Nevertheless, under S.30 (4) of the *Land Survey Ordinance* (Cap.473, *Laws of Hong Kong*), an authorised land surveyor has a duty to furnish a duplicate of the SRP and LBP to the Land Survey Authority in respect of the subdivision of land within seven days after the submission of the deed poll(s) or other instruments with the LBPs. These must be registered with the Land Registry under the *Land Registration Ordinance* (Cap.128, *Laws of Hong Kong*).

along with a good argument. That would, however, lead to a boundary dispute.

This system of "first come, first served" is undesirable in light of the following considerations:

First, there is no way to ensure that all affected landowners would be aware of the re-established boundary/boundaries, much less asking all of them to agree on the new boundary/boundaries.

Second, a single land surveyor has no power or duty to survey all adjacent lots, and what the surveyor does is only an ad hoc and confined assignment for a particular land parcel (bear in mind that "no property is an island"). The surveyor's assessment may be disputed for being incomplete and/or incompetent.

Third, there is no legal obligation for a land surveyor to adopt the same refined boundary segment. Such a requirement can generate conflict.

While there is simply no final re-established boundary, a boundary dispute may arise and the security of the landowner's property is at risk.

Accordingly, the lack of a binding legal status for a re-established boundary often leads to unwarranted claims of adverse possession. Hence, many public processes, such as building plan approvals and land resumptions, would be made more complicated and time-consuming, which would waste taxpayers' money and the speed of redevelopment, thereby harming the interest of the general public.

Still, increased demand for a precise boundary definition (whether in Hong Kong's urban areas or the New Territories) due to a growing awareness among landowners of the importance of land boundaries has generated a derived demand for properly dealing with land boundary redefinition exercises. However, a growth in the number of adverse possessions has not alerted the general public to the socio-economic significance of these cases.

Both the government and stakeholders certainly accept the need for a comprehensive, systematic land boundary survey for all of Hong Kong. Yet, similar to the resistance to a national survey of China's cultivated land during the Ming Dynasty, neither the government nor landowners dare to press for reforms. Their reasons are:

(1) "Let Sleeping Dogs Lie": an official boundary re-establishment system with statutory clarity may expose many cases of unauthorised land occupation.
(2) Lack of Government Commitment: many property boundary irregularities and associated squatting on government and/or

> private land would be exposed should a large-scale, systematic survey be carried out. The government, as the lessor of land and central organiser of cadastral records, has an unescapable responsibility to address tort claims that would arise because of erroneous and/or missing land boundary records.

Anybody who appreciates the present land boundary situation in Hong Kong realises that it is rare for two landlords to accept a boundary settlement drafted by independent land surveyors. If an owner is not satisfied with the boundary of one's property, regardless if it is redefined by a neighbour, the owner can take the neighbour and relevant surveyor(s) to court.

It could be inferred, at least from a cadastral land surveyor's perspective, that the most appropriate approach is that adjacent owners in dispute negotiate a solution. Yet, in Hong Kong, settling a boundary dispute outside of the court is rare because the dispute is often more than a rational economic calculation and its professional and legal costs often exceed the value of the land involved because usually only a small portion of the land is under dispute.

Some believe that the court system is a self-correcting mechanism that considers the evidence. A property owner, hence, has a higher possibility of obtaining a "correct" decision to safeguard one's property interests by having one's property boundary clearly delineated, legally recognised and protected, as well as enforced.

As cadastral land surveyors, the authors hope that property owners cooperate or negotiate when a conflict occurs instead of fighting it out in court. This is because, as stated earlier, most boundary disputes involve small plots of land (say, over only a few square feet/metres) or short segments (as little as a few centimetres long) that, from a land surveying perspective, are not worth the cost of litigation. Anger is a key reason for bringing a boundary dispute to court. Cadastral land surveyors are aware of this both in terms of the depth of knowledge and technicalities involved. However, those who work within the legal system may not know land boundary issues as well as cadastral land surveyors. Thus, they may not devise the best solutions to handle such disputes.

Indeed, there is the scenario of one client and a landlord accepting a boundary settlement, as advised jointly by two separate land surveyors. This happens when both parties are involved in an adverse possession process. In this instance, surveyors, as expert witnesses, have to agree on the land boundaries concerned before the case can proceed.

In an adverse possession case, the role of the land surveyor is two-fold:

(1) To identify the property boundaries.
(2) To ascertain the actual occupied area that was allegedly and adversely possessed.

The first deals with the original property boundaries, while the second deals with occupied areas. An occupier may have only occupied a part of the subject land and even other land parcels, be they government or private land.

During the proceedings, both parties have to agree to the answer of a crucial and primary question raised by the court: "Where is the land?" In practice, the two land surveying experts involved have to agree to a joint expert statement in which they have to list the issues on which they both agree and agree to disagree. The statement must also include the original lot boundaries and actual occupied area, as well as its physical features and, most importantly, the land's occupation history throughout the relevant period.

Under normal circumstances, both experts will generally agree on the property boundary, but may differ on the occupied area and physical features, as these depend heavily on extrinsic evidence such as old aerial photos and survey sheets, as well as witness testimony.

Land Boundary and Economics

Land is an immovable, spatially fixed entity (i.e., real property) on which an owner could carry out lawful activities and erect fixtures. There is a need to properly manage and invest in it, which may include erecting a valuable structure on it, farming, grazing, etc., before its value could be realised. If its boundaries are uncertain, investment in it and even its entitlement are at risk. Thus, this is the reason for a precise land boundary survey to clearly delineate a property, especially when the potential investment in it is huge.

The determination of compensation and loss is principally a matter for the court. But it is a costly and often inefficient process. All of the costs—financial, temporal, and emotional—involved in delineating boundaries and resolving boundary disputes are transaction costs and take resources away from making the land productive.

Litigation on boundary disputes is particularly severe in urbanised areas where:

(1) Land prices are bundled together.
(2) Land is either sold or granted with proper documentation.
(3) There is a rapid increase in land values, as well as an owner's awareness of the importance of correct boundary delineation.

Most importantly, when a dispute is adjudicated, the court's decision is final and definitive. Still, litigation as a means to resolve a boundary dispute occurs despite its transaction costs.

Lai et al. (2018) explained that there are two surveying factors (i.e., historical and map representation) that prevent landowners from settling their land boundary disputes by mutual agreement and have to rely on assistance from a firm (the government) and the law (the court) in terms of Coasian logic.

The former surveying factor refers to the ever-changing, contemporary property market. The boundary matters could be regarded as temporal by their nature and the modern boundary is most likely not identical to the customary boundary of old, while the modes of transacting real properties are dissimilar during different epochs. Clearly defined land rights could, therefore, facilitate land rights transactions and/or trades (i.e., buying, selling, mortgaging, and leasing land) in the contemporary property market.

Compared to the first factor, the second factor is more technical. The rationale behind this is the presence of errors, blunders, and fuzziness, as well as limitations in the personnel and/or surveying instruments employed. Thus, the interpretation of a map or plan's cartographical boundaries by different people could produce different results. It would, therefore, be practical to allow a trusted authority, such as the court, to offer a reasonable approximation that settles the differences.

The authors, as land surveying professionals with substantial experience in dealing with property boundary disputes, entirely concur with the propositions of Lai et al. (2018), who accurately elucidated and summarised recent tangible boundary dispute issues using sound economic theories. From the technical perspective of a cadastral surveyor, the ideas of Lai et al. (2018) relate to the following aspects:

(1) Incomplete/missing land grant records.
(2) Conflicting clauses within the land grant documents.
(3) Graphical and survey accuracies due to advancements in surveying technologies, which, in turn, could refine the rough graphical depictions of the lot boundaries in the old grant plans.

In fact, it is rare in Hong Kong for a cadastral land surveyor to be involved in the negotiation process for a land boundary dispute. Indeed, it would be very fortunate for owners of adjacent lots to the one under dispute to welcome any survey work carried on their properties. Even though negotiations are possible, it is doubtful that they could produce a fruitful result, which depends on the following factors:

(1) If the owners of the relevant adjacent lots are present during the field survey.
(2) If the owners present are amicable to the survey.
(3) If the owner who appoints the land surveyor would allow the surveyor to also be a negotiator or mediator.
(4) Most importantly, if the owners are ready to disclose their intentions regarding the property boundaries. In general, when an owner[3] appoints a land surveyor to redefine boundaries, the owner probably has two objectives:
    (a) To develop one's own land.
    (b) To check the extent of one's property boundary or a possible encroachment by an adjacent lot.

In both scenarios, the owner generally has no intention to encroach on adjacent land and, hence, has no initiative to disclose one's intentions regarding boundary determination unless s/he reached a consensus in advance. As Lai et al. (2018) pointed out, "the resolution of boundary disputes <u>is a pre-contractual process with a view to determining the *de jure* boundaries.</u> Hence the disputes cannot be resolved by mutual agreement."

[3] Currently, only the landowner or the owner's legal representative can request a boundary survey from an Authorised Land Surveyor/Registered Professional Surveyor (land surveying). As with the LBP and SRP, after the survey is performed, the results could be deposited at the relevant DSO.

The Need for Cadastral Reform

It is noteworthy that the property boundary problem is universal and that is why many developing countries have instituted cadastral reforms over the years to support economic and environmental development and stable society. These reforms required overcoming a vast array of legal, technical, and administrative problems. Each country either developed or renewed its own land management/deed registration system along with its corresponding cadastral surveying and mapping systems by implementing new laws to move from a structure of general boundaries to fixed boundaries based on a national coordinates system.

From a cadastral land surveyor's viewpoint, the fixed boundary concept better represents a plot's true land boundaries in terms of the title protection to secure its owner's interests and facilitate sustainable economic development given scarce land resources. In return, this provides substantial social and political benefits and ensures a more stable society because through formalising and implementing a centralised land records system, the management of a locale should become more efficient through the free and uninterrupted access to property information, the security of tenure, sustainable and environmentally friendly development, etc. Most importantly, the government is able to remind private landowners/occupants of their obligations.

These obligations stem from the social nature of private land property and do not merely refer to paying land tax. It is more important to impose additional tangential liabilities or restrictions on the landowner under a legal and regulatory framework, which only the government can do to oversee the safety and liabilities of third parties, the negative rights to not use through the town planning mechanism, etc.[4]

As an empirical study based on a set of novel data, which hypothesises that cadastral reforms should have a positive impact on economic growth, D'Arcy et al. (2021) concluded that, "a very strong correlation between

[4] In a District Court case (STS 7327/2021), the Court held that the defendant was not guilty of illegally building a road in a green-belt zone, which was government land. The Court referred to the evidence of an expert witness, who represented the Lands Department's Survey and Mapping Office and pointed out that the Lot Index Plan relied on by the Plaintiff, the Planning Department, might have been incorrectly surveyed. The Court had reservations over the relevant section of the road trespassing on government land, as the plaintiff alleged. It added that the plaintiff never proved that the road section involved belonged to the defendant and that the defendant engaged in illegal dumping there.

cadastral institutional reforms and economic growth at the cross-country level over a long run." In other words, there is a strong link between well-defined property rights over land and economic growth as "they imply more secure returns on investment, a reduction in the resources needed to defend the rights to land, facilitate land market transactions and increase access to credit."

The study of D'Arcy et al. (2021) produced a very long time series for GDP per capita. It justified that, except in Sweden, cadastral reforms were "associated with increased growth rates of GDP per capita" in the other three countries. D'Arcy et al. observed that the real interest rates in the United Kingdom and the Netherlands increased substantially, thereby signifying a comparatively strong boost in rural investment demand. In addition, they established that after five years of reform, the investment-GDP ratio increased by about 1.1 percentage points.

As the world further proceeds into its information era, cadastral reforms should be coupled with the rapidly growing waves of big digital data and smart-city trends. The development of future smart cities will definitely require access to inclusive services, technologies, and infrastructure. It should embrace the concept of "No one should be left behind"[5] to ensure that all efforts towards a sustainable, smart city will foster a better future for all.

Land boundary rights are undoubtedly a key factor in signifying the essential role of land administration in building sustainable, smart cities. A system of accurate and unambiguous land boundary recordings (i.e., a cadastre) is a critical and fundamental base information layer that could enable the integration of all property-related services administered by the government.

Unfortunately, Hong Kong, a comparatively mature city, lags behind much of the world in this regard due to its government's unwillingness to tackle the root cause of the property boundary conundrum. The government, as the lessor of all land lots in the city, should take a more proactive stance to upgrade and protect property titles by implementing statutorily assured boundaries to render Hong Kong a world-class smart city.

[5] *Leave no one behind (LNOB)* is the central, transformative promise of the United Nations 2030 *Agenda for Sustainable Development* and its sustainable development goals (SDGs).

Epilogue

With particular reference to Hong Kong's current situation, this chapter reviews the reasons behind its land boundary survey problems and limitations from land surveying and economic perspectives. Finally, the authors recommend timely cadastral reforms for Hong Kong to bring about a fixed boundary system that is accessible to the public to ensure certainty over lot boundaries and, hence, a reduction in the transaction costs of land property developments, greater public enjoyment, and heritage conservation.

Questions for Revision and Discussion

1. Discuss the difficulties when the government, as the landlord, must guarantee land boundaries or arbitrate over boundary disputes among private lot holders.

   Some difficulties are:

   - Land boundary records can be outdated or lost.
   - Inconsistent or poorly maintained documentation leads to ambiguities on land boundaries.
   - Changes in land uses and rapid land development: the resulting property law/regulations may lead to new interpretations of the land use and boundaries.
   - Changes in advanced surveying technology and supply of skilled professionals.
   - Rise in the economic values of land, which can fuel the propensity for conflict.
   - Lack of efficient coordination and bureaucratic readiness to deal with problems among government departments.

2. Discuss a Coasian way to resolve a boundary dispute over the alignment of a common boundary involving a disputed zone of less than one metre in width.

   Some useful means are:

- Focusing on negotiation and bargaining rather than legal adjudication.
- Aiming for win-win solutions in which both parties believe they have gained more than they have lost.
- Ensuring that the negotiation process is efficient to avoid costs due to litigation or prolonged disputes.
- Accepting monetary compensation: both parties in a dispute accepting money as compensation for a tiny disputed area.
- Accepting an exchange of another plot of land to make up for a disputed area.
- Agreeing to share in the use of a disputed land plot or grant. This is an easement that allows both parties to enjoy certain rights over the land without the need to change its boundary or ownership.

3. Discuss, with references to real-life examples, why government survey maps may not record all existing structures.

    - The rapid pace of development outstrips the pace of updating survey maps.
    - Illegal structures and informal settlements, such as those in the New Territories, may not be officially recognised or mapped by the government.
    - Structures of historical or cultural significance may not be fully captured in modern surveying methods.
    - Comprehensive and rapid surveying and mapping requires advanced technology, but resources may not always be available from the government, whose spending is not project oriented.
    - Legal procedures and administrative processes slow down the process of survey map updates.
    - Errors and omission.

References

Ching, Ken S. T., and Circle K. Y. Yuen. 2024. An Observation Post (OP) on a Private Land Parcel on Red Hill. *Survey and Built Environment* 33 (2): 13–28.

D'Arcy, Michelle, Marina Nistotskaya, and Ola Olsson. 2021. *Land Property Rights, Cadasters and Economic Growth: A Cross-Country Panel 1000-2015 CE.* Working Paper in Economics No.800. Department of Economics, University of Gothenburg, March.

Hallman, F. M. 1978. The role of the cadastral surveyor. *Australian Surveyor* 22 (3): 171–177.

Lai, Lawrence W. C. 2023. No Property is an island: The Private Lot as the Basic Unit of Landuse Planning & Management of a Wider World. *Cosmos + Taxis* 11 (1–2): 90–96.

Lai, Lawrence W. C., and Stephen N. G. Davies. 2020. 'Surveying was a Kind of Writing on the Land': The Economics of Land Division as Town Planning. *Planning Theory* 19 (4): 421–444.

Lai, Lawrence W. C., and Stephen N. G. Davies. 2023. Is Non-Zoning of Land Impossible? Eight Fundamental Propositions of Zoning. *Journal of Environmental Policy & Planning* 25 (3): 242–257.

Lai, Lawrence W. C., Stephen N. G. Davies, K. W. Chau, Ken S. T. Ching, Mark H. Chua, H. F. Leung, and Frank T. Lorne. 2018. The Determination of the "True" Property Boundary in Planned Development: A Coasian Analysis. *Annals of Regional Science* 61:579–599.

CHAPTER 12

Aerial Photos and Geo-Rreferencing

Ken S. T. Ching

This chapter describes the concept of geo-referencing, which is an essential technical technique in geographical information systems (GIS).

With reference to aerial photos kept and/or produced by the Lands Department, it explains the basic operation and limitations involved in practice and aims to serve as fundamental information for other non-land surveying/GIS professionals who interpret aerial photos during their land use analyses.

Aerial Photos Kept by the Lands Department

"Old aerial photo" refers to the photographs taken from an aircraft or other flying object. The Survey and Mapping Office (SMO) of the Lands Department (LandsD) periodically undertakes aerial photography at different altitudes in Hong Kong. Photos from 1924 to the present are kept and produced by the SMO and are available to the public upon request with payment.

K. S. T. Ching (✉)
Real Estate and Construction, The University of Hong Kong,
Hong Kong SAR, China
e-mail: kenching@connect.hku.hk

L. W. C. Lai et al. (eds.), *Principles of Land Administration at Work*, https://doi.org/10.1007/978-981-95-2972-8_12

There are various types of aerial photograph including colour, false colour infrared, and different oblique degrees, as well as orthophotos.[1] Since these aerial photos were taken with high-resolution film (recent aerial photos are captured in digital format in the form of a raster dataset) at relatively low-flying heights of about 2000 feet to 10,000 feet (about 609 metres to 3048 metres), they can be used to identify the ground's occupation and land use of the past. These photos can be purchased either in their original scales or as enlargements from the SMO.

It must be admitted that, despite aerial photographs faithfully record the ground features at their time of exposure, the photo images (i.e., the ground features shown thereon) were nevertheless subjected to various image distortions such as the tilting of photo angles, variations in flying height, the undulation of the terrain heights, and the weather at the time the photos were taken.

Despite the aforementioned technical, optical, and geographical limitations, these photos serve as the most objective records of the ground's occupational situation and history and hence are widely accepted by courts as evidence.

Principles of Geo-referencing

In the sphere of geographical information systems (GIS), individuals will **geo-reference** (or **ground-register**) their raster datasets using existing spatial data with respect to a known ground coordinate system. This is a technique whereby a digital image is processed so that the columns and rows of the resulting product are aligned with the north and east in the same ground coordinate system. The process involves identifying a series of ground control points (known x-y coordinates) that link the positions on the raster dataset to the locations in the spatially referenced data. The positions of the control points can be precisely identified on the raster dataset and in real-world coordinates.

The control points are used to build a polynomial transformation that will shift the raster dataset from its existing location to the spatially correct

[1] In photogrammetry, the term "relief displacement" refers to a feature position on a photograph radially displaced from the principal point, while the "tilt displacement" causes a photo to be displayed obliquely and its image is distorted. To rectify the original photo's distortions and obtain a map-like photo, all points on the photo must be of a uniform scale, which means measurements on it can be taken. Orthophotos result from a geometric rectification of the relief and tilt displacements.

location. During the transformation, a link will be established. This is the connection between one control point on the raster dataset (the "from-point") and the corresponding point on the aligned target data (the "to-point").

Aligning the Images in the Aerial Photos (Raster Data) with Known Control Points

When geographical data were collected through the optical scanning method (a digital aerial camera mounted on an airfreight to capture ground features), individual scans were based on an arbitrary spatial coordinate system. Thus, in order to use those different arbitrary scanning data in different positions, one must align their absolute positions and orientation (i.e., **geo-referencing**) so that the scanning geographical data use a common coordinate platform that should be based on a local grid.

In Hong Kong, this local grid is the Hong Kong 1980 Grid System (HK1980 Grid), which is a local rectangular grid based on the HK80 Geodetic Datum[2] and Transverse Mercator Projection. HK1980 Grid is used in land boundary surveys, engineering surveying, and large-scale mapping in the city.

A classic example of geo-referencing by a cadastral land surveyor in Hong Kong is when the surveyor is asked to present his/her aerial interpretations in Court. A land surveyor will generally geo-reference the relevant aerial photos s/he obtained from LandsD, which bears no coordinate system thereon, with respect to other relevant land boundary records that were produced with sound and measured coordinate systems so that an analysis of the results would be facilitated and, most importantly, be quantified.

Under normal practices, the processes of geo-referencing were conducted in office settings. One may geo-reference a raster dataset (aerial photos in raster format) using spatially known (target) data. Normally, it would involve using a "vector" data class that already exists in the coordinate system (for HK1980 Grid, a 1:1000 or other-scale basic survey sheets,

[2] Recently, two geodetic data were used in Hong Kong for horizontal control (i.e., the local datum—Hong Kong 1980 Geodetic Datum (HK80) and the global datum—the World Geodetic System (WGS84)). The origin of HK80 is the old Trig "Zero" (no longer in use) at the Hong Kong Observatory, while that for WGS84 is a Cartesian coordinate system for the centre of the Earth's mass.

survey plans, etc.). The process involves identifying a series of ground control points of known northing and easting coordinates, which could then establish a correlation between the positions on the raster dataset and the corresponding locations in the spatially known data.

As mentioned above, control points are locations that can be accurately identified on both a raster dataset and in the real-world coordinates grid. For a typical aerial photo taken from a low-flying height and possessing a low oblique, many different salient ground features can be used as identifiable controls such as building corners, road or stream intersections, stream openings, rock ridges, the end of a land jetty, the corner of an established field, sharp street corners, and the intersection of two hedgerows.

These control points are used to build a polynomial transformation that will mathematically shift the raster dataset from its existing location to the spatially correct location through the links generated. This spatial transformation involves a polynomial built on control points and a least squares fitting algorithm. This process has a classic technical name: "rubber sheeting".

As the number of links needed to perform the transformation is arbitrary, there is no definite quantitative measure of the dataset being aligned. The result is indeed highly dependent on the complexity of the transformation of the raster dataset to the map coordinates. Nevertheless, even one with added links would not return a better geo-referencing result, especially if these links cluster together.

The reason is simple. The control points that are used to align the raster dataset would be restrained or limited to an overlap area. Hence, areas outside the overlap area are unlikely to be properly aligned. Typically, the larger the overlap between the raster dataset and target data, the better the alignment because more widely spatially fixed points can be used to conduct the geo-referencing. This is, indeed, in line with the basic and well-known land surveying principle, i.e., "from whole to the part".

As a rule of thumb, it is preferable to spread the links over the entire raster dataset. For example, at least one link near each corner of the raster dataset of the aerial photo, along with a few links that evenly cover the inner areas of the same photo, will generally produce a more robust result. Yet, it should be noted that geo-referenced data are only as accurate as those data to which they are aligned. Given this limitation, the geo-referencing process should be at the highest resolution and largest scale, so as to minimise errors.

The Qualitative Measurement of Geo-Referencing: By Interpreting the Root Mean Square

When a general mathematical formula is derived and applied to a control point, a quantitative measure of the error, the "residual", is generated. The residual is the variance between the from-point generated and the actual location of the to-point. The total errors are then computed by taking the root mean square (RMS) sum of all the residuals.

This RMS quantifies the consistency among the transformation between the different links. The GIS users/operators are free to remove and/or add more control points to minimise the RMS value when it is considered too large.

It should be noted that despite the RMS value being a helpful indication of the measurement accuracy of a specific transformation process, one may note the fundamental concept that a relatively low RMS value does not mean that an image is perfectly geo-referenced. The transformation process would contain significant errors due to inadequate control points being inputted (garbage in, garbage out). The basic principle is that the more equal quality control points are used, the more a polynomial can convert the input data into a more accurate and robust result for the output coordinates.

Questions for Revision and Discussion

1. Discuss the values of old aerial photos for land studies.

The Lands Department holds many aerial photographs dating back to 1924. They are available for public use. These photos are invaluable resources for researchers, planners, and anyone interested in the following historical and environmental aspects of land use in Hong Kong:

- Urban and environmental monitoring of changes in land use and development of vegetation, water bodies, and other natural features.
- Land Use Analysis: analysing past land use patterns, which can help urban planners and designers decide on future land uses, management, and conservation.
- Use as evidence in boundary disputes or to verify claims to land ownership and usage.
- Documentation for cultural and heritage preservation.

2. How are aerial photos used for geo-referencing?

Aerial photos are essential for geo-referencing, which involves assigning real-world geographic coordinates ("Vector" data class) to photo images ("Raster" data class). The following are major processes:

- Identifying Ground Control Points (GCPs) such as road intersections, building corners, and survey markers, which are specific locations on the ground with known geographic coordinates and visible in aerial photos. It is preferable to spread the links over the entire raster dataset to ensure better geo-referencing results.
- Using the control points to build a polynomial transformation that will shift the raster dataset from its existing location to a spatially correct location through the links generated during the transformation.
- "Rubber sheeting": Forming the raster dataset from its existing location to a spatially correct location through the links generated.

3. Discuss the importance of BO No.4 in mapping Hong Kong.

- A relic of the first systematic land survey of Hong Kong territory by Lt. T.B. Collinson, R.E.
- An example of the early use of cadastral markers in Hong Kong.
- The only known Hong Kong example of a Board of Ordnance marker.
- Rare: similar markers in Canada and the UK are rare.
- Highlights the importance of Hong Kong's built historical heritage, in particular the significance of the ungraded and unprotected Saiwan Redoubt during the Battle of Hong Kong.

CHAPTER 13

Aerial Photo Interpretation of Change in Use of Land

Lawrence Wai Chung Lai

Introduction

This chapter, an extract of Davies et al. (2018), presents some theoretical criticisms of photographical information and some issues in aerial photo interpretation for enforcement against unauthorized land use.

Aerial photographs are, for many environmental planners and land use managers, something to be turned to without question as a useful resource (Bowden & Brooner 1970). Such photographs, scrupulously taken using carefully designed systems, give and are assumed to give a clear, exact, detailed depiction of terrain. With the use of such tools as orthophotography, infrared filters or today's additional tools like LIDAR (Light Detection and Ranging), AVIRIS (Airborne Visible and Infrared Imaging Spectrometer) and SAR (Synthetic Aperture Radar), seemingly 'invisible' data can be 'seen', extending our understanding of the surface world being depicted. If such images cannot offer Thomas Nagel's 'view from

L. W. C. Lai (✉)
Department of Real Estate and Construction, The University of Hong Kong, Hong Kong, China
e-mail: wclai@hku.hk

L. W. C. Lai et al. (eds.), *Principles of Land Administration at Work*, https://doi.org/10.1007/978-981-95-2972-8_13

nowhere' (Nagel 1986), they are, as 'bird's eye views', by definition not a normal human's eye view.

Theoretical Context: Subjectivist Attacks on Maps and Photos

Like many other social practices, the use of maps has not been immune to subjective critical analysis (Monmonier 2018). The idea behind this is that maps are not free from the biases and preferences of their authors or commissioning authority.

Recently, photos, championed by artists for being heritage items (Arijs 2014), have been subjected to similar criticism. It is a criticism that can be dated back to the ever-controversial Viollet-le-Duc, who preferred maps over photographs (O'Connell 1998). Interestingly, no such accusation of bias or authorial preference has been made with respect to the use of aerial photos. Perhaps the reason is the same as that which we can infer from animated Viollet-le-Duc. For what he actually hoped to obtain was "a series of photographs taken perpendicularly from the surface of the earth" to represent Mont Blanc because what he wanted—in anticipation of photogrammetry—was to make an accurate map. The bird's eye view, in short, promised accuracy, not bias or distortion.

Some theorists, taking a social perspective, probably under the undue influence of de-constructionism, have critiqued maps and/or photos as inevitably subjective things. Sometimes this stance reflects an *ideological presumption* that tends to rule out any *possibility* that maps and photos, as social products, can correspond to objective reality, supposing such a reality to exist. Such a stance is weakened by the same theorists' admission that maps and photos can be 'useful.' Accepting that minimal 'usefulness' reduces the claim of radical subjectivity to little more than the hardly controversial—indeed commonplace—claim that a map or photograph in some way reflects the values of its producer. But it also stresses, if *sotto voce*, how much a map or photograph may also serve as an instrument that helps to give a realistic understanding of the place(s) it shows.

A sober attitude is that map and photo users, who very much want an objective understanding of reality, however difficult that might in theory be, would not waste time playing with merely subjective things, especially when it is truly "a matter of life and death" rather than imaginary killing and saving. This will be the nub of our argument for why critical strictures aimed at ground level photography have not been extended to aerial photography.

For it is not without strong relevance that aerial photography was born, as a critically useful tool, over the trenches of World War I battlefields as a natural 'child' of a long tradition of what we might style 'overview reconnaissance' that dates back millennia via the first military observation balloons in the eighteenth century (Gillispie 2004: 372–373) to the commonplace of 'seizing the high ground' to command an overview of a battlefield (Corson & Palka 2004: 403). When the object is to kill or be killed, however repugnant such a misuse of human genius may be, of one thing we can be sure; everyone involved has a very lively interest in avoiding merely seeing what they want to see.

Put very simply, looking down above the heat and dust of battle allows a commander to see the relationship between his own and enemy forces and make his dispositions accordingly. The clearer the view, the better. So a progression from real-time but imperfect direct observation from an advantageous hilltop through time-delayed 'bird's eye' verbal and sketch reports from a balloon and time-delayed scaled photographs to today's real-time satellite and battlefield drone 'eyes' makes clear sense. We want that view from the empyrean, detached as it is from the shortcomings of a merely earthbound perspective.

It follows that maps and photos produced and/or used by the military or police in their operations, whatever may be the 'bias' in choosing this area to photograph or map rather than that, can hardly be intentionally "made beliefs" that are in some sense displaced or disconnected from the real world they are intended to represent. Indeed critics who would argue for such an ineradicable shortcoming find it extremely difficult clearly to expound the displacement or disconnect their critique suggests.

Government Aerial Photos and Maps

Aerial photos taken by the state/government form a carpet of images of a territory targeted for reconnaissance, regardless of the need to place the visual information so gathered.

With the passage of time, these photos become relics representing a 'frozen' moment in the appearance of a given territory and, thus are prima facie heritage pieces, as well as indispensable primary sources for exploring, rediscovering, and ascertaining present propositions raised over ground features and even underground matters in the territory.

Prior to the rise of remote sensing devices that can be used as aerial surveying tools for the private collection of ground data in digital form that today constitute what has become part of "big data," aerial photos were initially largely the monopoly of military and governmental agencies, which used these photos for mapping (Dawe 1969) and surveillance purposes, whether routine or task specific. For at least the last fifty years this monopoly has been broken. Today there are many private firms operating in co-opetition with government and state agencies and, with the rise of satellite and drone imagery, their numbers are set to grow ever more rapidly. Many of these private concerns have put their data into the public domain or sell them in digital or other forms for a charge. A good example is the Earth Resources Observation and Science (EROS) Center of USA, though to most people the most immediate example will be Google Earth.

Aerial Photos *Versus* Other Photos: A Methodical Inquiry

"All photography is propaganda." So Martin Parr described any published image that appears as an ***individual*** piece intended to tell some specific message. Possibly. However, aerial photographs as a set of data can hardly be said to fit Parr's understanding at all well. Parr's "Propaganda," upon closer analysis, simply means communication of a specific message. But that message, as a photograph simpliciter, need not necessarily misrepresent or distort but instead *highlight* or *expand* reality.

Possibilities of Subjectivity

Where the objective/subjective issue is involved, the image itself is what it is, whatever subjectivity there may be would come only in:

a. processing: supposing that someone is deliberately using processing to impose a way of seeing (q.v. cropping, air-brushing, photoshopping)
b. interpretation: what we think we can see/are seeing or wish to persuade others to see or believe they are seeing

Of course there is a possible 'subjective' element in the choice over what to photograph and from what height with what resolution. But other than, for example, decisions like not to include sensitive military/security sites, the sense of 'subjectivity' here seems to be much attenuated and probably unrelated to the aerial photograph as a record of what is photographed. The variables would be more likely to be concerned with economy, speed (i.e., urgency of purpose for which the image was commissioned (q.v. wartime reconnaissance photos)), available technical resources (quality of camera, stability of platform, quality of film, quality of image processing system, etc.), and so on, rather than, for example, wilful ideological bias.

Primarily developed for military and associated mapping purposes, aerial (or generically "remote sensing") photographs have been widely applied to scientific research from geology and soil analysis.

Indeed we may repeat that the photograph is what it is—an image of a given tract of the Earth's surface of a certain resolution at a certain scale—and, depending on whether it has been taken with a plain lens or with some filtering, may be used by any scientist, geographer, historian or even visual artist for whatever purposes he or she has in mind.[1] It follows that such photos may be used to study landscape, land use, transportation; urban development; and heritage and land economics.

Bocking's (2009) treatise on Canadian aerial surveys during the Cold War consolidated the core sociological interpretation of aerial photos. This draws attention to the view, common also as a general critique of the practice of mapping, that the technology enables scientists to assert greater authority over ground researchers and surveyors, replacing knowledge of local particulars with "a synoptic, universal view." However, this critique seems to presume that the aerial photographic view is always a substitute rather than a complement. We shall revisit this point in a thought experiment later.

Critical Stance Towards Aerial Photography

The essays by Dorrian and Pousin (2013) are an excellent introduction to a social understanding of aerial photography but the collection is generally

[1] In an era in which aerial photography is moving entirely into digital acquisition, the data gathered can extend far beyond the bounds of the visual spectrum out into other areas of the electromagnetic spectrum in what is known as multispectral remote sensing. Extending the term 'aerial photograph' to include such a multispectral 'picture' merely takes the next logical step from that initial grasp of the importance to improving one's understanding of the terrain before one that impelled history's first hunter or soldier to seize the high ground.

exploratory, with a focus on the visual history of the genre, rather than an analytical treatment of aerial photography as a social product. Wickstead and Barber (2012) have an excellent survey of the two positions one might take towards aerial photography, the technical and the critical, and seek to offer a social view of aerial photography, though this reduces to no more than the outcomes of "fragmentation" and "attention to detail" as points of importance. However, no frontal attack on aerial reconnaissance as in some sense 'subjective' is hinted at.

Reasons for Immunity of Aerial Photography from Attacks

So why have aerial photos not been subject to critical treatment as "propaganda"?

Unfamiliarity

The first reason is that most theorisation of photos by media researchers deals with their use in mass media and/or political communications rather than in 'dry' empiricist research in "other fields of studies" like geology or ecology. It is probable that such theorists may not have focused on, or even have been significantly aware of aerial photos or of the scientific use of them. As such this chapter may serve as a basis for them to exploit, bettering the works of the much-cited works by Cosgrove (1994), Castro (2009), and Amad (2012), who focused on *individual* aerial photos massaged for wartime publicity purposes.

Disinterested Mass of Data

The second reason is that aerial photos exist in a databank as a "disinterested" data source. As long as they are not "published" or rendered for specific purposes, they are not placed in any context explaining this or defending that, so represent no threat to anyone. In this sense of the mere physical existence of a repository of aerial photographs (let us say the entire aerial photographic survey of Hong Kong of 1963 and 1964, or any of the 13 specific collections held by NCAP in the UK), it is accordingly likely to be considered as less inherently 'biased' or 'interested' than, for example, released census statistics, as little obvious manipulation is apparent.

That any government may have kept aerial photographs as "secret," "confidential" or "restricted" in the past, denying access to the public, or charging at prices beyond reach of an average student may be seen to pose some difficulty for the claim of absolute neutrality. To understand why that might not be the case, it is necessary to distinguish between the photographic image and the information it contains. What motivated governments to restrict access was not the bias of the aerial photographs but, surely, the very absence of bias. And that cut two ways. On the one hand the aerial photographs, as a record of what was there at the moment the image was taken, may have recorded what the government would not have wished would be seen had it known what the photograph could reveal.[2] On the other, the aerial photographs, in recording what was there at the moment the image was taken, may have recorded what the government did not know about but could have been expected to know and so would be embarrassed to see revealed as evidence of its incompetence or indifference. Either way, the problem is not one of bias but, if anything, its opposite.

To pursue the census analogy further, the aerial photographs so understood are to be understood as we understand the raw data of a census. Even there, however, the analogy is less helpful than it immediately appears.

We can come at why this might be so by noting an important difference that can be put this way. A census sets out to enumerate a population, but in fact does more than that. It is not merely a head count, since for census data to be useful the 'heads' need to be more fully understood in terms of which heads count, where the heads live, how young or old the heads are, what sex and gender they consider themselves to be, what ethnicity they claim, their education levels attained, their occupations and so on and so forth. But these questions are not entirely 'innocent', perhaps more in respect of the qualitative discriminations that are omitted as in the qualitative distinctions that are recorded (the literature is vast but, for example, Mezey (2004)). In short, there are presumptions as to what the 'facts' are about a citizen body that a census ought to gather and these presumptions inform the format and the questions on the census form.

By contrast an aerial photograph is simply the mechanical outcome of the passage of a camera-equipped aeroplane passing across a territory in multiple, overlapping sweeps, taking images at set intervals. In that sense there are no prior 'questions' that have to be formulated. What is captured

[2] See, for example, the 2005 *New York Time's* story "Governments tremble at Google's bird's eye view": http://www.nytimes.com/2005/12/20/technology/governments-tremble-atgoogles-birdseye-view.html?_r=0 (accessed on 13.6.2017).

is what is there at the time. That is everything visible to whatever bands of the electromagnetic spectrum the imaging device covers that falls within the footprint of the succession of sweeps of the aircraft or satellite.

It might be objected that there are still choices with respect to the quality of camera, lens and film chosen, the height at which the pass is made and so forth and that these are, in some sense, 'subjective'. On one level one can agree with that objection because clearly any such survey must have competed for funds with other public or private projects. It follows that even if the protagonists of an aerial photographic survey would have wished for the best possible equipment available that would yield images with the best possible resolution, a political or business judgement may have been made that prioritised some other project over the survey, reducing the funding available. That would evidently in turn require cost-saving compromises, perhaps a lower-quality camera and film, a higher flight path increasing the 'footprint' of each photograph thereby reducing the number of shots taken and, hence, the resolution of the resulting images. That would entail less information (in the technical sense) in each photograph, so in some attenuated sense we could see this as a probably indirect rather than deliberate 'bias' imposed on the resulting photographs: they tell us less than they could have done.

But in most cases this would have been an accidental outcome rather than a deliberate one. In the example above, the intention was to save money in order to spend it elsewhere, not to reduce funding to make sure that photo resolution was so poor that some object or objects could not be identified. This is not to deny that such an intention is possible and that where there is evidence of such an intention, we have grounds for supposing some sort of 'bias' in the resulting images. But this bias is not something inherent in the photographs themselves.

We can see that this is so by considering the distinction between 'man-made image' and 'machine-made image' by Gombrich (1980), who showed how an image is lit before being photographed as an example of a 'man-made image'. That is how it can be 'made' to 'look' one way or another in the resulting developed image by manipulation of the appearance of the image that the camera subsequently captures. Gombrich could have added the additional 'man-made' elements of the choices of the graininess and colour bias of the film, the depth of field and shutter speed of the camera and, in the development phase, how long the film is developed and how the image is cropped.

In our case, where issues of subjectivity are clearer, a typical 'man-made' image is one taken by photo-journalists, official or corporate photographers, etc. But consecutive photos taken by an automatic camera from an aeroplane flying along a survey path are perfect examples of Gombrich's 'machine-made image'. The light is what it is. The imaging equipment and the height of the survey are the best that funding can pay for and so on. In short, the intention is always to remove the 'man' in the image-capturing process. Put simply, there is no one looking through the viewfinder.

Upstream Data

The third reason is that in many fields of study or industries, aerial photos from disinterested sources are used primarily for GIS purposes as part of a larger big data project. This is too far 'up stream' in any publicity or propaganda production line. By contrast, ground-level site photos could be used to serve far better propaganda functions as they show images "on the spot," down to earth and, by definition, are examples of Gombrich's 'man made' images. Aerial photos, as noted above, are structured to remove the 'photographer'. Theirs is not an earthbound human's view, but that of the disinterested, mechanical bird.

Remoteness from Any One: Two Thought Experiments

The fourth reason which conditions the above factor is the density of information in a series of high-level (say above 3000 feet or 914 metres) aerial photos taken automatically along a set flight path by a reconnaissance aeroplane. It is hard to find any particular "gaze" or "frame" for such data compared to say a ground photo taken only a few metres away from a photographer in the agony or thrill of the moment, especially when the photographer has either been able to pre-select a shooting position or is able to move to an 'optimal' spot as an event unfolds. The aerial photos taken are by contrast "unfocused" sources of information. Where the ground photo is itself a message about the object or person, event or moment, the aerial photo is simply what it is, displaying what was there at the time.

We can make that contrast more vivid by a *thought experiment* in which, at the very same moment, a photographer on the ground is recording an event and the highest quality imaginable aerial survey is passing overhead. By definition the event will appear on both resulting photographs. Yet it would seem reasonable to argue that were we to use the extremely high quality of the aerial photograph to zoom in on the 'event', so that it is revealed at the same scale as it is in the photo-journalist's 'scoop', we would have two very different images. One would be the news image, full of intention and meaning that speak immediately to us if, perhaps, with ambiguities and uncertainties. The other would be a curiously bland juxtaposition of viewed objects that are unlikely immediately to be obvious. If we came upon the aerial photograph with no knowledge of its simultaneity with the 'scoop', would we recognise what we are seeing? After analysis and perhaps contextual research in archives we would begin to be able to 'decode' what we are seeing. But, quite unlike the 'scoop' image, the aerial photograph, taken without any intention to record THAT moment, has to be interrogated closely using resources external to the photograph, to release this unexpected and unintended additional meaning.

This brief thought experiment reveals the very different stances we understand as between the two images (Dennett 1998: 43–68), the photo-journalist's image in terms of the intentional stance, the aerial photo image more in terms of Dennett's physical stance. This view can be argued to be supported, with respect to aerial photographs, by the institutional contexts in which they are used. An example would be how the common law courts in Hong Kong and elsewhere readily accept expert interpretation of government aerial photos sold by the Survey and Mapping Office, or its equally authoritative equivalents in other jurisdictions, which are adduced by parties in adverse possession and in planning enforcement prosecutions. To overcome challenges in Hong Kong that these photos are hearsay evidence in criminal proceedings,[3] the *Town Planning Ordinance* was amended to deem them to be "public documents" to save the trouble of calling the reconnaissance plane pilot, the photographer, the film developer and other technical officers as prosecution witnesses.

We might indeed take this Dennettian 'stance' approach to a further extreme by extending the idea of a photograph understood from a physical stance from the aerial photograph to any photograph. For when, as historians, for example, we look at a photograph of a streetscape, building or landscape, what matters to us is precisely not the message the photographer may have intended. In short, we are not, or not necessarily interested in the intentional stance the photograph inheres. Rather we approach

[3] The aftermath of *Keen Lloyd Limited and Cheung Kam Tong v. A.G.* (1996, Magistracy Appeal No.266), in which the Defendant raised the issue.

the photograph *as if* it were an aerial photograph: merely a record of what was there.

We may engage in a second thought experiment to illustrate the point here. In the previous thought experiment, we had a single event and two photographs. In this thought experiment we have a single event and a single photograph. But that photograph of event X has two ways in which we may look at it. We may understand it as in the previous thought experiment, namely as a photograph of event X. On that understanding our eyes are drawn to all elements of the scene relevant to X that may help further understanding of the event, which of course exposes us to the possible biases inherent in the photographer's 'view' of X. But we can alternatively simply see it, as we saw the aerial photograph in the previous thought experiment, as just a photograph of WHERE X took place. We see it, that is, *as if* that X is happening is irrelevant such that our eyes switch to identifying things in the image that may be irrelevant to X but full of information about the location as it was at that time. That is, once one has grasped via aerial photographs the possibility of approaching a photograph from the physical stance as something machine made, then with more or less facility *any* photograph can be approached similarly.

To clarify, in such an approach to a photograph of X in which X per se is ignored, what our eyes focus on would be such things as the variety of makes of car in the scene, the haircuts and clothing of any people in the scene, the names of any shops in the scene, the streetscape in general, etc. That is, we treat the photograph, as we treat an aerial photograph, as a repository of information that, by interrogation, we can extract and put to such non-X-related purposes as putting a date on the image, if it does not come with such data, and with such a date understanding traffic flows in that place at that time, identifying a moment in the evolution of a streetscape, identify the state and use of a specific building of interest at that moment and so on.

In summary, what aerial photographs represent, other than what in and of themselves they may be used for, to which we shall turn next, is a way of seeing that any photograph inheres in it, namely both the qualities of the man-made and machine-made images. That this is so may well be the underlying explanation for why aerial photographs have not been deemed inherently subjective. This is a twenty-first-century echo of the perceived promise of photography in the decades after its invention and before the advent of the more sceptical temper of the late twentieth century (Mnookin

1998: 1–7 and especially 4). Aerial photography reminds us of how a photograph can be read as other than the product of the intentional stance.

Use of Government-Held Aerial Photo Data in Environmental Management and Land Use Planning and Enforcement in Hong Kong

Because aerial photographs are machine-made images replete with information about the surface of the world we inhabit, they have great significance for our decision making with respect to our lived environments. It follows that where there are repositories of aerial photographic images of our home territory—whether we understand that restrictively as the territory of our polity or expansively as the territory of our species—there is a presumption that access to those repositories should be open to all.[4] Unlike China, the government of Hong Kong makes available to the public all aerial photos and survey maps for free inspection and, given its belief in the 'user pays' principle,[5] duplicates them as required according to a published price list.

History of Government Aerial Photography 1924–1962

All the earliest examples of such photos had a military origin and were taken by the British Royal Navy's Fleet Air Arm. The first territory-wide air survey of this kind in what was then a British colony occurred in 1924. It was taken by four Fairey IIID seaplanes equipped with aerial cameras aboard HMS *Pegasus*, eventually producing the new 1:20,000 topographic maps of 1930 (Empson 1992). Intermittently, the US Air Force took reconnaissance aerial photographs of Hong Kong also during World War II (Empson 1992). Thereafter the Royal Air Force took over the role and was responsible for the second exercise 21 years later, in winter of 1945, after the surrender of Japan in World War II. The third was undertaken by low-flying planes in 1949 when China became communist in the wake of

[4] Reference has already been made to Google Earth, which in the light of the argument in the text must stand as a global instantiation of this belief in our right to see with the bird's eye what our landbound species would otherwise be denied. The high ground is always an advantageous spot and its denial to others always a hostile act.

[5] http://www.fstb.gov.hk/tb/en/policy-programmes.htm (accessed on 13.6.2017).

the Cold War in a context of uncertainties over border security. The last major British military aerial survey exercise was taken in 1956.[6]

R.C. Hunting Aerial Survey of 1963 and 1964 and Subsequent Mapping

The rapid development of aviation as a result of the two major global conflicts in the first half of the twentieth century resulted in the explosion of civil aviation. Whilst for most of us the impact of this has been felt in passenger transport, its effects also transformed aerial photography (Mott 1963). In Hong Kong, this was coupled by an amazing pace of change ranging from public/private housing for the fast-growing population to industrialisation, especially in the new town developments of its former agricultural areas. Maps were surely needed but the conventional ground survey simply could not cope with the speed of change. Accordingly, only in 1963 and 1964 did the colonial government daringly commission the private British aerial surveying firm Hunting Surveys Ltd., to conduct a low-altitude (mainly 2700 feet to 3900 feet or 823 metres to 1189 metres) aerial photo survey of the whole of Hong Kong to map it in a short span of time. This successful survey from January 1963 to February 1964 was one of the largest contemporary aerial surveys in the British Commonwealth and cost the Hong Kong Government HK$2 million in 1962/1963 financial year.[7]

This set of photos[8] was used to calibrate the first large-scale (1:600 in urban areas and 1:1200 in the New Territories) survey maps of Hong Kong (Cooper 1968 and Empson 1992), an earlier large-scale survey having been made in the years before the publication date of the complete survey map set in 1922. Cooper (1968) and Dawe (1969) attribute the Hunting survey's success to the excellent ground control points provided by the Crown Lands and Survey Office and PWD. The Photogrammetric and Air Survey Section of the Survey and Mapping Office, set up in 1972 (Ho et al. 2006), provided services for engineering design/calculations, environmental studies, assistance in the investigation of flooding, air crashes and other emergency situations (Hong Kong Government 1990).

[6] The photos produced were rectangular.

[7] Sub-head 316 "Photogrammetric Survey of Hong Kong and the New Territories" (Hong Kong Government 1963).

[8] This set had photographs square in shape.

The year after they were able to install a Wild RC10 camera on a Royal Hong Kong Auxiliary Air Force Short Islander aircraft (Hong Kong Government 1963). At that time it was the British military which held copies of all these photos and maps. Thereafter all aerial photos were taken by the Hong Kong government[9] for civilian and security purposes and for updating the survey maps for land use and development control purposes. Before the turn of the millennium, advanced digital photogrammetry equipment replaced the 1970s analogue stereo-plotters, enabling the mapping office to produce orthophoto-maps, 3D modelling and image analysis (Hong Kong SAR Government 2000). Orthophotos are mosaics of vertical aerial photographs wherein geometric distortions have been rectified to a uniform scale. A complete set of high-resolution orthophotos using aerial photos taken by the 1963 Hunting Surveys Ltd. aerial survey were published in 2013 (Hong Kong SAR Government 2013).

Security Classification of Government Aerial Photos

Throughout the period from the earliest aerial photographs until recently there had always been some concealment of data on public security grounds. Photos that had been taken over, and maps that covered military land, were classified as "Restricted" documents and were not made available to the general public until the 1990s. This policy has not entirely ceased. Since 1997, photos taken in any years of the area across the border in Shenzhen have not been available for public consultation; indeed their existence was not publicly made known, likely for political reasons. With those exceptions, instances indeed of a 'bias' though not one of the photographs but of their accessibility, the aerial photos and the maps produced according to them have been used in day-to-day development work and in litigation as noted (Tang and Zhang 2012).

Use of Government Aerial Photos for Engineering, Land Use and Environmental Planning

Aerial photographic surveys of Hong Kong have also been used for public policy and academic research purposes.

[9] Until 31 March 1993 by the Royal Hong Kong Auxiliary Air Force, thereafter by the Government Flying Service.

In land use planning for new towns in the New Territories and renewal projects in the old urban cores of Hong Kong, aerial photos and survey maps have been used by town planners and their surveyor officers as a basic input since the early 1970s. The engineers use these photos for site formation and highway construction purposes according to the administrative plans prepared by planners. In the 1990s, the Geotechnical Control Office started to use aerial photos systematically for detecting earth movements in actually and potentially problematic hillside areas (Franks 1999) and planning preventive or remedial measures.

In a 1982 exercise the government used helicopter aerial surveys for the identification of marine squatters before assigning licences to them to regularise a rising primary industry under the *Marine Fish Culture Ordinance* (Lai et al. 2014). These photos were taken by hand-held cameras and can be inspected and purchased from the Information Services Department by the public. Local researchers used them for their specific thematic studies.[10]

Use Government Aerial Photos in Planning Enforcement Against Change in Use of Land

A good illustration of the use of aerial photographs, highlighting at the same time the 'neutrality' of an aerial photograph, albeit one subject to bias in interpretation is its application to planning enforcement.

Under the *Town Planning (Amendment) Ordinance* 1990, any owner or occupier of land who is found to have carried out work or development on land or has changed its use without planning permission, if such permission is required by the plan, is liable to enforcement action. This provides the "teeth" of town planning law in Hong Kong much desired by planners. In the run up to that amendment to the Ordinance, New Territories' land interests had become agitated, so to pacify them, the government assured them in the legislative process that 'existing uses' up to a 'certain date' (as defined) were exempted and this concept was imported into the Ordinance. It can readily be seen that this is a perfect occasion for the invocation of aerial photographs. Would an "existing use" as shown in an aerial photo really protect the rural interests?

Let us assume that the 'certain date' is date D and that the plan makes use U a use requiring planning permission. Aerial photographs of a tract

[10] See, for instance, Lo (1979) on squatting, Franks (2009) on geology and Lai et al. (2009) on military relics.

of land T_L at dates D_{-1}, D and D_{+1} give unequivocal evidence of the use of T_L (D_{-1}), T_L (D) and T_L (D_{+1}). If at D_{-1} the use of T_L is E and at D it is also E, then at D_{+1} U can be determined to be an existing use at D and therefore exempt. Table 13.1 shows the sequence of events on lot T_L.

That is the theory. In practice, in cases in court where such issues are deliberated, the prosecution typically adduces aerial photos taken on diverse days as evidence to show that such work, development or change occurred. But contrary to theory, this is not always simple, as defendants discover, given that it is they who bear the onus of rebutting the evidence.

On a series of days when such aerial photos were taken, two key days are important. The first 'relevant day' is "immediately before the date of the plan" first made under the ordinance: so for a plan published in the *Gazette* on 2 July 1990, the first 'relevant day' would be 1 July 1990. What is shown on a first 'relevant day' photo is therefore the 'existing use' of land. The second 'relevant day' is the day of the most recent photo that is produced in court by the prosecution. This by definition would be a day after 2 July 1990, the day the plan was published and the requirement for permission for alterations, etc., came into force. It is this second photograph that the prosecution relies on to compare with the first to convince the court that the work that had been done (for instance, pond filling or excavation) constituted a development or change in use, because it is contended that what the photograph on the second relevant day shows was not present on the photograph taken on the first 'relevant day'. This sounds reasonable and scientific, and it is unless the target of the prosecution is a use that is not always photographically manifest.

Table 13.1 Two scenarios of planning enforcement in Hong Kong

Time code (Date: event)	*Scenario 1 on Lot T_L*	*Scenario 2 on Land T_L*
D_{-1} (30 June 1997)	Use interpreted to be E from an aerial photo taken on that day	Use interpreted to be E from an aerial photo taken on that day
D (1 July 1997: Non-existing use becomes one that needs planning permission)	Use interpreted to be E from an aerial photo taken on that day	Use interpreted to be non E, for example, F, from an aerial photo taken on that day
D_{+1} (2 July 1997: decision about a use on T_L)	E needs no planning permission	F needs planning permission

For example, the typical prosecution target in such cases in Hong Kong has been the use of land for open storage, especially of containers (as back up for the Hong Kong's international container terminal at Kwai Chung). But 'storage' is not a simple visual entity like, for example, a pond. It is a use that naturally *fluctuates* in turnover. We can see the problem by looking at a simple and a less simple case.

The simple case is where, in 1990, the land was vacant farm land or a fish pond but in 1997 a container yard. The photographic evidence is unequivocal and the case is straightforward: there was a field or a pond, there is now a storage yard. The judgement will go against the defendant.

However, the case is more complicated where the site was a storage yard with containers in 1990 and also in 1997 but in the second instance had more containers. In such a case the prosecution could submit that there was an "intensification" of use. Here again there is a simple and a difficult situation.

The simple situation, readily resolved by an aerial photograph, is if the site has expanded in area. Here again the photographic evidence will be unequivocal. Before the storage footprint was F_p m^2, afterwards it was F_{p+n} m^2.

But there could be a situation in which the site did not change in size but the level or "intensity" of use fluctuated. For example, the number of containers identified on a 1 July 1997 image, F_t, may be fewer than on aerial photos taken on 1 July 1994 (F_n) and 1995 (F_o), but the number on those intermediate days may be greater than those on the site on the first relevant date, 1 July 1990 (F). In that case, even if the level of use on 1 July 1997 happened to the same as 1 July 1990 ($F_t = F$), the prosecution would hold that because of the evidence of there having been more after the first 'relevant day', even if all of the more were not present on the second 'relevant day', there had been intensification, meaning that the "existing use" as of 1990 was no longer useful in defence. A summary of the scenario is shown in Table 13.2.

This thinking, as used in the unreported magistracy case FLS 6333/95 (December 1995),[11] is an example of how the use of aerial photographic evidence, whilst in one sense manifest (given use → greater/intensified use since the first relevant day) may actually be unreasonable because the photographic evidence itself is insufficient to elucidate the point at issue. The

[11] In this case, the defendant was acquitted of the charge "pond filling" based on evidence as shown on government survey maps.

Table 13.2 "Intensification of use" in planning enforcement in Hong Kong

Relevant data	*Amount of containers interpreted (Scenario X)*
1 July 1990	(F) 150 units
1 July 1994	(F_n) 200 units
1 July 1995	(F_o) 250 units
1 July 1997	(F_t) 150 units

use of a magistracy court decision was conditioned by the availability of cases. Though aerial photos were used by the prosecution to establish its case, as there was no appeal to the High Court concerning the admissibility or interpretation of photo images. It is for this reason that we have resorted to magistracy cases.

The simple point is that storage varies in amount as a matter of business life and a 'use' as a storage facility at time T does not entail a use of that facility at T for a fixed quantum of goods stored $G_{q(T)}$. The quantum of goods stored at T will have been a function of market demand at T and, had the market at T been at a peak, then the quantum of goods shown by the photograph taken on the first relevant date would have been $G_{q+n(T)}$. So a crude enumeration from aerial photos, whilst in one sense 'accurate', in this case fails to allow for a normal variation of business on a site of a given location. "Use" is not always a simple visual quantity.

To illustrate, we have three aerial photographs taken of the same CityBus bus depot, held under a short-term tenancy in a "Government, Institution or Community" (GI/C) zone in the statutory town plan. Those taken by government's Surveying and Mapping Office in 2009, 2013 and 2017 have been compared. The first photo of 2009 shows only six buses (including four which were used as a noise screen). In the photo taken about 4 years later, the same site had 13 buses. The more recent 2017 photo shows 21 buses parked. Following the simple enumeration logic described in the previous paragraph, this increase in the number of parked buses would have been deemed an "intensification" of use and the occupier liable to planning enforcement prosecution but for the fact that there is no enforcement provision in the relevant statutory town plan. But let us assume that the town plan has enforcement provisions. In that case, should enforcement follow the narrow 'intensification' logic, the depot would not be viable in planning terms as it is quite normal that the number of buses in a depot varies from time to time within the quanta the three photographs reveal, depending on such variables as the time of day, route changes, shifting demographics and employment locations, the economic cycle, etc.

The aerial photos in such cases would thus be produced to the court as if they told a story that, in fact, they cannot tell. Here the issue is not any bias in photos but a bias in *interpretation*. A contrast between the diachronic evidence provided by an aerial photograph and the synchronic evidence required for the 'proof' needed in this particular case makes this point clear. In our container yard example synchronic evidence would be a motion picture taken from 1 July 1990 to the date of prosecution. This would show clearly, supposing this to have been the case, that the site had been continuously in business and that the number of containers on site was never constant, rising and falling from what was on site on 1 July 1990 (and may possibly have been on the site before that date) through peaks and troughs of business, as the fortunes of the logistics market changed, to the state of affairs on 1 July 1997. The temporally disjunct, diachronic 'snapshots' provided by aerial photographs cannot 'prove' anything so complex as 'intensification' in this sense. The same argument obtains with our bus station example. The problem here is the same which led De Jong et al. (2000: 64) to consider "aerial photos a suitable medium to study the dynamics of the city of Ouagadougou" in Africa. There, aerial photos are only taken every 10 years.

Equally, however, there is a diachronic response to this. For were there to have been presented in court a set of aerial photographs covering, say, a full year of operations if not day by day, then at sufficiently close time intervals to ensure the capture of *normal fluctuations in business*, then such a judgement could be arrived at whether in favour of prosecution or defence.

Discussion

In daily life, aerial photo imagery and data, whether taken by balloons, planes, satellites or drones, have become ever more accessible. They have become widely used and accepted as credible data by the public and various businesses and industries as well as in evidence in legal proceedings.[12]

[12] In a recent US case, *Unites States v Jones*, the Fourth Amendment was invoked as a police GPS to follow a suspect was challenged for digital trespass.

The vehicle by means of which a 'neutral' aerial photo is taken should not affect our analysis. What matters, and has been the case since fairly early days, is that the 'decision' to take a 'shot' is entirely automated as, after the initial decisions for the photographic sortie have been made, are the 'settings' (shutter speed, focus, depth of field, distance from subject, film speed). An aerial photograph platform piloted by a human pilot is in this sense conceptually no different from a drone. Had early aerial photographers been able to use drones, they would have done, q.v. the early use of unmanned balloons to carry cameras.

Any discussion of the use of aerial photos in planning may profit from an examination of the terms of art in geography education at secondary school and degree level as planning schools have a good supply of students from geographers and have geography as one of its learning pillars.

In geography education, the rise of human geography promoted by such scholars as Hall (1978) has marginalised the teaching of aerial photogrammetry and mapping in upper high school curricula, which leads to some difficulties for spatial analysis by university students as the authors have discovered in their own teaching. However, the pendulum is swinging back. Education psychologists have found young children learn a lot from aerial photos used as learning aids.

Conclusion

This chapter offers four reasons why any critical attack on aerial photos in the land use, environmental and planning study arena as 'subjective' or 'biased' would be an uphill battle for those who would mount it. To recapitulate, aerial photos are taken by mechanical means operated by disinterested parties, are neutral in data presentation and show things "from above" rather than here on ground. They lack the 'intentional stance' that informs any 'man made' photograph taken at ground level.

The Hong Kong study on planning enforcement is illustrative of the fact that aerial photographs, as static records of given moments, can be asked to prove no more than they can prove, which was the state of affairs at the moment the image was taken (Lai 1998). Within those constraints, their 'machine made' objectivity holds good. What we learn is that between a given photograph's 'moment' until the next photograph's 'moment' there is silence and the photographs themselves can tell us nothing determinate about what occurred during that lapse. Something may have done, and the photographs will tell us what that something has resulted in. What they cannot tell us is when change occurred, who was responsible for it, why it happened and so on. The human dimension is missing, and in an important sense, in that lies the objectivity of the photographs.

Aerial photographs have to be understood for what they are. When they are so understood they can be used in the manner the Hong Kong government and other governments, businesses and individuals have sought to use them. But they can only be used within the restricted sense we have outlined. Should any information more than that given by a 'freeze frame' moment in time be sought, aerial photographs can provide it if and only if there are sufficient aerial photographic sets to establish the diachronic case that needs to be made. At that point, however, we can see a critical step occurring from the coldly objective world of a frozen frame to the warmer and more problematic domain of human interpretation. The photographs are what they are. It is in the story we tell to weave them together that their objectivity may be compromised.

Questions for Revision and Discussion

1. Discuss the importance of obtaining ground truths in aerial photo surveys for resolving cadastral boundary disputes.

   Remember that land users use land on the ground, not from the air.

   - Ground truths help verify the precision of aerial photos by cross-referencing them with physical measurements taken on the ground. This process ensures that the aerial images, which may be distorted by camera angles, terrain or atmospheric conditions, are correctly aligned with actual geographical coordinates, thus making these photos more trustworthy for all stakeholders involving land analysis or dispute.
   - Small features such as fences, walls or trees, which mark boundaries, are critical for accurate cadastral mapping, but could not be too fine to be captured accurately in aerial photos without ground truths.

2. Discuss the values of old aerial photos for built heritage conservation.

Current or new photos do not contain information on heritage buildings that might have existed in earlier times.

- Contextual appreciation of developers: Old aerial photos provide the historical context for new buildings by helping developers interested in conversation efforts understand their original settings. For example, developers of recent projects in Sheung Wan extensively used historical aerial photos to understand how their constructions could coexist with the historical buildings without damaging or altering their character.
- Curating the history of a place: Old photos as visual aids could raise public awareness of the importance of heritage conservation by showing a location's earlier appearance. Exhibitions and educational programmes can use aerial photos to showcase the transformation of a location's built environment over the decades and help future generations appreciate its built legacy. Such a practice has been used to curate the Blue House in Wanchai and Central Market.
- Admissible documentary evidence in court: In legal proceedings during the government's enforcement of Government Leases, planning law, building law and private boundary disputes, aerial photos are admissible evidence adduced by expert witnesses.

3. Discuss the contribution of drones to surveying.

They are of immense help because they can show inaccessible locations of existing features unconcealed by plant cover. Some contributions of drones are:

- Increased efficiency and speed: Drones can cover large areas quickly and capture data faster than traditional surveying methods.
- Enhanced accuracy and precision: Equipped with high-resolution cameras, LiDAR sensors and GPS capabilities, drones provide extremely accurate data and can capture detailed aerial imagery and generate precise 3D models, digital elevation models (DEMs) and orthophotos. This level of accuracy helps reduce measurement errors and improves the overall quality of surveys.
- Cost effectiveness: Traditional surveying methods often involve significant costs related to field labour, equipment and safety measures. Drones can significantly reduce these expenses by minimising the need for manual labour and expensive equipment. In addition, drones reduce the need for repeated site visits, thereby lowering transportation and logistical costs and improving safety.

- Real-time data and rapid processing are useful for areas undergoing rapid development, hazardous areas and emergencies.
- However, vegetation covers can conceal structures unknown to the surveyors and hence they are no substitutes for field inspection and surveys.

List of Court Cases

Keen Lloyd Limited and Cheung Kam Tong v. A.G. (1996, Magistracy Appeal No.266).

References

Amad, Paula. 2012. From God's-Eye to Camera-Eye: Aerial Photography's Post-Humanist and Neo-Humanist Visions of the World. *History of Photography* 36 (1): 66–86.

Arijs, Hilke. 2014. Images of Value: Why Assessing the Value of Image Collections is Worthwhile. In *CoMa 2013: Safeguarding Image Collections*, ed. Arijs Hilke, 21–45. New Castle upon Tyne: Cambridge Scholar Publishing.

Bocking, Stephen. 2009. A Disciplined Geography: Aviation, Science, and the Cold War in Northern Canada, 1945–1960. *Technology and Culture* 50 (2): 265–290.

Bowden, Leonard W., and William G. Brooner. 1970. Aerial Photography: A Diversified Tool. *Geoforum* 1 (2): 19–32.

Castro, Teresa. 2009. Cinema's Mapping Impulse: Questioning Visual Culture. *Cartographic Journal* 46 (1): 9–15.

Cooper, J. T. 1968. The Large-Scale Mapping of Hong Kong by Air-Survey. In *Report of Proceedings of the Conference of Commonwealth Survey Officers 1967*, 473–479. London: Her Majesty's Stationery.

Corson M. W., and E. J. Palka. 2004. Geotechnology, the US Military and War. Chap. 18 in S. D. Brunn, S. L. Cutter, and J. W. Harrington Jr., *Geography and Technology*, 401–430. Springer Nature.

Cosgrove, Denis. 1994. Contested Global Visions: One-World, Whole-Earth, and the Apollo Space Photographs. *Annals of the Association of American Geographers* 84 (2): 270–294.

Dawe, H. G. 1969. Aerial Survey: Colony of Hong Kong. *Photogrammetric Record* 6 (34): 335–347.

Dennett, D. C. 1998. *The Intentional Stance (6th Printing), Cambridge.* Massachusetts: The MIT Press.

Dorrian, Mark, and Frédéric Pousin, eds. 2013. *Seeing from Above: The Aerial View in Visual Culture.* IB Tauris.

Empson, Hal. 1992. *Mapping Hong Kong: A Historical Atlas*. Hong Kong: Government Information Service.
Franks, C. A. M. 1999. Characteristics of Some Rainfall-Induced Landslides on Natural Slopes, Lantau Island, Hong Kong. *Quarterly Journal of Engineering Geology and Hydrogeology* 32 (3): 247–259.
Gillispie, C. C. 2004. *Science and Polity in France: The Revolutionary and Napoleonic Years*. Princeton UP: Princeton.
Gombrich, Ernst H. 1980. Standards of Truth: The Arrested Image and the Moving Eye. *Critical Inquiry* 7 (2, Winter): 237–273.
Hall, Robin. 1978. Teaching Humanistic Geography. *The Australian Geographer* 14 (1): 7–14.
Ho, Hoi-Yan, Jonathan King, and Mark Wallace. 2006. *A Basic Guide to Air Photo Interpretation in Hong Kong*. Applied Geoscience Centre, Department of Earth Sciences, University of Hong Kong.
Hong Kong Government. 1963. *Accountant General Annual Report*. Hong Kong: Government Printer.
Hong Kong Government. various years. *Hong Kong Annual Report (*1990*)*. Hong Kong: Government Printer.
Hong Kong Special Administrative Region Government. 2000, various years. *Hong Kong Annual Report (2000)*. Hong Kong: Government Logistics Department.
Lai, Lawrence W. C. 1998. The Use of Aerial Photographs in Planning Enforcement Against Unauthorized Development. In *Lai Zoning and Property Rights: A Hong Kong Case Study*, ed. W. C. In Lawrence, 2nd ed., 157–174. Hong Kong: Hong Kong University Press.
Lai, Lawrence W. C., Stephen N. G. Davies, Y. K. Tan, and P. Yung. 2009. The Gin Drinker's Line: Reconstruction of a British Colonial Defence Line in Hong Kong Using Aerial Photo Information. *Property Management* 27 (1): 16–41.
Lai, Lawrence W. C., Mark H. Chua, and Frank T. Lorne. 2014. The Coase Theorem and Squatting on Crown Land and Water: A Hong Kong Comparative Study of the Differences Between the State Allocation of Property Rights for Two Kinds of Squatters. *Habitat International* 44:247–257.
Lo, C. P. 1979. Surveys of Squatter Settlements with Sequential Aerial Photography – A Case Study in Hong Kong. *Photogrammetria* 35 (2): 45–63.
Mezey, N. 2004. Erasure and Recognition: The Census, Race and the National Imagination. *Northwestern University Law Review* 97 (4): 1701–1768.
Mnookin, Jennifer L. 1998. The Image of Truth: Photographic Evidence and the Power of Analogy. *Yale Journal of Law and the Humanities* 10 (1): 1–74.
Monmonier, Mark. 2018. *How to Lie with Maps*. 3rd ed. Chicago: University of Chicago Press.
Mott, P. G. 1963. Aerial Methods of Surveying for Civil Engineering. (Includes Plates). *Proceedings of the Institution of Civil Engineers* 26 (4): 497–512.

Nagel, T. 1986. *The View from Nowhere.* Oxford: Oxford University Press.
O'Connell, Lauren M. 1998. Viollet-le-Duc on Drawing, Photography, and the 'Space Outside the Frame'. *History of Photography* 22 (2): 139–146.
Tang, Conrad H. W., and H. D. Zhang. 2012. Direct Georeferencing and Orthophoto Correlation with Demarcation District. *Surveying & Built Environment* 22:73–86.
Wickstead, Helen, and Martyn Barber. 2012. A Spectacular History of Survey by Flying Machine! *Cambridge Archaeological Journal* 22 (1): 71–88.
De Jong et al. 2000: De Jong, S.M., Bagre, Alain, Pieter, B.M., Teeffelen, Van, Deursen, Willem P.A.Van, 2000. Monitoring trends in urban growth and surveying city quarters in Ouagadougou, Burkina Faso using SPOT-XS. Geocarto International 15 (2), 63–70.
Hong Kong SAR Government 2013: Hong Kong Special Administrative Region Government. (various years). Hong Kong annual report book (1997-2015). Hong Kong: Government Logistics Department.

PART III

Development Issues

CHAPTER 14

The Small House

K. T. Liu and Lawrence Wai Chung Lai

This chapter explains the historical origin, salient features, and some social and planning issues of the small-house policy.

The history of building on private land in the New Territories is complicated. Before Britain leased the New Territories, villagers living there could build without the need for government permission so long as they paid taxes on the land. The colonial government took all land and re-granted it as leasehold interests. From that point onwards, new construction other than the re-building of existing houses on old scheduled lots needed government approval. (Otherwise, villagers had to buy New Grant Lots in order to build a dwelling.)

Originally, the permission was granted by the District Offices. From 1959 to November 1972, permission was obtained from the Director of Public Works. The small-house policy implemented in December 1972 reverted the granting of permission to build a house to the District Offices until 1982, when the District Lands Offices took over land administration.

K. T. Liu (✉) • L. W. C. Lai
Department of Real Estate and Construction, The University of Hong Kong, Hong Kong, China
e-mail: wclai@hku.hk

L. W. C. Lai et al. (eds.), *Principles of Land Administration at Work*, https://doi.org/10.1007/978-981-95-2972-8_14

The requirements an applicant needs to provide on the government form for a small house have changed over time.

The Small-House Policy

The small-house policy applies only to "indigenous villagers" in "recognised villages" in the New Territories.

Under this policy, any male indigenous villager (in some situations his spouse) of a recognised village, whether or not he resides in Hong Kong, is entitled to a once-in-a-lifetime right to build a house on his own plot of land or land granted by the government to him and his family.

An applicant should be at least 18 years old.

Indigenous villagers are villagers who can trace their ancestry through the male line back to 1898, when the British took over the New Territories, and are members of "recognised villages".

Not all villages in the New Territories are recognised villages. Recognised villages are those that are not located in New Kowloon or Cheung Chau:

(1) Pre-1898 villages in existence since 1898.
(2) Pre-1898 villages re-sited before 1945.
(3) Post-1898 villages within "village environs" and approved village extension areas (VEAs).

The site applied for must be within the "Village Environ" (VE) or VEA of a recognised village or within a "Village" (V) Zone in an outline zoning plan (OZP) or development permission area (DPA). The VE is the area within a 300-foot radius, as measured from the outermost edge of the last village-type house built on or before 1 December 1972. VE plans could be found at the Lands Department website, HKMS 2.0.

A V zone is common in the OZP for any area in the New Territories outside New Kowloon. The planning intention for this zone demarcates both existing recognised villages and the land considered suitable for village expansion. The boundaries of the V zones are drawn up with regard to the village "environs" boundaries, local topography, existing land-use patterns, the provision of infrastructure, previously approved planning applications for small-house developments, and small-house demand forecasts.

Specifications for a Small House

A small house is a New Territories Exempted House (NTEH). It is called an "exempted house" because it is exempted from the need for building permission under the *Buildings (Application to the New Territories) Ordinance* if it does not exceed 700 square feet (65.03m^2) in coverage, 27 feet (8.33 m) in height, and three storeys plus two balconies.

An NTEH is defined in the Notes of the OZP as:

> a domestic building other than a guest house or a hotel, or a building primarily used for habitation other than a guest house or a hotel, the ground floor of which is used as a retail shop or restaurant, in respect of which the Director of Lands, or any person authorised by him under Section 11 of the *Buildings (Application to the New Territories) Ordinance*, has issued a Certificate of Exemption pursuant to Part III of the said ordinance.

To obtain permission to build a small house, the provision of Emergency Vehicular Access (EVA) must not be less than 4.5 metres[1] in width or of a lesser width acceptable to the Fire Services Department with a headroom clearance of 4.5 m to allow emergency vehicles to reach within 30 metres of the NTEH. For site constraints, alternative fire safety measures may be allowed, such as the provision of an automatic sprinkler system or fire detective system and hose reel system.

Land for Small-House Developments

The government would grant a building licence to an applicant to build on his own agricultural land at a concessionary premium. In case government land is obtained by a land exchange (a surrender [of private land] and a re-grant [of government land]). In both building licence and surrender and exchange, a site must be held in the name of the applicant.

If the applicant has no private land and government land is available, the government will grant the land to the applicant at a concessionary premium by Private Treaty Grant (PTG).

The terms and conditions of a building licence and PTG are similar. There is a recital of the background of the land grant as the exercise of the building right of the grantee as an indigenous villager.

[1] Previously, it was 3.75 metres.

Use of the Small House

The applicant is allowed to build a three-storey NTEH either as a single residence or planned with three flats divided vertically. Each NTEH should stand on its own with its own staircase. In other words, two NTEHs sharing a communal staircase are unacceptable.

The "use" of the house is restricted to non-industrial purposes. In other words, other than residential uses, commercial uses are allowed.

According to the Notes of the OZP, in addition to an NTEH, which is the use always permitted, a selective range of uses, including commercial, community, and recreational, may be permitted within a "V" zone upon an application to the Town Planning Board on the basis that these uses will serve the need of villagers and would not adversely affect the character of these villages. This means the small house can have non-domestic uses on application to the Town Planning Board.

Restrictions on Alienating and Removing These Restrictions

There are restrictions on alienation. In the case of a PTG, there is a perpetual restriction on alienation. In the case of a building licence, a five-year-restriction is imposed.

However, the grantee may:

(1) Underlet the lot if the underletting:
  (a) is at a rack rent;
  (b) does not charge a premium or fine;
  (c) is for a term not exceeding five years; and
  (d) comes without the right or option to renew or extend.
(2) Assign it to another indigenous villager with the prior written consent of the District Lands Officer.

The applicant may apply to remove the restrictions on alienation within the restricted period and, if approved, will be charged a premium by the government.

The government will not entertain an application to remove the restrictions on alienation until the building is completed (i.e., after the issuance of the Certificate of Compliance).

In case of a PTG in a VEA or a re-site area, no application will be entertained until three years have elapsed after the completion of the house.

The premium to remove the restrictions on alienation, as assessed by the government, is the difference between (a) the market value of the land as of the date of application without restrictions of alienation and (b) the premium already paid, as stated in the Building Licence or New Grant when the land was granted.

Application Procedure for a Small House

The development of an NTEH by an indigenous villager must go through the following procedures:

(1) Make an application—endorsed by the village representative.
(2) Post a notice.
(3) Obtain a land grant: a Building Licence or a New Grant.
(4) Apply for a Certificate of Exemption.
(5) Setting out the land boundaries.
(6) Commence the building works.
(7) Serving a notice of completion for the building works.
(8) Applying for a Certificate of Compliance.
(9) Applying for the removal of the Non-alienation Clause.

Upon applying to develop a small house (whether or not it is an NTEH) outside the "V" zone, an applicant must give a brief account as to why suitable private land could not be identified within the "V" zone.

Town Planning Board's Considerations

Some considerations of the Town Planning Board in respect of a proposed small-house development, expressed as "house" under Column 2, are that:

(1) it should not frustrate the planning intention of the particular zone in which the application site is located;
(2) it should be compatible, in terms of land use, scale, design, and layout, with the surrounding area/development;
(3) it should not encroach upon the planned road network lest it has an adverse traffic, environmental, landscape, drainage, sewerage, and geotechnical impact on the surrounding areas; and
(4) the provision of fire services installations and emergency vehicular access, if required, is appropriate for the scale of the development and complies with the relevant standards.

Public Concerns over the Small-House Policy

Four main public concerns over the small-house policy are:

(1) Legality of the pre-sale of small houses.
(2) Availability of land resources to sustain the policy.
(3) Entitlement of female indigenous villagers to small houses.
(4) The fact that small houses have become part of an actively traded housing market instead of purely satisfying the residential needs of indigenous villagers.
(5) The introduction of a period ousting applications for the removal of the alienation clause.

A Challenging Question: What's Wrong with Building on One's Own (Ancestral) Land?

Many criticise the small-house policy, as a land policy, for:

(1) sexual inequality;
(2) social inequality; and
(3) unfair subsidy.

The real planning issue is really the shortage of suitable land for such houses.

The Small (as a form of NT Exempted) House can only be applied for, under a government policy introduced in 1972, by an adult male villager of a recognised NT indigenous village to build a house (of a standard design of no more than 2100 square feet (195 square metres) and not more than 3 storeys on a flat site of 700 square feet (65 square metres) once in his life) without the need to obtain approval under the *Buildings Ordinance* on (a) private land (Scenario 1) within the "village environ"; (b) government land in a village re-siting exercise (Scenario 2); (c) government land other than (b) (Scenario 3).

This policy replaced and streamlined the former practice of the District Office granting on an ad-hoc basis Crown land licences for erection houses on the private agricultural lots under Block Crown Leases.

Though the policy involves sexual discrimination against female villagers, it does NOT (none of the three scenarios) involve any unfair transfer of wealth or government subsidy (Lai 2000a, b, 2017; Lai and Ho 2001; Lai and Lorne 2014; Lai et al. 2014).

The first scenario is simply a partial return of property rights to the NT landowners to build on their land, which had been confiscated by the British when they began their lease of the NT in 1898. This point has not been considered by those who argue that the villagers should pay lease modification premia before they could build on the farmland. These critics forget that NT leasehold lots under Block Crown (government) leases were not allocated by sale, but by legal fiction. The second scenario involves a subsidy until a villager sells the land, under which a premium would be levied. Here, critics hold that such land should not be sold for gain, a stand that actually perpetuates the subsidy.

The conflict of interest between indigenous villagers and urban people must be resolved as a matter of strategic planning, and this requires "solution spaces" on reclamations, unless government can assemble massive amount of private flat land in the New Territories. Drastic constitutional and legal changes in Hong Kong since Summer 2019 have however overwhelmed such planning.

The most significant and interesting finding on the small-house question is that, despite so many polemics for and against its status, the small house is a widely accepted product in the local housing market and much sought after by expatriate (now local) residents. Backed by the housing market, the common law is an effective constraint on the behaviour of villagers and is needed to sell properties with good titles. Therefore, unauthorised developments occur only along the vertical, not horizontal, dimension of space, as the latter cannot be easily rectified without demolishing the whole structure and having to trespass on the land of other villagers (Lai and Lorne 2014).

Some Safety Problems of Small-House Developments

There is a Lands Department policy that requires a development of more than nine small houses to be served by emergency vehicle access with a standard of not less than 4.5 metres in width. To avoid this road provision requirement, small-house builders tend to build no more than nine houses along an existing access passage that is less than 4.5 metres. Often some properties abut the access walls for privacy and security purposes even though they, by default, create obstacles for emergency vehicles. These walls may violate several legal provisions summarized in Appendix 3.

Questions for Revision and Discussion

1. Discuss why unauthorised building works in small houses tend to have extra floors or cellars rather than greater footprints.

Unauthorised horizontal expansion would be easily felt, detected, and opposed by neighbours or impossible due to the presence of adjoining buildings that have no sideway setbacks.

2. Discuss, with the help of survey maps and aerial photos, the differences between small-house development in the absence of a government layout and the development of the Kowloon (Walled) City.

Basically similar: site unlevelled, though a small-house site usually has a perfectly rectilinear footprint.

3. Discuss and explain why there was no "recognized indigenous village" in "New Kowloon".

Study the relevant law, *Ordinance No.8 of 1900.*

References

Lai, Lawrence W. C. 2000a. Housing 'Indigenous Villagers' in a Modern Society: An Examination of the Hong Kong 'Small House' Policy. *Third World Planning Review* 22 (2): 207–230.

Lai, Lawrence W. C. 2000b. Not Small (on the Small House Policy). Letters to the Editor. *South China Morning Post*, July 2, p. 11.

Lai, Lawrence W. C. 2017. Solving the 'Problem' of the Small House Policy. *Hong Kong Economic Journal*, August 21, p. B07.

Lai, Lawrence W. C., and Winky K. O. Ho. 2001. Small Is Beautiful: A Probit Analysis of Planning Applications for Small Houses in Hong Kong. *Environment and Planning B: Planning and Design* 28 (4): 611–622.

Lai, Lawrence W. C., and Frank T. Lorne. 2014. Ambiguous Property Rights: A Taxonomic and an Exploratory Account of Post-Colonial Rural Housing in Chinese Hong Kong. *Urban Studies* 51 (10): 2052–2067.

Lai, Lawrence W. C., Mark Hansley Chua, and Frank T. Lorne. 2014. The Coase Theorem and Market for Squatting on Crown Land and Water: A Hong Kong Comparative Study of the Differences Between the State Allocation of Property Rights for Two Kinds of Squatters. *Habitat International* 44:247–257.

CHAPTER 15

Heritage Conservation of Government and Private Built Heritage

Lawrence Wai Chung Lai

Introduction

Hong Kong's approach to build heritage conservation involves government-appointed experts deciding the fate of a building appointed by the Antiquities and Monuments Office (AMO). The AMO's mission is to conserve both government and private archaeological and built heritage. Its legal tool for doing so is the *Antiquities and Monuments Ordinance.*

Those buildings deemed worthy of conservation, including private buildings, can be declared monuments under the *Antiquities and Monuments Ordinance* (Cap.53), enacted in 1976 and amended in 1982, and are protected against demolition.

Historical buildings, which are not declared monuments, are usually graded 1 to 3 by the Antiquities Advisory Board (AAB). Until these buildings are declared monuments, they are not legally protected from demolition or extensive alteration.

L. W. C. Lai (✉)
Department of Real Estate and Construction, The University of Hong Kong, Hong Kong, China
e-mail: wclai@hku.hk

L. W. C. Lai et al. (eds.), *Principles of Land Administration at Work*, https://doi.org/10.1007/978-981-95-2972-8_15

As in the case of statutory zoning under the *Town Planning Ordinance*, the enforcement of an administrative grading made by AMO or statutory monument designation under the *Antiquities and Monuments Ordinance* also relies on the *Buildings Ordinance*. The reason is that a private building cannot be lawfully demolished without prior permission from the Building Authority under the *Buildings Ordinance*.

In September 2007, the Executive Council formulated a heritage policy:

> To protect, conserve and revitalise as appropriate historical and heritage sites and buildings through relevant and sustainable approaches for the benefit and enjoyment of present and future generations. In implementing this policy, due regard should be given to development needs in the public interest, respect for private property rights, budgetary considerations, cross-sector collaboration and active engagement of stakeholders and the general public.

In 2008, the Commissioner for Heritage's Office (CHO) was established under the Development Bureau. One of CHO's functions is to provide policy support for and guidance to the AMO.

Built Heritage on Government Land and Private Land

There are two types of built heritage in terms of Hong Kong's land tenure: built heritage on government land and built heritage on leasehold land. The former is not "common property", although access to it may be "open" or "restricted" to various degrees. It is the *private* property of the government. The latter is private property, access to which is usually highly restricted. While the conservation of the former is a matter of government knowledge and determination, which is definitely influenced by public awareness and support, the conservation of the latter only entails resentment by its proprietor, who often prefers to maximise the economic value of his/her land by redevelopment.

Designation of Monuments and Proposed Monuments Under the *Antiquities and Monuments Ordinance* (Cap.53)

The Antiquities and Monuments Authority (the Authority), being the Secretary for Development, may after consulting with the Antiquities Advisory Board and with the approval of the Executive Council, declare any place, building site, or structure to be a "Monument" by placing a notice in the Gazette.

Where a *private* building of historical value is *under threat of demolition*, the Antiquities and Monuments Authority may, after consulting with the Antiquities Advisory Board and with the approval of the Executive Council, declare it as a "proposed monument". The declaration shall be in effect for a period of 12 months, unless it is withdrawn earlier, which cannot be extended.

Whether a private building is declared a "Monument" or "Declared Monument", the owner may apply to the Authority to withdraw the declaration, and if refused, may appeal to the Chief Executive, who may decide that:

(1) The declaration shall stand;
(2) The declaration shall stand, subject to such variations or conditions as he thinks fit; or
(3) The declaration shall be withdrawn.

The Chief Executive's direction shall be final. The Authority may then, again after consulting with the Board with the approval of the Chief Executive, place a notice in the Gazette to declare any place, building, site, or structure a Monument. (Until now, there were 101 "declared monuments".)

Except with the permission of the Authority (in the form of a permit), no person shall demolish, remove, obstruct, deface, or interfere with a proposed monument or monument.

Not all declared monuments are open to the public for reasons of public safety or operational needs.

The designation of a private building as a "proposed monument" or "declared monument" takes away its owner's right to alter its existing appearance or demolish it for redevelopment.

Compensation to the Owner Whose Property Is Declared a Monument

The Authority may, with the prior approval of the Chief Executive, pay the owner compensation in respect of the financial loss suffered. Should the owner and the Authority fail to reach an agreement, the compensation shall be assessed by the District Court. The District Court may compensate the applicant an amount that it thinks is reasonable under the circumstances.

In *Land Compensation and Valuation Law in Hong Kong (Second Edition), Judge* Gordon Cruden stated:

> The Court would no doubt seek to ascertain the market value of the land which had been diminished as a consequence of the declaration under the [Antiquities and Monuments] Ordinance (p.40)... Declaration under the Ordinance may adversely affect the market value including loss or reduction of development rights (p.41).

Historical Buildings

Between 1996 and 2000, the AMO conducted a survey of buildings in Hong Kong built before 1950 that might have historic significance. This survey identified some 8800 buildings, from which the AMO selected 1444 buildings with "higher heritage value" for assessment. After public consultation, these buildings were assessed using six criteria:

(1) Historical interest.
(2) Architectural merit.
(3) Group value.
(4) Social value and local interest.
(5) Authenticity.
(6) Rarity.

An appointed assessment panel commenced this exercise in 2005. The definitions of the grades it used are:

Grade 1: Buildings of outstanding merit, which every effort should be made to preserve, if possible.

Grade 2: Buildings of special merit, for which efforts should be made to selectively preserve.

Grade 3: Buildings of some merit, the preservation of which in some form would be desirable, while alternative means could be considered if preservation is not practicable.

Government buildings with grade or monument status are usually maintained by the Architectural Services Department (ASD). Private buildings in the same situations are maintained by their owners.

The AMO carries out restoration and maintenance for private buildings that are declared as monuments on the condition that the owners agree to accept arrangements for public access to their buildings.

The March 2009 Announcement of Historical Building Grades

In March 2009, the Assessment Panel of AAB, which reports to the Secretary of Development, announced the following proposed gradings of the 1444 buildings.

Proposed Grade 1: 212.

Proposed Grade 2: 366.

Proposed Grade 3: 576.

Proposed No Grade: 290.

In September 2009, the AAB decided that any newly referred premises for grading would be considered in a separate exercise after all of the first 1444 buildings, except those at risk of demolition, were assessed.

By 20 February 2013, the grades of the original 1444 buildings were mostly confirmed after adjustments and removals. Fifty-three of them were declared monuments. In addition, the AMO received public referrals to assess 202 other buildings.

Effects of Grading

The Grade of a building does not immediately affect its ownership status. The demolition, alteration, and renovation works of Grade 2 and Grade 3 buildings are not encouraged, but neither are they prohibited. There exists an internal monitoring mechanism in which the Buildings Department, Lands Department, and Planning Department will alert the AMO when threats of demolition exist.

If a Grade 1 building is threatened by demolition, it may be re-assessed so that it can become a "proposed monument" or even a "monument" under the *Antiquities and Monuments Ordinance* to give it statutory protection.

The AAB is considering a proposal to review public resources for preservation and conservation through town planning.

Practical Issues of Heritage Conservation

Two practical issues of heritage conservation are:

(1) The revitalisation of historic buildings, especially adapted for re-use and be open to the public, needs to comply with the current provisions of the Building Regulations, fire services requirements, and access for the disabled. This often jeopardises the authenticity of the building, as the additions of enforcement works, passenger lifts, and sprinkler systems may be required. A good example is the Central Market.

(2) High maintenance costs and running costs, e.g. the Central Police Compound.

Government Policy Initiatives Regarding Government and Private Historical Buildings

The government has agreed to:

(1) Conduct a *heritage impact assessment* of any new capital project.

(2) Implement the "Revitalizing Historical Buildings through Partnership Scheme" for government-owned historical buildings. This scheme seeks to strike a balance between sustainable development and heritage conservation, as well as designate historical buildings for good, adaptive re-use. The government would invite non-profit organisations to submit applications to use historical buildings to provide services or run their businesses as social enterprises.

(3) To provide economic incentives for the conservation of privately owned historic buildings by means such as land exchanges and the "transfer of development rights" to compensate owners for their loss of development rights. A good example is King Yin Lei, Stubbs Road.

Government Initiatives Regarding the Maintenance of Privately Owned Graded Historic Buildings

To facilitate the maintenance of privately owned graded historic buildings, the government will only provide financial support in the form of grants with a ceiling of HK$1,000,000. Maintenance works are the owner's responsibility and s/he also has to abide by a number of conditions, including promising to not demolish any building or transfer ownership and to allow reasonable public access.

Did AAB Discriminate Against Colonial Built Heritage?

Two interesting cases that attracted public attention involved obvious lease breaches that restricted development to "European-type house" due to statutory and racially discriminatory zoning that predated the *Town Planning Ordinance* (Lai et al. 2011).

Ho Tung Gardens, 75 Peak Road Lost as a "Proposed Monument"

Ho Tung Gardens was built in around 1927. The site originally consisted of RBL's 26 and 28 and was subjected to Crown Lease covenants that only allowed for the development of a "European-type house". The sites were surrendered after the war in exchange for a re-granted plot of land designated RBL 670. It had an area of about 11,520 square metres and was zoned R(C)2 with a maximum plot ratio of 0.5 and a maximum building height of four storeys. Its market value was estimated at $8 billion in 2012.

Under the threat of demolition, Ho Tung Gardens was declared a "proposed monument" in October 2011. The heritage assessment document in support of the site's designation as a "proposed monument" describes the property as such:

> three buildings (including a basically two-storey main building in **Chinese Renaissance style**, a servants' quarter and a garage) and structures including Chinese pavilions, a Chinese pagoda, etc. (Emphasis authors)

The owner objected to the designation and petitioned the Chief Executive to overturn it. On 4 December 2012, the Chief Executive in Council directed that the intended declaration should be dropped. To pacify conservationists, the government announced that it would not demolish the West Wing of the Central Government Offices on Ice House Street.

King Yin Lei, 45 Stubbs Road Made a Declared Monument

This was officially a private building built in 1937 on Inland Lot No.7327 and was praised for its unique Chinese architectural style. The government entered into a 75-year lease for it in 1957. The Crown Lease restricts future construction at the site to "a **European-type house**" and any development would be subjected to a design-disposition-height (DDH) clause. Its Chinese Renaissance style (a mix of Chinese and Western architecture) partly contravenes these provisions. (Emphasis authors)

After a public outcry against its demolition while it was in progress, the government quickly negotiated with the landowner who eventually surrendered the whole property in exchange for an adjacent site of roughly the same size for private development. King Yin Lei was declared a monument in 2008.

Statistical Analysis of AAB Grading

A statistical study by Chau et al. (2022) found no evidence of nationalistic bias against British or Japanese built military heritage buildings and structures after the handover of Hong Kong to China in July 1997. The study found no evidence of bias in favour of imperial Chinese architecture in the postcolonial period. There was some evidence that suggests AAB's assessments of heritage value for military heritage buildings and structures have actually increased while those for imperial Chinese architecture have decreased after 1997, which is somewhat puzzling and merits further investigation.

However, it should be noted that many World War II–built heritage structures in the countryside, such as pillboxes built by the Japanese occupier in the Northeastern NT (Davies et al. 2022), those along the Gin

Drinker's Line (Tan et al. 2022), and on Hong Kong Island (Lai et al. 2021), were left ungraded and/or unmanaged, even though they are educational and tourism assets.

The Public and Built Heritage Conservation

Members of the public, with different skills and knowledge levels, can contribute to heritage conservation on government land under dense vegetation cover by discovering heritage buildings such as pillboxes and shelters, sharing them in the media, and mapping them (Davies et al. 2024). Though some of these structures appear on old maps, whether they have survived the test of time can only be ascertained by actual visits to them, as the use of LIDAR technology in Hong Kong is still new. Figure 15.2 shows how the public can contribute to military heritage mapping, which differs from the conventional model shown in Fig. 15.1. Such a model assumes official experts know everything.

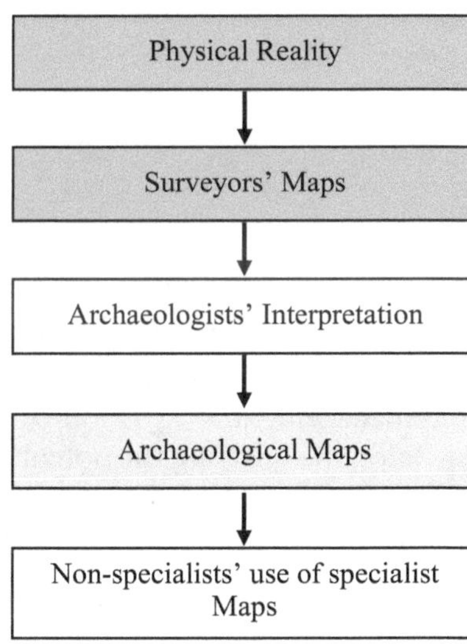

Fig. 15.1 Mapping information transmission model of Gupta and Devillers (2017) adopted for Hong Kong terminology

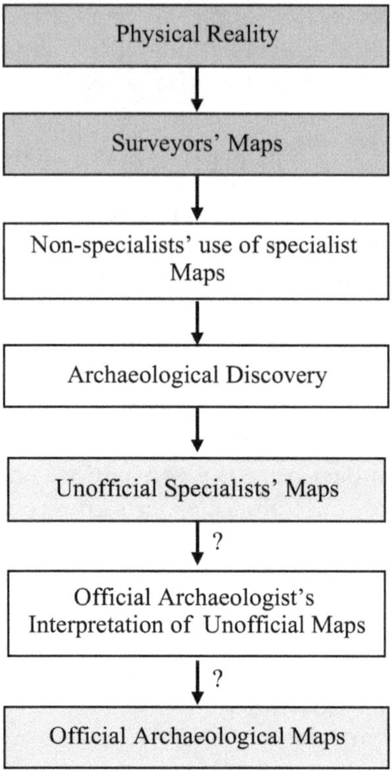

Fig. 15.2 Mapping information transmission model of Hong Kong for military heritage

The Surveyor and Built Heritage Conservation

How can a surveyor contribute to built heritage conservation planning and management?

Before recollecting the potential role of the modern surveyor in conservation, it is necessary to trace the history of the surveyors who actually shaped the modern urban and rural environment throughout the world. At the street corner of the junction of Perth, Australia, stands a statue of a nineteenth-century naval officer: John Septimus Roe (1797–1878), the first Surveyor General of the Swan River Settlement (today Perth) in Australia. In Roe's day a surveyor like him was usually the first to determine the layout of a town or region and the lot plans for its settlement: in effect a town planner. So in the past, especially in what is today the developing world, when many of the old buildings that are today our heritage were planned and built, the land surveyor, who was as much also a bona fide town planner, often had a military background. Roe was a classic example of this. Thus, any heritage study or assessment of buildings that ignores cadastral details, details that usually have a long history, will likely be incomplete and even inauthentic.

While built heritage conservation surely requires special knowledge and ways of appreciation that go beyond the skills and training of most surveyors, this does not make the surveyor a peripheral agent in conservation planning and management.

Even at the most basic level where heritage conservation is treated as just *another form of real estate* to plan for, develop, and manage, there is still a need to include all surveying specialties in the picture.

Built heritage is after all *built property* with spatial, cadastral, structural, facility, land tenure, and value dimensions, some of which are historical and, hence, actually part of the heritage in question.

The overall project conceptualisation in any heritage conservation exercise would be a task for the planning and development surveyor. For what is involved is coordinating land, building, and estate surveyors, especially when the conservation project in question forms part and parcel of a wider scheme.

The ascertaining of the spatial, cadastral, and even structural dimensions of the building in question is the domain of the *land surveyor*. The interpretation of maps and aerial photographs and other remote-sensing images, along with the identification and appreciation of the location and functions of a building, are areas in which a land surveyor can assist a heritage conservation expert. The presentation of conservation concepts in map and other media based on GIS data is also something to which a land surveyor can make a big contribution.

The examination of the physical status of a building and recommendations for and supervision of its rehabilitation and/or adaptation with the proper facilities for a modern viable use is the domain of a building surveyor. In turn the building surveyor may need the assistance of a quantity surveyor for project control when the scale and magnitude of the project are large enough. For cost control and administering contracts are important elements in ensuring heritage projects stick within budget.

An estate surveyor is indispensable for investigating land ownership matters, conducting a feasibility study, writing a valuation report on an existing and/or adapted use, drafting lease documents, selecting tenants, and overseeing a property's management for its new role as a heritage site.

Knowledge, skill, technique, and an awareness of all surveying branches are indispensable for sound heritage conservation research. Research on

Hong Kong's built heritage conservation efforts, informed and conducted by surveying, is gathering momentum.

Questions for Revision and Discussion

1. Facadism is a way to retain some memory of a historic building. Discuss why it is uncommon in private residential or office development in Hong Kong.

Hong Kong developers have traditionally not paid attention to the value of heritage conservation. However, they have quickly learned to make use of built and non-built heritage in their redeveloped sites.

2. How does a valuer assess the value of a heritage building near a popular trail in a country park?

It is not easy to assess the value of a heritage building due to the limited transaction and rental records of similar properties, i.e. comparables. In some circumstances, it is difficult to dedicate a heritage building for any beneficial use that the cost approach (contractor's basis), usually regarded as "a method of last resort", may be applied.

In the present case, it could be practical to use the heritage building, which is near a popular trail, for some income-generating tourism-related purposes. If the building, upon suitable fitting out, can be leased to earn rental income, and assuming that the tenant is responsible for the rehabilitation, conservation, upkeeping, and maintenance of the building, the income approach would be applicable in the valuation. There is however no generic answer and the value, if any, is to be assessed on a case-by-case and location-by-location basis.

3. Discuss the value of public opinion expressed in social media concerning built heritage conservation in Hong Kong.

Public opinion has a heavy impact, as in the case of the declaration of King Yin Lei as a monument and the development of an open museum in the Shing Mun Redoubt area.

References

Chau, K. W., Lawrence W. C. Lai, and Mark H. Chua. 2022. Post-Colonial Conservation of Colonial Built Heritage in Hong Kong: A Statistical Analysis of Historic Building Grading. *Environment and Planning B: Urban Analytics and City Science* 49 (2): 671–686.

Davies, Stephen N. G., Y. K. Tan, and Lawrence W. C. Lai. 2022. Japanese Occupation Period Military Structures near Hong Kong's Northeastern Border: An Initial Survey. *Surveying & Built Environment* 31 (2): 64–147.

Davies, Stephen N. G., Lawrence W. C. Lai, Y. K. Tan, and H. C. Chiu. 2024. Discovery Flows From Mapping for Conservation Planning: The Case of the Unofficial Finding and Mapping of World War II British Hong Kong Defence Structures. *Town Planning Review*. in print.

Gupta, N., and R. Devillers. 2017. Geographic Visualization in Archaeology. *Journal of Archaeological Method and Theory* 24:852–885.

Lai, Lawrence W. C., Valerius W. C. Kwong, and Jason W. Y. Kwong. 2011. Segregation Legal and Natural: An Empirical Study of the Legally Protected and Free Market Housing Ownership on the Peak. *Habitat International* 35 (3): 501–507.

Lai, Lawrence W. C., Y. K. Tan, and Stephen N. G. Davies. 2021. *Pillboxes on Hong Kong Island in the Era of World War II*. Hong Kong: Hong Kong Institute of Surveyors.

Tan, Y. K., Stephen N. G. Davies, and Lawrence W. C. Lai. 2022. *Pillboxes Along the Gin Drinker's Line, 80 Years After World War II*. Hong Kong: Hong Kong Institute of Surveyors.

PART IV

Capturing Land Values

CHAPTER 16

Assessment of Development Potential of a Site

Daniel Chi Wing Ho

Introduction

This chapter is the domain where the development market faces the Building Authority (BA), one of the three most powerful development approval decision makers, as a regulator. Regulations grow in number and complexity over time, increasing the entry and other transaction costs of the development industry. As discretionary power is inevitable and must be exercised, this naturally favours bigger and hence more resourceful players in the development market.

Ignoring the political economy of building regulation, this chapter shall confine itself to the basics of development potential assessment with reference to the *Buildings Ordinance* (BO), *Building (Planning) Regulations* (B(P)R), and Practice Notes for Authorized Persons, Registered Structural Engineers and Registered Geotechnical Engineers (PNAPs).

D. C. W. Ho (✉)
Department of Real Estate and Construction, The University of Hong Kong, Hong Kong, China
e-mail: danielho@hku.hk

L. W. C. Lai et al. (eds.), *Principles of Land Administration at Work*, https://doi.org/10.1007/978-981-95-2972-8_16

Technical Meaning of Development Potential of a Site

Technically, the development potential of a site in Hong Kong is the potential value (the difference between the achievable value under regulations and the current value) to the owner/prospective developer upon (a) renovation or redevelopment of an existing building or (b) construction of a new building on a vacant site for profit or other benefits.

A number of factors determine the Gross Development Value (GDV) of a site. These include the proposed use, configuration, design and quality of construction, prevailing market price, and the maximum GFA that can be developed.

The GFA for a site is determined with reference to the permissible plot ratio (PR), site coverage (SC), and other inter-related factors of a proposed building under the *Town Planning Ordinance* (via the outline zoning plan [OZP]), conditions in the land lease, and the *Buildings Ordinance* (BO).

Under the BO, the PR and SC of a site can be obtained according to the First Schedule of the *Building (Planning) Regulations* (B(P)R), with reference to (a) 'class' of site, (b) building height, and (c) use(s), of the proposed development, subject always to any applicable lease conditions and restrictions under a statutory town plan (e.g. an OZP or a development permission area (DPA) plan under the *Town Planning Ordinance* (TPO)).

The maximum development potential of a site is derived from the joint interpretation of the applicable lease conditions, statutory town plan, and the BO, whichever is the more restrictive.

Plot Ratio

The plot ratio is the ratio of total GFA to the area of the site on which the building is erected. In other words:

$$\text{GFA} = \text{Plot Ratio} \times \text{Site Area}$$

It is rigidly controlled under the BO by maximum permissible plot ratio specified in the First Schedule of the B(P)R. Site area to be used for the calculation of GFA is the gross site area enclosed within the lot boundary *less* the areas of roads and lanes, usually *include* areas of slopes and non-building areas.

To find out the permissible plot ratio for the site under the BO, one should first establish the **class of site** (Class A, B, or C), determine the **use** of the building proposed (either domestic or non-domestic) and building **height** proposed, then look up the permissible plot ratio from the First Schedule.

For the purposes of calculating the total permissible GFA, the area of the **site** shall exclude the area of any new and existing internal streets or service lanes in the area defined by the boundary of the site.

Site Coverage

Site coverage is the area of site that is covered by the building at respective levels, usually expressed in percentage of the accountable site area.

A procedure similar to PR determination can be adopted to find out the maximum permissible site coverage for the site. Note that 'street shadow area' evident in buildings in the 1960s and 1970s was repealed in early 1980s.[1]

Class of Site

Building sites are classified into **Class A, B,** and **C** depending on the degree of 'openness' and their intrinsic site characteristics. The more open is the site and the longer is public street frontage enjoyed, the higher the density of development can be permitted.

Refer to Reg.2(1) B(P)R and Reg.18A B(P)R[2] for definitions. For this application, the boundary of the site must abut and touch the edge of the street in question:

[1] Building design affects the "street shadow area", which shaped old buildings in Hong Kong. While this parameter is insignificant to new building designs, it is a reminder of the former control of natural lighting provision by the BO according to Hong Kong's geographical latitude.

[2] Under Reg.18A(3)(i) of B(P)R, a street is regarded as a specified street only if it is vested in the government and maintained by the Highways Department. A village road, which is not maintained by the Highways Department, although it belongs to the government, is ineligible for street classification under the BO unless it meets other criteria under Reg.18A(3).

(1) A Class A site means a site, not being a class B site or class C site, that abuts on one specified street not less than 4.5 m in width or on more than one such street.
(2) A Class B site is a corner site that abuts two specified streets, neither of which is less than 4.5 metres wide.
(3) A Class C site is a corner site that abuts three specified streets, none of which is less than 4.5 metres wide.

Note that a corner site shall not be regarded as abutting two specified streets unless at least 40% of the site boundary abuts the streets.

A corner site shall not be regarded as abutting three specified streets unless at least 60% of the site boundary abuts the streets.

It is worth mentioning that building sites abutting more than one 'specified street' at more or less that same level or with big difference in levels but not being a corner site shall always remain as a Class A site.

Building Heights

Building height control under the TPO and a Government Lease may be stipulated as the (a) maximum permissible height (in metres), (b) number of metres above the mean principal datum (mPD), or (c) number of storeys. Joint Practice Note No.5 (JPN05) elaborates on building height restrictions commonly applied by government, as specified in statutory town plans and Government Leases, but not the BO. However, building height under the BO is used to determine the development intensity and fire safety requirements, which are not a 'restriction'.

Under the BO, the top of a building for the purpose of measuring its height is the *mean* height of the main roof, whose *highest* level is for measuring the top of the building under the other two control regimes. The definition of main roof is the roof over the highest usable floor space, where the three control regimes align.

Also under the BO, the bottom of a building shall be measured from the mean street level of the lower or lowest specified street that the building abuts. For the TPO and lease, however, the bottom of a building is measured from its mean site-formation level to its basement, if any.

Building height measure under the *Hong Kong Airport (Control of Obstructions) Ordinance* (Cap.301) included all projecting structures e.g. water tanks, machine rooms, etc.

Table 16.1 An example of a Class C site's development control parameters

Example: A Class C site for domestic use		
	Max. plot ratio	*Max. site coverage*
Height of building **under 30 m**	**5.5**	**55%**
Height of building **over 61 m**	**10** (max. for domestic use under BO)	**40%**

If the widths of all adjoining streets[3] are less than 4.5 m (i.e. the site cannot be classified), the scale of development and details shall be determined by the BA. Usually, the plot ratio and the number of storey (height) are taken not to exceed the existing bulk.

If the width of any one of the adjoining streets is ≥ 4.5 m, there will be no restrictions on height under the B.O. (Table 16.1)

Subject to PNAPs APP-101 and APP-132, the site coverage of non-domestic building (or non-domestic part of a composite building) may have 100% site coverage to a height not exceeding 15 metres. This is the reason why there are many buildings with a 100% SC commercial podium for malls, car parks, etc. (non-domestic) with residential towers (domestic) above.

Lease Conditions

It is stipulated under s.14(2) BO neither the approval of any plans nor the consent to the commencement of any building works or street works shall be deemed to confer any title to land. Lease conditions, which govern the use of the land and building bulk in accordance with public interest and government policies, usually take precedence over the provisions of the BO.

Examples of lease clauses are 'maximum 6 storeys for domestic use'; 'building height not to exceed 65 metres above the Hong Kong Principal Datum'; 'the design, disposition, and height of the proposed building shall be subject to the prior written approval of the Director', etc.

[3] An adjoining street must physically overlap and touch the boundary of the private lot without any intervening green area or planting strip that does not form part of the gazetted street.

The developer should apply for lease modifications if the proposed building will exceed the specified height and a premium is normally payable on negotiation.

Statutory Town Plan under TPO (e.g. an OZP)

The OZP may specify certain block or site not to exceed certain height (in mPD), no. of storeys, or not to exceed the height of the existing building upon redevelopment. Similar to that of the lease conditions, the provisions of an OZP, or any other type of statutory town plan under TPO, dictate use of the land, building bulk, and environmental impact and they always take precedence over the provisions of the BO due to s.16(1)(g).[4]

Use of the Proposed Building

Generally the use on a particular site is restricted under the respective OZP or user clause in the lease. For checking of plot ratio and site coverage under First Schedule of the B(P)R, use of a building is classified either 'domestic' or 'non-domestic'.[5]

For composite buildings with mixed uses, e.g. G/F with shops, 1–2/F as office, and domestic flats above, the plot ratio of a particular use (e.g. domestic) shall be determined as a *residual* of the other use (e.g. non-domestic), taking the different plot ratios in account.

Permitted PR for domestic use (residual) = (A – B) × C / A, where:

A = maximum permitted PR for non-domestic use.
B = actual PR for non-domestic use.
C = maximum permitted PR for domestic use.

[4] The BA has the authority to reject building works that would result in buildings that differ in height, design, type, or intended use from buildings in their vicinity or those that previously existed at the same sites.

[5] The exception is a hotel, which, unless otherwise exempted, is regarded as a "non-domestic" use, in which case s.23A B(P)R applies.

Parameters Affecting Development Potential

Gross Floor Area

GFA under Reg.23(3) B(P)R is the total floor areas contained within the outer surface of external walls of a building measured at each floor level (PNAP APP-2). It includes features and elements such as staircase and corridor areas, toilets and bathrooms, internal walls, service ducts, lift lobbies, lift shafts, balconies, etc. In general, all 'covered' areas within the site including floor areas at basement levels (underground), unless otherwise exempted.[6]

Areas Generally Excluded from GFA Calculation

There are '*exempted*' GFA under Reg.23(3)(a) B(P)R and '*disregarded*' GFA under Reg.23(3)(b) B(P)R.[7] Both of which can be excluded from GFA calculations and usually welcome by developers as sites are subject to caps on PR and hence total GFA.

'Exempted' *GFA Under Reg.23(3)(a) B(P)R*

Areas of voids at each floor level are normally accountable for GFA, though the actual floor plates do not exist. According to PNAP APP-2, exemption of GFA calculations would be allowed on application, such as the front of cinema and theatre balconies, banking halls and shopping arcades,[8] auditoria, sporting halls, school halls and religious institutions, main entrance lobbies to hotels and non-domestic buildings, etc.

Other examples of '*exempted*' GFA which required application for modifications include:

(1) In duplex domestic flats or houses if they satisfy certain criteria.
(2) Green and innovative features, utility platforms, sun screens, etc.

[6] Unless otherwise exempted, a space on the G/F covered by a projection 20 floors above it is included in the GFA calculation.

[7] Note that GFA concessions granted under s.23(3)(a) of B(P)R require an express modification permit issued by the Building Authority with powers under s.42 of the BO, whereas GFA concessions accepted under s.23(3)(b) of B(P) require no written modification or approval.

[8] That is as long as the total area of the voids in the shopping arcade does not exceed 10% of the arcade's total GFA.

(3) Bay windows.
(4) Area occupied by legitimate curtain walls.
(5) External walls constructed of prefabricated units.
(6) Recreational facilities such as squash courts, gymnasia, indoor swimming pools, roof trellises, etc.
(7) Areas covered by canopies and covered walkways.
(8) Area for picking up and setting down persons departing from or arriving at the hotel by vehicle.
(9) Supporting facilities for a hotel (i.e. legitimate 'back-of-house' accommodations).
(10) Refuge floor including refuge floor cum sky garden.
(11) Covered area under large projecting/overhanging feature.
(12) Public transport terminus.[9]
(13) Buildings adopting Modular Integrated Construction.
(14) Non-essential plant rooms, filtration plant rooms for swimming pools in hotels.

These exemptions do not apply to luxury clubs with restaurants and other facilities obviously meant for an exclusive membership and commercial takings, rather than for the general benefit of residents and occupiers.

'Disregarded' *GFA Under s.23(3)(b) B(P)R*

Subject to stipulated criteria fulfilled and demonstrated to the satisfaction of the BA, no modification or approval is required from the BA and direct application of Reg.23(3)(b) B(P)R will suffice[10] for the following areas to be *disregarded* in GFA calculations:

(1) Permitted car parks and driveways.[11]
(2) Parking motor vehicles, loading or unloading of motor vehicles.
(3) Refuse storage and material recovery chambers, material recovery chambers, refuse storage and material recovery rooms, refuse

[9] The provision of a public transport terminus normally comes with lease conditions for a 'Comprehensive Development Site'. The design and disposition of the public transport terminus must have policy support from the Transport Department.

[10] See Footnote 9 *ante dictum*.

[11] Only the minimum provision of car park spaces, which form part of the lease conditions with the expressed support from the relevant government departments, will be eligible for consideration by the Building Authority for a GFA concession under s.23(3)(b) B(P)R.

chutes, refuse hopper rooms and other types of facilities provided to facilitate the separation of refuse to the satisfaction of the BA.

(4) Access facilities for telecommunications and broadcasting services.
(5) Air-conditioning plant rooms and rooms for other similar services, including lift, machinery rooms, plant rooms, boiler rooms, electrical switch rooms, meter rooms, transformer rooms, generator rooms, pump rooms, telephone equipment rooms, CO_2 rooms, water tanks, etc.[12]
(6) Sewage treatment plant rooms.
(7) Chimneys shaft.
(8) Staircase and lift shaft passing through floors constituting a refuge floor or consisting completely of non-accountable floor areas.[13]

There have been changes in recent years on GFA concessions given to projects which demonstrated sustainable and green building designs and incorporation of amenity features. Please refer to PNAP APP-2, APP-42, APP-151, and JPN1 to JPN8 for the latest development of the issue and related concessions and caps.

'Bonus' GFA Under Reg.22 B(P)R

Subject to related lease conditions and the OZP, the development potential of a site may be increased via the granting of bonus plot ratio by the BA under Reg.22 B(P)R. Bonus PR and SC may be permitted for areas dedicated to public for the purposes of passage[14] or road widening[15] or for areas permanently surrendered to the government on resumption or on demand.[16]

[12] Refer to PNAP APP-151 for details.

[13] The horizontal area of staircase, lift shaft, and vertical duct that solely serves floors is accepted as not being accountable for GFA and can be disregarded in GFA calculations. In case a small floor area is accountable for GFA, all associated horizontal areas will automatically resume their statuses as GFA accountable spaces.

[14] The government must request that areas in private sites be dedicated to public access for the purpose of passage. Otherwise, policy support for the relevant government departments must be secured. A deed of dedication must be signed and registered prior to the issue of an Occupation Permit for occupants of the new building to enjoy the bonus plot ratio.

[15] The government must request that areas in private sites be dedicated to public access for the purpose of street widening. Otherwise, policy support for the relevant government departments must be secured.

[16] Areas within private sites that are permanently surrendered to the government for returning vacant possessions or for the purpose of street widening must be required by the

Detail considerations of granting bonus GFA and the requirements are stipulated in PNAP APP-20 and APP-108.

Saleable Floor Area

Floor area is often used to describe the size and scale of a building and flat units to the general public, but often mean different things to different people. In the past some developers included the common areas as part of the area sold to individual owners. The result was the total 'area' sold becomes much larger than the approved GFA.

The Hong Kong Institute of Surveyors (HKIS) jointly published a booklet in 1999 (updated in 2008) together with the Consumer Council, which contained standards of measurement of floor areas known as 'saleable floor areas' (SFA). The *Residential Properties (First-hand Sales) Ordinance* (Cap.621) was enacted since 2013 to regulate calculations of SFA for first-hand sales of residential properties. It has become a standard for the general public and the real estate development industry in measurement of floor areas.

Questions for Revision and Discussion

1. Discuss which parameter, building bulk, GFA, or building height is the best to reflect development potential.

The plot ratio (PR) is the best proxy to measure/gauge development potential. The PR of a site may be subject individually to a statutory town plan (OZP, DPA Plan) and/or the Crown/Government Lease, and more generally under the *First Schedule* of the *Building (Planning) Regulations.*

2. Discuss the justifications for exemption of GFA.

Most exemptions are related to essential facilities/services for a building such as refuse collection and materials recovery chambers, refuge floors, car parking, plant rooms, underground carparks, and club houses.

government or, if proposed by the landowner, must be accepted by the relevant government departments. The official cession of a site area must be completed and gazetted prior to the issuance of an Occupation Permit for the new building to enjoy the bonus plot ratio.

Other exemptions are for green and environmental benefits that building facilities/features, like balconies and utility platforms, can bring about.

In normal cases, Planning Department would follow Buildings Department's (or the Building Authority's) decisions in GFA calculations. Lands Department would calculate the GFA with reference to the conditions of each land lease. The GFA definition by Lands Department may also be different from Buildings Department.

3. Discuss the rationale and problems of site class classification.

Site classification is about the number of specified street(s) a site abuts. Generally the greater the number of streets a site abuts, the more 'open' is the site, and the higher is the plot ratio allowed under the *Buildings Ordinance*.

For sites with irregular shapes/boundaries, it may be difficult to ascertain the site classifications. Under such situations, the classification will be determined by the Building Authority.

Also, there are many sites in Hong Kong which do not abut on any 'specified street'. The Building Authority will also determine the development potential of these sites upon submission of General Building Plans.

CHAPTER 17

Land Readjustment: Reforming Property Boundaries and Proportional Reallocation of Rights and Obligations

Lawrence Wai Chung Lai and Lennon H. T. Choy

This chapter deals with a means of replanning an urban layout with a lot of individually owned lots or an area under traditional land tenure with lots not allocated according to any formal layout.[1] This means has many names.

Land readjustment (or replotting) is adopted here as the better last name for many other names of land conversion such as (1) land adjustment, (2) land consolidation, (3) land modification, (4) land parcellation (re-parcelling/re-parcellization), (5) land pooling, (6) land reconstitution, (7) land redistribution, (8) land re-dividing, (9) land repatriation,

[1] This chapter is an abridged version of Lai et al. (2020). For a textual review of literature from 1919 to 2019, see Lai (2023).

L. W. C. Lai (✉) • L. H. T. Choy
Department of Real Estate and Construction, The University of Hong Kong, Hong Kong, China
e-mail: wclai@hku.hk; lennonchoy@hku.hk

L. W. C. Lai et al. (eds.), *Principles of Land Administration at Work*, https://doi.org/10.1007/978-981-95-2972-8_17

(10) land replotting, or (11) land sharing because it focuses on the planned realignment of cadastral boundaries (some of which are also road boundaries) and is an old term that can be traced in the English literature to the 1920s.

Dr Edward G. Pryor (1976), who retired in 1999 as Principal Government Town Planner of the government of Hong Kong Special Administrative Region, shows how private rural land lots in an area of the New Territories of Hong Kong, which retain the irregular cadastral boundaries typical on customary Chinese land holdings, were readjusted to conform to an urban layout using an ingenious government issued interest-bearing "I O U" (called Letter A/B) which can be freely traded. This work was discovered from the citation by Archer (1981).

Introduction

Land readjustment as a planning tool has been referred to by Alterman (2012: 11), as cited by Muñoz-Gielen (2016: 78), as "the sleeping beauty" among planning instruments and land management strategies. From a different perspective, which sees "planning as boundary delineation" (Buitelaar 2021; Lai 2021), it is worthwhile scrutinizing land readjustment, as it is all about replanning by re-delineating formerly laid down boundaries.

From a Coasian transaction cost reasoning (Coase 1960, 1988), this chapter focuses on land readjustment (i.e., "land adjustment" or "readjustment of property lines" (Ehlers 1928:8)) as a town planning method, *a special case of the transfer of development rights*, that seeks to overcome the *constraints for redevelopment posed by existing cadastral boundaries.* This focus is informed by recent works on boundaries in the planning and urban studies literature by such authors as Arruñada (2018), Bobkova et al. (2019), Ellickson (2012), Kalbro (2019), and Lai and Davies (2017, 2020, 2022). The Coasian neo-institutional *perspective* is intended to pin down land readjustment in terms of boundary re-delineation. Hence such spatial property rights dimensions as "use of neo-institutional economic terms" and the use of "maps." Maps are of special professional interest as maps and plans manifest the "beauty of town planning" (Schubert 2017).

The neo-institutional paradigm is sensitive to private and communal property rights, tacitly understood as a dimension of human rights, and to the costs of alternative policy or legal approaches to any public policy issue. It articulates well with concepts like value capture, public-private sector participation (PPP), and transfer of development rights (TDR). Value capture can be an empirical or ideological concept. Doebele (2007) summarizes the history of land readjustment with reference to Henry George's idea and the stance of the Lincoln Institute of Land Policy:

> Land readjustment seemed to be the most ingenious method yet devised for the capture of socially created value for public purposes. Unlike Henry George's single tax and most other instruments, it executed the recapture while the rural-urban transformation was taking place, eliminating the unpopular task of extracting money from landowners after the process was complete. It seemed that a mechanism capable of operating on a scale commensurate with the pace of urbanization in third world cities and with a built-in self-financing capability had finally been found. (Doebele 2007: ix)

As a historical overview, the origin of land readjustment can be dated back to the eighteenth century when President Washington established the capital of the US in Washington (Deuskar 2013). However, in terms of land use policy, land readjustment has a German beginning (Frankfurt in the nineteenth century and later developments); followed by a large-scale adoption by Japan and dissemination to her imperial sphere of control (Manchuria) and colonies (Korea and Taiwan) with lasting effects; and after WWII spreading to Western Australia (Perth), Western Europe, Southeast Asia, Africa, and the Americas.

Theoretical Perspective

This chapter, as a contribution to town planning as boundary ordering and reordering, invites readers to pay attention to the rigidity of land boundaries from a new neo-institutional economic perspective as informed by the Coase Theorem. While it is tempting to use a single work as the key to a framework, the book chapter of Alterman (2012) that highlights "value capture" is a useful prelude to what is to be discussed below.

Boundaries in the Town Planning Context

Boundaries succeed in terms of "value accumulation"[2] (Lai et al. 2020b), the condition for "value capture" by third parties (including the state), if they help orderly exclusion for greater and truly mutually beneficial exchanges. Boundary delineation, in a sense, is town planning (Buitelaar 2021; Lai 2021). This is so whether such demarcation is for an apartment, a house, or a vast piece of land.

The recent rise of Airbnb, which challenges zoning control, has been wrongly treated by some as the rise of a new "sharing" or "communal" way of "post exclusion" living (Fennell 2019). In fact, on close analysis, it is an intensely *commodified and exclusive* use of private properties partitioned minutely in terms of both time and space.

Although recent works by Home (2003, 2007, 2018) reveal that land readjustment has a pre-WWI British Indian planning legislation relevance, by and large, land readjustment in the literature is mainly represented up to the early 1980s as a German-Japanese land assembly and layout regulation practice that has spread to Taiwan and Korea, in parallel to Western Australian town planning endeavours.

Laws that enabled land readjustment in Turkey can be traced (as revealed in works in the past 20 years) to 1858 and British India to 1915. In terms of practice, however, the idea was first adopted by Meiji Japan borrowing German practice as a means of rural land reform to enhance agricultural productivity and development. In 1917, such readjustment was applied to Korea under Imperial Japanese control. It was also massively used to modernize the urban layout of Tokyo-Yokohama after the Great Kantō earthquake (Kantō dai-jishin) of 1923, which burnt down much of the capital. After WWII, land readjustment was pursued in Japan and South Korea for both rural and urban development. From the 1970s onwards, land readjustment was increasingly seen as an interventionist solution to imperfections and failures of the land market with a concern for equity in housing. Then it became a tool for urban development in the early 1980s.

Absent from the above landscape of research is a discourse of land readjustment in terms of the boundaries of the very land that it adjusts. Boundaries in the planning literature were given little regard in the

[2] In a wider context of capital accumulation, de Soto (2001) pointed out the significance of land registration. However, the prior issue of land surveying and boundary determination in rural areas was not mentioned.

beginning. British town planner Geddes (1908: 257) dismissed them as school book "rubbish." He did not connect his understanding with the fact that property boundaries were as old as *property (law)* if not human civilization and that by 1908 many former British colonies, including United States, Canada, and Australia, had got a lot of well-laid-out cities and towns (Home 1997).

In terms of *physical planning*, land readjustment seeks to bring about a *better environmental-land use-transport pattern, plat or layout* for a place by re-delineating existing proprietary boundaries and reallocating ownership according to a new plat or layout (Lai et al. 2020a, b). A transfer (vertical or horizontal) or reallocation of property rights without any change to cadastral boundaries of lots should not be treated as land readjustment, though it may qualify as a TDR.

Neo-institutional Economic Framework

In terms of *neo-institutional economics*, unlike land taking or resumption with or without due compensation to implement the said better plat or layout, such re-delineation of boundaries and reallocation of ownership does not involve expropriation *but planned reassignment of private and/or communal property rights*. Yet, it calls for the formation of some *organization* (i.e., by a Coasian firm (Coase 1937)) which is essential to coordinate such project tasks as persuading and assisting proprietors to join a scheme, drafting a new layout and reallocating rights according to the plat or layout and scheme.

On social and community planning grounds, land readjustment is superior to the taking of land or *eminent domain* as affected owners and even occupiers are all *re-accommodated in-situ* within the confines of the plat or layout rather than displaced. It involves lower transaction costs in terms of litigation, political confrontation, social dislocation, or even human lives while overcoming the problems of private negotiation due to the vast number of proprietors involved.

However, as the process of land readjustment calls for much more land *coordination* work by the state or an NGO, it incurs the specific transaction costs of land registration, proper administrative and legal and arrangements, project implementation, and building trust in the state or NGOs as social capital not relevant for private negotiation or taking.

To readjust land boundaries and reassign revised lots to original landowners means there are known existing cadastral boundaries to realign and this presupposes the existence of property boundaries and titles, cadastral registration, and the rule of law that supports the exercise.

Transaction costs are costs other than those captured by a neo-classical production function.

Land readjustment as a policy alternative to taking of land is a special case of "transfer of development rights" (TDR), as elucidated by Lai and Davies (2017: 16) as a way of freeing development rights from their existing legal boundaries, by which:

(a) a property owner transfers land coverage, (residential) development rights, and (residential) allocations from one part of a site he owns to another part of the same site (Maraist 1995) or to another site;
(b) on elaboration, a predetermined maximum level of development within a specified region is distributed as "development rights" to landowners within the region such that landowners who keep their development levels below their allotted development rights level can sell their surplus development rights to other landowners, or they can use them to offset development on other properties (Shogren et al. 2003);
(c) a way used by the state to compensate a landowner deprived of his property by exchanging with him/her another piece of government/private land of comparable economic value by mutual agreement; or
(d) a tradable and redeemable land certificate which can be used to obtain a certain ratio of new sites planned and serviced by the state.

Land readjustment is a form of (c) described, with the proviso that the land received after readjustment is within the project locality, as in the case of "rights conversion" (Archer 2000).

The Coase Theorem and Property Boundary Revision

A reference to the Coase Theorem according to George Stigler's interpretation (which might be said to be the "official version" in so far as it is endorsed by Coase (1988)) of a hypothetical example of a land use conflict between cattle ranching and crop culture is relevant to appreciate the application of property rights concept embodied in boundaries to town planning. This externality is demonstrated by Coase (1960) to be resolvable by a private and *voluntary exchange* of rights, in the absence any third-party mediation, that rearranges the area of land under the two conflicting uses, thus an alternative to litigation or zoning.

This private solution is often called one of a Coasian market that needs no assistance of the court or intervention by a visible hand. Both the court and government planning alternatives suppress the interaction of the two economic activities and are hence sub-optimal to cooperation between the two land users. The Coasian market rearrangement of rights entails a readjustment of the common property boundary. However, the actual pre-contractual and contractual *alignment* of this boundary is irrelevant other than as a factor for working out the area of land involved.

Under the so-called invariant version of the "Coase Theorem" of Stigler, institutional arrangements or designs do not affect resource allocation under the assumptions of zero transaction costs and clearly defined property rights.[3] At a social order level, capitalism and socialism, so much criticized by Hayek (1960) for its knowledge problem, are indistinguishable in terms of economic performance (Cheung 1982).

Lot or property boundaries, as part of a plat or layout as governance, are a form of institutional design. As such, according to Stigler's interpretation, (a) the way land was platted/laid out should not affect urban or rural land use efficiency; and (b) all means to revise a plat or layout are identical in terms of resource outcome. Any form of plat or layout (say gridiron) is as good as any other (say radial or double loop) and any means of changing the pattern is equally good. In other words, land readjustment is a non-issue. In any event, as mentioned, the Coasian market solution to the land use conflict example does not bother with the exact alignment of property boundaries, but only the right amount of land. Conceptually, TDR but for land readjustment is in tune with this solution.

In reality, the transaction costs of revising a plat or layout as a web of proprietary boundaries, formally defined by streets and lanes or informally by field bunds under customary tenure, in a place where the rule of law prevails are gigantic (Lai et al. 2020a). Indeed, the process of platting or laying out land, once implemented, is like a physical production process that is as irreversible as cleaving a raw diamond (Lai et al. 2020b) and creates what has been called a "conflict of zoning" by Lai and Davies (2017), who reviewed the meaning of zoning. This is due to legal recognition and protection of, and social respect for, *de jure* proprietary rights and *de facto*

[3] Cheung holds that the second assumption is subsumed under the first.

communal interests as spatially delineated by property boundaries as private planning units. These accessible bounded land units (residential, commercial, industrial, and community) form the backbone of a market economy predicated on private property and enterprise.

The economic need to revise such plat or layout, whether traceable to a colonial surveyor like George Washington or being a legacy of Roman centuriation, is that the gain in land value of altering it exceeds the costs of compensating those adversely affected according to the Kaldor-Hicks principle (Ellickson 2012: 489). From another angle, such revision is economically efficient when the transaction costs of adhering to the old plat or layout far exceed those of changing it due to a new mode of land use, new transport technology, cross (property) boundary environmental problems, and so on. In practical terms, this method must be market viable in order to cater for the interest of the landowners and occupants.

As regards an institutional mechanism of revising the plat or layout, different methods incur different transaction costs, shaping the outcomes differently. As explained previously, private negotiation, taking and TDR (land readjustment being a special case) involve different sets of transaction costs. Where transaction costs prohibit a Coasian market solution, land readjustment may be a means to capture development potential constrained by property boundaries.

Land Readjustment Possibilities in Hong Kong

Researchers have proposed the use of land bonds (Lai et al. 2018a) as a means to facilitate land readjustment in Hong Kong. This may prevent the problem of land resumption (Lai et al. 2018b).

Questions for Revision and Discussion

1. Discuss the mechanism of Letter A/B.

A landowner surrenders his agricultural land in exchange for a certificate that entitles him to be compensated with a smaller plot of (usually more valuable) urban land when the government offers such land for sale. The certificate is transferrable and entitles the holder to a guaranteed annual payment. This mechanism allows the government to obtain land without heavy upfront compensation and the retention of land rights for those affected.

2. Explain why land readjustment is largely a civil law country policy?

Probably, the civil law countries have the tradition of greater obedience to civil authorities. This requires further and better research (See Lai et al. 2022).

3. Explain the prerequisites for a "successful" land readjustment.

A credible and trusted organizer/mediator, rule of law, and respect for property rights.

References

Alterman, Rachelle. 2012. Land Use Regulations and Property Values: The 'windfalls capture' Idea Revisited. In Ch.33. *Oxford Handbook on Urban Economics and Planning*, eds. Nancy Brooks, Kieran Donaghy and Gerrit-Jan Knapp, 755–789. Oxford University Press.

Archer, Raymon Walter. 1981. Bibliography on Land Pooling/Readjustment/ Redistribution for Planned Urban Development in Asia and West Germany.

Archer, Raymon Walter. 2000. Urban Redevelopment with Landowner Participation with the Land Pooling/Readjustment Technique. In *Planning for a Better Urban Living Environment in Asia*, ed. G. A. Yeh and M. K. Ng, 252–277. Aldershot: Ashgate.

Arruñada, Benito. 2018. Evolving Practice in Land Demarcation. *Land Use Policy* 77:661–675.

Bobkova, Evgeniya, Lars Marcus, Meta Berghauser Pont, Ioanna Stavroulaki, and David Bolin. 2019. Structure of Plot Systems and Economic Activity in Cities: Linking Plot Types to Retail and Food Services in London, Amsterdam and Stockholm. *Urban Science* 3:66.

Buitelaar, Edwin. 2021. Planning Is Zoning: A Response to Lawrence W.C. Lai. *Planning Practice & Research* 36:1–3.

Cheung, Steven N. S. 1982. *Will China Go Capitalist?* London: Institute of Economic Affairs.

Coase, Ronald H. 1937. The Nature of the Firm. *Economics* 4 (16): 386–405.

Coase, Ronald H. 1960. The Problem of Social Costs. *Journal of Law and Economics* 3:1–44.

Coase, Ronald H. 1988. *The Firm, the Market and the Law*. Chicago: Chicago University Press.

De Soto, Hernando. 2001. *The Mystery of Capital*. London: Black Swan Book.

Deuskar, C. 2013. George Washington and Land Readjustment. July 31, 2013 https://blogs.worldbank.org/sustainablecities/george-washington-and-land-readjustment

Doebele, William A. 2007. In *Analyzing Land Readjustment: Economics, Law and Collective Action*, ed. Foreword Yu-hung Hong and Barrie Needham. Lincoln Institute of Land Policy, vii–xiii.

Ehlers, J. H. 1928. *Reconstruction and Development of the Tokyo-Yokohama District*. Washington: Department of Commerce.

Ellickson, Robert C. 2012. The Law and Economics of Street Layouts: How a Grid Pattern Benefits a Downtown. *Alabama Law Review* 64:463–509.

Fennell, Lee Anne. 2019. Property Beyond Exclusion. *William & Mary Law Review* 61:521–572.

Geddes, Patrick. 1908. Boundaries and Frontiers. *Westminster Review* 169 (3): 257–260.

Hayek, Friedrich A. 1960. *The Road to Serfdom*. Chicago: University of Chicago Press.

Home, Robert. 1997. *Of Planting and Planning: The Making of British Colonial Cities*. London: E and Spon.

Home, Robert. 2003. 'An irreversible conquest'? Colonial and Postcolonial Land Law in Israel/Palestine. *Social and Legal Studies* 12 (3): 291–310.

Home, Robert. 2007. Land Readjustment as a Method of Development Land Assembly: A Comparative Overview. *Town Planning Review* 78 (4): 459–483.

Home, Robert. 2018. Why Land Readjustment in the British Former Colonies, But Not in the United Kingdom? In *Land Readjustment: Solving Urban Problems Through Innovative Approach*, ed. Felipe Francisco De Souza, Takeo Ochi, and Akio Hosono, 189–203. Tokyo: Japan International Cooperation Agency (JICA).

Kalbro, Thomas. 2019. Economics of Property Formation-Adjustment of Property Boundaries with Examples from Swedish Legislation. *Nordic Journal of Surveying and Real Estate Research* 2 (1): 82–95.

Lai, Lawrence W. C. 2021. A Dialogue on Town Planning and Boundary Delineation. *Planning Practice & Research*1–8.

Lai, Lawrence W. C. 2023. A Neo-institutional Economic Centennial Literature Review (1919–2019) of Research Publications on Land Readjustment. *Surveying & Built Environment* 32 (1): 6–84.

Lai, Lawrence W. C., and Stephen N. G. Davies. 2017. A Coasian Boundary Inquiry on Zoning and Property Rights: Lot and Zone Boundaries and Transaction Costs. *Progress in Planning* 118:1–28.

Lai, Lawrence W. C., and Stephen N. G. Davies. 2020. Surveying Was a Kind of Writing on the Land: The Economics of Land Division as Town Planning. *Planning Theory* 118.

Lai, Lawrence W. C., and Stephen N. G. Davies. 2022. Is Non-zoning of Land Impossible? Eight Fundamental Propositions of Zoning. *Journal of Environmental Policy & Planning*1–16. https://doi.org/10.1080/1523908X.2022.2098096.

Lai, Lawrence W. C., K. W. Chau, and Lennon H. T. Choy. 2018a. Stock and Flow of Land: Freeing Land from Rigidities for Urban Development in Hong Kong. *Editorial, Surveying & Built Environment* 27 (1): 5–9.

Lai, Lawrence W., C. Lai, K. W. Chau, Alwin Chan, and Lennon H. T. Choy. 2018b. Two Dialogues on Land Readjustment in Hong Kong. *Surveying & Built Environment* 27 (1): 5–9.

Lai, Lawrence W. C., Stephen N. G. Davies, Edwin H. W. Chen, Mark Hansley Chua, and C. L. Lin. 2020a. The Production and Consumption of Land Use Planning: A Neo-institutional Economic Perspective and Three Taiwan Case Studies of Planning Layering. *Land Use Policy*.

Lai, Lawrence W. C., Stephen N. G. Davies, Frank T. Lorne, K. W. Chau, and Lennon H. T. Choy. 2020b. A Neo-institutional Economic Analysis of Revising Informal and Formal Proprietary Boundaries. *Journal of Environmental Policy & Planning*1–18.

Lai, Lawrence, W. C. Stephen, N. G. Davies, K. W. Chau, Lennon H. T. Choy, Mark Hansley Chua, and Terry K. W. Lam. 2022. A Centennial Literature Review (1919–2019) of Research Publications on Land Readjustment from a Neo-institutional Economic Perspective. *Land Use Policy* 120:106236.

Maraist, Patrick W. 1995. A Statutory Beacon in the Land Use Ripeness Maze: The Florida Private Property Rights Protection Act. *Florida Law Review* 47:411–458.

Muñoz-Gielen, Demetrio. 2016. Proposal of Land Readjustment for the Netherlands: An Analysis of Its Effectiveness from an International Perspective. *Cities* 53:78–86.

Pryor, Edward G. 1976. The Acquisition of Land for Urban Development by Exchange in Hong Kong and Taiwan. *Town Planning Quarterly, Auckland* 41 (Dec.): 27–29.

Schubert, Dirk. 2017. Review of Manuale zum Städtebau. Die Systematisierung des Wissens von der Stadt 1870–1950: edited by Vittorio Magnago Lampugnani, Katrin Albrecht, Helene Bihlmaier and Lukas Zurfluh, Berlin, Dom Publishers, 2020. (*Planning Perspective* 35 (2): 392–394.)

Shogren, Jason F., Gregory M. Parkhurst, and Chad Settle. 2003. Integrating Economics and Ecology to Protect Nature on Private Lands: Models, Methods, and Mindsets. *Environmental Science and Policy* 6 (3): 233–242.

CHAPTER 18

Rates and Crown (Government) Rent

Castor T. C. Wong and Polycarp C. W. Cheung

Rates as a Tax on Ownership/Occupation of Land

Until now, rates have had a misleading Chinese translation, "police salaries" (差餉), which suggests that they are user charges for law and security. This was true from the beginning of Hong Kong's status as a British colony until 1888, when their proceeds became general Government revenue and stopped having a direct relationship with policing (Hong Kong SAR Government 2018).

Rates as a property tax are a tax on the ownership/occupation of land and are drafted in relevant ordinances as a tax on land occupation. The *South Australia v Commonwealth* court case, which dealt with s.144 of the Australian Constitution on commonwealth taxes on states, held that, "whilst the taxpayer pays tax because he/she derives income that may be identified with a chose in action of which he/she is the owner, the correct character of the tax is that of a tax on income rather than a tax on ownership or holding of property" (Morabito 1998: 49). The *Rating Ordinance*, introduced in 1845, is one of the oldest laws in Hong Kong.

C. T. C. Wong (✉) • P. C. W. Cheung
Department of Real Estate and Construction, The University of Hong Kong, Hong Kong, China

L. W. C. Lai et al. (eds.), *Principles of Land Administration at Work*, https://doi.org/10.1007/978-981-95-2972-8_18

The economic advantages of a system of private ownership, together with intense political reaction against the abuses of state control, frequently conflict with deeply held beliefs in the need for a continuing public interest in the permanent and irreplaceable heritage of immovable property. This conflict can arise most strongly in the case of land, whose supply cannot be expanded and whose existence is not the result of individual effort, but similar issues arise with regard to the privatization of buildings. (Youngman 1996: 266)

From time to time, the abolition of domestic (O'Hagen et al. 1985) and commercial (Timothy 1984) rates has been proposed, especially when a pro-market political climate prevails.

This chapter does not dwell on this property rights issue as (a), in any case, rates have long been understood to be payable for properties (under *Ordinance No.2 of 1845*) when the early lots were sold, which meant that rate payments were an implicit pre-contractual condition and (b) most, if not all, lease conditions specify rate payments.

The assessment of rates is a kind of property valuation and, hence, the Rating and Valuation Department (RVD) is a major employer of GP surveyors.

Hong Kong property owners typically pay two types of payment to the government in relation to properties: rates and government rent. Although the two payments share similarities in terms of assessment and the collecting party RVD for a substantial number of properties in Hong Kong, they are principally different in nature.

Rates

Rates are "a tax on the occupation of the property" (Hong Kong SAR Government 2024). There is a common misunderstanding that vacant properties are not subject to rates payment. In fact, whether the property is vacant or occupied will not affect its liability and the level of assessment. In Hong Kong, rates are charged, at a certain "specified percentage" of the rateable value, and collected quarterly by the RVD. According to the *Rating Ordinance*,[1] both the owner and occupant of a tenement are liable for the payment of rates.

Historically, rates were not levied on land properties in the New Territories until 1935, when the rates were levied on the capital value of

[1] Section 21 (1), *Rating Ordinance* (Cap.116).

buildings. In 1955, this separate system was replaced by the system applied to urban rating (Hong Kong SAR Government 2021).

Under the Rating Ordinance 1973, rates collected from Hong Kong's urban areas were divided into two parts: general rates to be transferred to the general revenue and Urban Council rates to the Urban Council. Upon the establishment of Regional Councils in 1986, a similar arrangement was introduced to the New Territories. Since the abolishment of these two municipal councils on 1 January 2000, all rates collected have become part of the government's general revenue (Hong Kong SAR Government 2021).

Rates are now payable quarterly in advance on the first month of each quarter (i.e., January, April, July, and October) of each year. Demand notes are issued by the RVD.

The "specified percentage" was set at a flat rate of 5%[2] of a property's rateable value from the 1999–2000 to 2023–2024 financial years. Starting from the 2024/2025 financial year, while the specified percentage has been kept at 5% for non-domestic properties, a progressive rating system was introduced for domestic tenements in which the rates were set at 5% for the first $550,000 of rateable value, 8% for the next $250,000, and 12% for the remainder.

Since the 2007–2008 financial year, the government has offered rates concessions (capped at a prescribed amount) of different amounts to each tenement, in light of the prevailing social-economic conditions and affordability of payers. This is discretionary in nature and the amount, if any, is subject to review each year and anounced during the Budget Speech.

Except for certain types of properties listed under Section 36 of the *Rating Ordinance*, for example, agricultural land, re-site villages, and purpose-built religious worship premises, all properties in Hong Kong, including parking spaces, vending machine sites, and advertising signs, are liable to rates assessment.

Government Rent

Government rent is the rent property owners pay under their relevant land leases. It is not a statutory "tax," but a contractual liability under a lease, and resembles a material part of the "Leasehold" system in Hong Kong.

[2] Rate concessions of 7.5% will be granted if there is no filtered water supply from government mains, or 15% if the property is not covered by fresh water supply.

Government rent is collected either by the RVD or the Lands Department (LandsD). The most common types of Government rent are shown below:

(i) Zonal Government Rent: This applies to the older land leases granted by the British government, mostly on Hong Kong Island. The amount of rent is specified on the Lease Document, usually a nominal amount, throughout the lease term and shown in the land register.
(ii) Cap.515 Government Rent: This is currently the most common type of government rent in Hong Kong, accounting for over 70% of properties. The amount of rent is calculated at 3% of the rateable value. Details will be discussed later.
(iii) Cap.40 Government Rent: This applies to a specific type of renewable land leases in the urban area. Similar to Cap.515, government rent is still calculated at 3% of the rateable value assessed by RVD, whilst the amount of payment is fixed at the date of lease renewal until redevelopment of the building. Upon completion of assessment, the amount of Government rent for payable for the lot will be shown under the Remarks in the land register.

Cap.515 Government Rent

For properties with government rent payable under the *Government Rent (Assessment and Collection) Ordinance* (Cap.515), the amount to be paid is assessed at 3% of the property's rateable value and collected by the RVD. This covers properties located in the New Territories (including New Kowloon), north of Boundary Street, as well as the new grant lots on Hong Kong Island or in Kowloon, which are held under land leases granted or extended on or after 27 May 1985 under the *Sino-British Agreement*. While a fixed percentage of 3% is charged throughout the duration of lease, the rateable value will be "revalued" annually to concur with the prevailing market level.

Government rent for items (i) and (iii) are collected by LandsD. RVD, on the other hand, is responsible for the collection of government rent under item (ii). RVD charges Government rents on a quarterly basis, together with the demands for rates. On the other hand, the frequency of

Government rents charged by LandsD varies according to the billed amounts, rather than being set at fixed intervals.

It is worth noting that government rent is payable for properties situated on private lots only. For government let-outs (such as swimming pool kiosks and public rental housing units) and land under Short Term Tenancies, collection of government rent is not required because the rent is already included in the periodic rental payment to the government.

Rateable Value

Rateable value is the basis of assessing the rates and government rent of a property. According to the *Rating Ordinance*, rateable value is "an amount equal to the rent at which the tenement might reasonably be expected to let, from year to year, if:

(a) The tenant undertook to pay all usual tenant's rates and taxes and
(b) The landlord undertook to pay the Government rent, the costs of repairs and insurance and any other expenses necessary to maintain the tenement in a state to command that rent."

Rateable value is assessed at the valuation reference date ("the relevant date" under the *Rating Ordinance*). Starting from 1999–2000 fiscal year, the date is fixed at 1 October immediately before the effective financial year. For instance, the relevant date for the 2024–2025 financial year is 1 October 2023.

Since 1999, assessment of rateable value is conducted annually.

The rateable value of each property unit in an estate was assessed individually by the RVD according to saleable area (SA) and measured unit by unit (now by AutoCAD) from approved building plans. Ratepayers are notified of their rating assessments and quarterly payments through the "Demand for Rates and/or Government Rent." The rateable value of a tenement is available for viewing online for free from mid-March to late May every year. Outside this period, a fee is required to access the information.

Public Inspection, "Proposal," and Appeal

After the annual revaluation, the new rateable values of all properties will be included in the new *Valuation List and Government Rent Roll*, which is available for public inspection free of charge after declaration (on or before 31 March) until 31 May. Beyond the period, the public can obtain the rateable value of a property from the RVD, at a charge of $9 per record (the fee is subject to change from time to time).

Subject to Section 37 of the *Rating Ordinance*, any person who is aggrieved by the new Valuation List or Government Rent Roll may serve a proposal in a specified form (Form R20A) to the Commissioner of Rating and Valuation (the Commissioner) to alter the Valuation List or Government Rent Roll on or before 31 May every year.

If there is no agreement with the Commissioner, s/he will notify the proposer on another specified form (Form R22A) before 1 December of the same year, specifying if and what alteration is to be made to the Valuation List or Government Rent Roll. Anyone who is not satisfied with the decision may appeal to the Lands Tribunal ("rating appeal") within 28 days of Form R22A's issuance, at a fee of $235 per Notice of Appeal (the fee is subject to change from time to time).

Interim Valuation

For newly completed tenements or tenements that have undergone structural alterations, interim valuations need to include such properties on the Valuation List.

The interim valuation date depends on the completion/occupation of the subject property. There are fewer disputes over newly completed buildings because the RVD could refer to the Occupation Permits / Certificates of Compliance issue dates to establish the building completion dates. However, for properties with major alterations, it may be difficult to determine the alteration completion dates or the dates fit for rateable occupation. Further supporting documentary evidence may be required to prove the completion of such works.

Computer-Assisted Mass Appraisals

On the 2024–2025 Valuation List are about 2.7 million assessments (including block assessments) covering around 3.5 million properties.

During an assessment of the rateable values of units for a block of residential apartments, a reference unit is identified. Upon deciding on the unit rate of the reference unit (usually by the comparison method, which references market rents for similar properties in the locality), the RVD will make horizontal and vertical adjustments to cover all units in the same building to reflect their differences in size, floor level, etc.

However, it may have been difficult to assess rateable value for special properties. Rental evidence is hardly available, for example, for harbour tunnels and container terminals, so RVD surveyors may need to resort to valuation methods, such as the Receipts and Expenditure and Contractor's Methods, to assess their rateable values.

Relevant Land Tribunal Cases

Tenement

The unit of assessment for rating purposes is a "tenement," which is defined in Section 2 of the *Rating Ordinance* as *"any land (including land covered with water) or any building, structure, or part thereof which is held or occupied as a distinct or separate tenancy or holding or under any licence."*

In the rating appeal case, *Yiu Lian Machinery Repairing Works, Ltd. & Others v Commissioner of Rating and Valuation [1982] HKDCLR 32*, the Lands Tribunal observed that the above definition consists of two "limbs." It ruled that:

(a) The first limb concerns the subject matter to be rated, namely land, buildings, and structures and
(b) The second limb makes even those three species of property rateable, if they are held or occupied as a distinct or separate tenancy, holding, or licence.

Rating Appeals

The *Rating Ordinance* provides for the lodging of rating appeals to the Lands Tribunal. In the High Court case, *Yiu Lian Machinery Repairing Works, Ltd., and Others v Attorney General HC MP 179-181/80*, the Court held that the Lands Tribunal had jurisdiction to decide on rating appeals, so the ratepayer's appeal to the Court failed (Hong Kong SAR Government 2021).

Illegal Extensions/Use of Properties

Some properties may have illegal structures called unauthorized building works (UBWs). Their owners might have also violated their lease conditions.

In *Cheung Man Yee v Commissioner of Rating and Valuation* (RA 41/84), the Lands Tribunal argued that it correctly included the value of an illegal extension to assess the property's rateable value. However, the value must reflect the calculated risk of renting the subject property including its UBWs (Hong Kong SAR Government 2021).

For any property, the impact of any contract or agreement restriction, including a Government Lease, imposed on or which affects the use of its premises, should be ignored in the valuation, but statutory restrictions must be considered. The Lands Tribunal case, *Commissioner of Rating and Valuation v Lai Kit Lau Mutual Aid Committee and Another [1986] HKLR 93*, confirmed this rule.

Questions for Revision and Discussion

1. Discuss the conceptual differences between rates, government rent, property tax, and stamp duties.

Rates are a tax on the occupation of private properties, government rent is a tax on ownership of Leasehold interest, while property tax is a tax on the rental income received for leasing a property and stamp duties are taxes on effecting property transactions.

2. Discuss the effect of the *Sino-British Joint Declaration* (19 December 1984) on Crown (Government) rents in Hong Kong before and after 30 June 1997.

Properties everywhere in the New Territories (including New Kowloon) and in the rest of Hong Kong in which the conditions of sale/grant/re-grant, etc., commenced after the Sino-British Agreement are subject to an additional 3% land rent in rating.

3. Explain if and how the following property types are subject to rates:
   (a) A site newly tendered

(b) A shop that has no tenant for its whole rating year due to a market downturn
(c) An illegal rooftop structure

(a) In general, a newly tendered site with building works in progress is not liable to rates (*London County Council v Wilkins (Valuation Officer) (1957), Commissioner of Rating and Valuation v Agrila Limited & 58 others (2001)*). This is because a building site does not fall under the four criteria of "rateable occupation": (i) actual, (ii) exclusive, (iii) beneficial in the sense of being of value to the occupant, and (iv) not too transient. These requirements were established in *Yiu Lian Machinery Repairing Works v Commissioner for Rating and Valuation (1984)*.
(b) Historically, refunds for rates were once allowed for vacant properties in Hong Kong. However, this practice was abolished in 1973 (for domestic properties) and 1995 (for non-domestic properties). Nowadays, there is no exemption or concession granted to a vacant property unless it becomes vacant because of a government-initiated court order (s.31ba of the *Rating Ordinance*). This policy aims to boost the cost of holding vacant properties and encourage owners to optimize their use of land resources.
(c) One important prerequisite for a rating assessment is that it should reflect the existing condition (i.e., the *status quo*). Therefore, any illegal structure or extension that a tenant enjoys should be included in a rating assessment. However, the assessment must also consider the risk of enforcement by government authorities. This is in line with the "*rebus sic stantibus*" (fundamental change in circumstances) principle (*Commissioner of Rating and Valuation v Lai Kit Lau Mutual Aid Committee and Another (1986)*).

Nevertheless, it's important to note that any property that undergoes a rating assessment must fall within the definition of a "tenement," as stipulated in Section 2 of the *Rating Ordinance*. A tenement is defined under this section as any land plot (including that covered by water), building, structure, or part thereof that is <u>held or occupied as a distinct or separate tenancy or under any license</u>. Hence, an illegal structure erected on an area allocated with an undivided share or land held under a proper lease, licence, or tenancy would qualify as a tenement. In contrast, a standalone illegal structure on unallocated government land or one without a proper land title (such as a housing unit in the Kowloon Walled City, demolished during the early 1990s) may not be rated.

References

Hong Kong SAR Government. 2018. *Chronology of Events, 7th edition*. Hong Kong, Rating & Valuation Department.

Hong Kong SAR Government. 2024. *Your Rates and Government Rent*. Hong Kong, Rating and Valuation Department, February (Pamphlet).

May, Timothy. 1984 The businessman's burden: rates and the CBI. *Politics* 4, no. 1: 34-38.

Morabito, Vince. 1998. The Constitutional Restriction on Taxes Imposed on Crown Property. *Journal of Australian Taxation* 1:41–56.

O'Hagan, J., P. McBride, and P. Sanfey. 1985 Local government finance: The Irish experience. *British Tax Review*, no. 4: 235-254.

Youngman, Joan M. 1996. Tax on Land and Buildings. In *Tax Law Design and Drafting*, vol. 1, 264–291. International Monetary Fund.

Appendix A: Searching for Conditions of Sale/Grant/Exchange/Regrant/Extension and Crown (Government) Leases

The Conditions of Sale/Grant/Exchange/Regrant/Extension (Conditions) refer to the written contracts of sale by and purchase of Crown/Government land. They entitle land purchasers/successors to obtain Crown (government) leases once they fulfil all positive covenants specified in the Conditions.

Copies of most Conditions and Crown (government) leases can be found at the Land Registry's online platform, Integrated Registration Information System Online Services (IRIS).

Searching for the Conditions of Sale/Grant/Exchange/Regrant/Extension

Instead of inputting a lot name for the concerned lot(s) in the case for A Crown (Government) Condition, a researcher should input the lot's condition/new grant number when searching the Conditions.

Researchers can start with searching for a lot's land register on IRIS if they are unfamiliar with conditions/new grant numbers. Figure A.1 shows a sample of a land register. Its first page lists the lot's property particulars, such as the lease term, Crown (Government) rent, and lot number. Most importantly, it tells the condition/new grant number (see the arrow).

Again, if the researcher cannot find the conditions in IRIS, the next place to search is the Government Records Service (GRS). However, if

L. W. C. Lai et al. (eds.), *Principles of Land Administration at Work*, https://doi.org/10.1007/978-981-95-2972-8

土地註冊處 THE LAND REGISTRY
土地登記冊 LAND REGISTER 印製編號 PRINT CONTROL: ESN[redacted]

印製於 PRINTED AT: INTERNET SEARCH (E-MAIL)
查冊日期及時間 SEARCH DATE AND TIME: 27/03/2023 18:56
查冊者姓名/名稱 NAME OF SEARCHER: [redacted]
查冊種類 SEARCH TYPE: CURRENT

本登記冊列明有關物業截至 27/03/2023 07:30 之資料
THE INFORMATION SET OUT BELOW CONTAINS PARTICULARS OF THE PROPERTY UP TO 07:30 ON 27/03/2023.

備存土地紀錄以供市民查閱旨在防止秘密及有欺詐成分的物業轉易，以及提供容易追溯和確定土地財產及不動產業權的方法。土地紀錄內載的資料不得用於與土地紀錄的宗旨無關之目的，使用所提供的資料須符合<<個人資料（私隱）條例>>的規定。
The land records are kept and made available to members of the public to prevent secret and fraudulent conveyances, and to provide means whereby the titles to real and immovable property may be easily traced and ascertained. The information contained in the land records shall not be used for purposes that are not related to the purposes of the land records. The use of information provided is subject to the provisions in the Personal Data (Privacy) Ordinance.

進行任何交易前，應先向土地註冊處查閱最新的土地紀錄。
BEFORE ANY DEALINGS, UP-TO-DATE LAND SEARCH SHOULD BE CONDUCTED WITH THE LAND REGISTRY.

物業資料
PROPERTY PARTICULARS

物業參考編號
PROPERTY REFERENCE NUMBER (PRN): [redacted]

地段編號
LOT NO.: LOT NO. [redacted] IN [redacted]

批約 HELD UNDER: NEW GRANT NO.[redacted]
年期 LEASE TERM: 99 YEARS
開始日期 COMMENCEMENT OF LEASE TERM: 01/07/1898
每年地稅 RENT PER ANNUM: $3,940.00

所佔地段份數
SHARE OF THE LOT: -

ADDRESS: TUEN MUN
NEW TERRITORIES

地址: -

物業參考編號 PRN: [redacted] (27/03/2023) 第 1 頁・共 3 頁 PAGE 1 OF 3

Fig. A.1 Property particulars for a search for Conditions of Sale/Exchange/Grant

this also produces no results, the last resort is the notifications published in the *Government Gazettes*.

For land sales on or before December 1908,[1] the government published details of the particulars and the conditions of sale on Gazette Notices. They include the general and special conditions, if any, but exclude sale plans. Printed copies of the *Government Gazettes* are available in public libraries and the Hong Kong University Libraries, while digital copies can be found on Hong Kong Government Reports Online (1842–1941), a digital initiative of the HKU Libraries, and are free.

Searching for Crown (Government) Leases

To start with the search, searchers need to know the Lot Type and the Lot Number of the concerned lot(s). When the Lot Type and the Lot Number combine, they are called Lot Name or Lot Details. They look like the following examples (short form in the bracket): Marine Lot No.23 (ML 23),

[1] GN 248, *The Hong Kong Government Gazette*, 24 June 1893.

Remaining Part of Section A of Inland Lot No.8790 (IL 8790 S.A.R.P.), Tuen Mun Town Lot No.54 (TMTL 54), and Kowloon Permanent Pier Lot No.8 (KPP 8).

In the case that the Lot Name has not yet been identified, the searcher should take a step to identify it first. It can be found by browsing the digital map appeared in the search function "By Map" in "Search Land Register". This map is produced by Survey and Mapping Office (SMO), LandsDepartment, which manages cadastral survey records of land in Hong Kong, particularly those records of private land parcels, and offers products for public use. Like Lot Index Plan, a typical type of cadastral survey records, the digital plan identifies the approximate lot boundaries and location, the Lot Type and Lot Number.

With the Lot Type and Lot Number, the researcher can begin the search by going to the page "Order Land Document" and entering the Lot Type Code (a short form of Lot Type[2]) and the Lot Number. The searcher should be careful that the Lot Type Code used by Land Registry can be very different from the short form of Lot Type appears on a Lot Index Map.[3] The Code can be found by using the "Find Lot Type" toolbox on the same page and entering the Lot Type in full form. Meanwhile, when entering the Lot Number, the searcher shall disregard the section number and the sub-section number of the lot.

Once entered a correct set of the Lot Type Code and the Lot Number, the system will return to a page for ordering with options such as certified or plain copies, if the Government (Crown) Lease is held by the Land Registry. Copies of the Lease can be delivered by mail, email, or collected by hand. However, if the Lease is not held by the Land Registry, such as in the cases of lease surrender or exchange, the searcher may search at the Government Records Service, Public Record Office.

The Government Records Service (GRS) of the Public Record Office manages the archives of government records, which are not in current use. Their holdings can be searched online through their online catalogue, @ PRO. Similar to searching at Land Registry, the searchers may input the lot name to search for the records about the lots. However, records in

[2] It is also called Lot Abbreviation by Survey and Mapping Office, and Lot Designation by Buildings Department.

[3] For example, the IRIS system contains five different APML to differentiate Lot Types with similar but different spelling: APML1 stands for Apleechow Marine Lot, APML 2 stands for Ap Lei Chau Marine Lot, APML3 stands for Aplichow Marine Lot, APML4 stands for Appleechow Marine Lot, and APML 5 stands for Applichow Marine Lot.

GRS use different spelling systems for Lot Types to Land Registry, so searchers should try with different combinations. For example, a Farm Lot is called "FL" in the system of Land Registry, but "F.L." or "Farm Lot" in GRS. In addition, since GRS holds many records other than land documents, the searchers may employ some strategies to limit the search results. One of the ways is to look for the related series. While HKRS265 is concerned with records related to surrendered titledeeds, HKRS57 is about Japanese titledeeds. Another way is to start the "New Search" with the Lot Type and then search the Lot Number by using "Search within Results". Once the record and its record ID are located, the searcher can request to inspect the records by visiting Hong Kong Public Records Building. Currently, online inspection for these records is almost unavailable. Lastly, searchers should understand that there may be possibilities that the Government (Crown) Leases cannot be found in GRS as one must first identify the correct record title, sometimes by chance, which is not always the case.

Appendix B: Definitions of Land Use Terms in Statutory Town Plans

Lawrence Wai Chung Lai

Properly interpreting the meaning of land uses in a statutory zoning plan in Hong Kong is not always an easy professional task. This technical note provides basic facts regarding the dates of three administrative definitions produced by the Town Planning Board. To the extent that at least one of the versions can be browsed on the government's website and most of (but not the latest) the versions can be inspected by the public at the Planning Department at the time of this note's writing and because the Court of Appeal in Civil Appeal No.231 of 2011 (the Hero Case) made reference to such definitions, we shall regard them as published planning documents relevant to the interpretation of land uses in statutory town plans.

Unlike those under the British planning system, but like those under the New South Wales planning system, statutory town plans in Hong Kong are "zoning plans". That is, land uses have been grouped under various "zones".

Land uses that are (a) always permitted in all zones, (b) "always permitted" in a specific zone, and (c) "may be permitted" in a specific zone are itemised and listed in the "Notes" of a statutory plan, which may be an outline zoning plan (OZP) or a Development Permission Area (DPA) Plan.

There is no statutory definition of each of the land use items within a specific statutory plan or, generally, under the Town Planning Ordinance

L. W. C. Lai et al. (eds.), *Principles of Land Administration at Work*, https://doi.org/10.1007/978-981-95-2972-8

or Town Planning Regulations. The Town Planning Board has, however, administratively issued definitions of land uses from time to time.

The three types of definitions are (A) those that deal with those areas without a history of an Interim DPA (IDPA) or DPA Plan (these mainly cover the areas [including new towns] with OZPs prior to the 1990 amendment to the Town Planning Ordinance); (B) those that deal with those areas with a history of an IDPA or DPA Plan; and (C) those that deal with all areas. The titles and dates of these three distinct groups of definitions are shown in the chart (Fig. A.2).

Type (A) was originally called "Definitions of Terms used in Statutory Plans", but has been called "Definitions of Terms Used in Statutory Plans (for Areas not Previously Covered by Interim Development Permission Area Plans or Development Permission Area Plans)" since July 2000.

Type (B) was originally called "Definitions of Terms for Interim Development Permission Area Plans/Development Permission Area Plans", but has called "Definitions of Terms Used for Rural Outline Zoning Plan (for Areas Previously Covered by Interim Development Permission Area Plans or Development Permission Area Plans) and Development Permission Area Plans" since July 2000.

Type (C) was introduced on 28 February 2003 and is called "Revised Definitions of Terms/Broad Use Terms used in Statutory Plans".

A version of each of the three types was revealed on the government website on 16 May 2003.

As far as the author is aware, the last updates of these three types of definitions were on 6 January 2005, 6 January 2005, and 27 September 2010, for Types A, B, and C, respectively. These latest versions can be inspected in the public enquiry office of Planning Department with permission of the Town Planning Board secretariat. The file reference for the 27 September 2010 version of Type C is M:/PSOTA200707/PEC Operation C'lists as at 27.9.2010.doc. It is bilingual and has 45 pages. Type C definition of a "shrine" was referred to in the decision on the Hero Case.

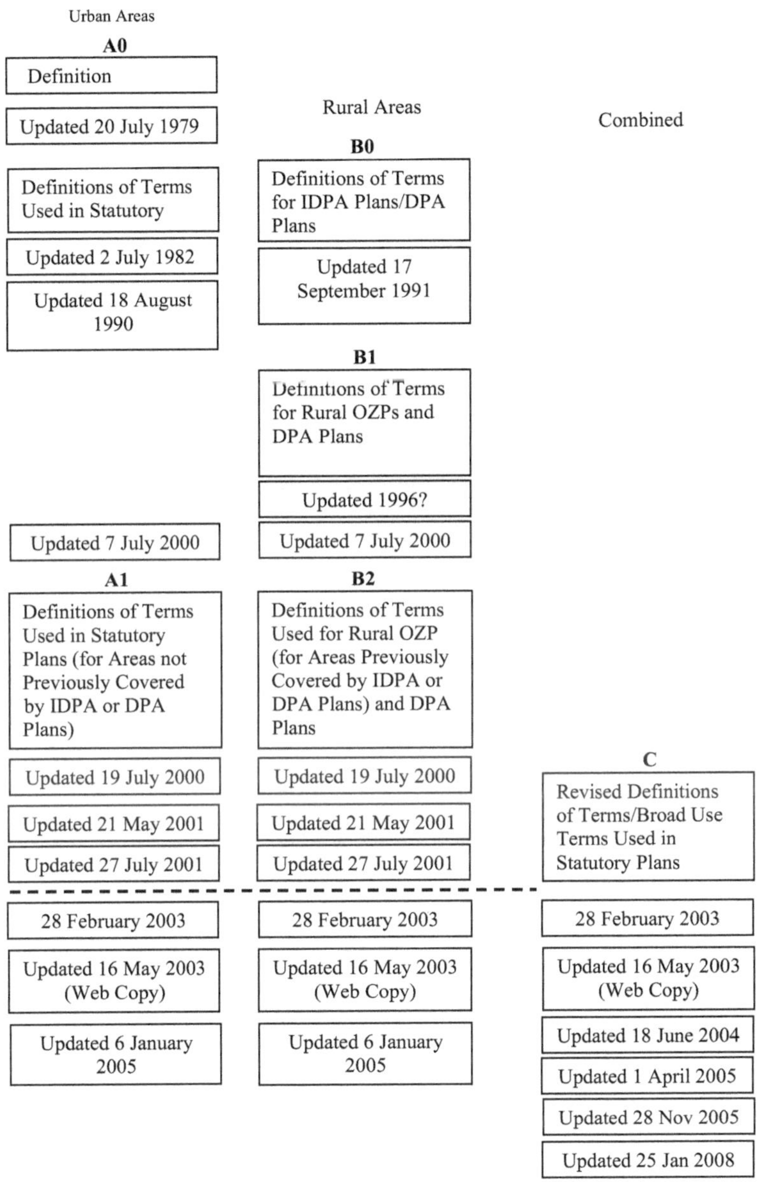

Fig. A.2 Three types of administrative definitions of terms used in statutory town plans

Appendix C: Possible offences of free-standing walls of a house in the New Territories with a history of an IDPA Plan

Planning matter	*Land matter*	*Building matters*
The redevelopment of the free-standing walls of House XXX (to become House WWY) in 2011/2012 might have violated the statutory OZP, which originated from a 1990 IDPA Plan, in effect at the time	The development of the free-standing walls of the development was not authorised by any building licence	The development of the free-standing walls of the development was "unauthorised building work" (UBW), as no building plan for them had been submitted for approval
	The development of the free-standing walls violated the building licence for each house of the development because they exceed the total built-up area specified	The redevelopment of the free-standing walls of House XXX (to become House XXY) from 2011 to 2012, in particular, might have violated the statutory OZP and, hence, could not be approved under the *Buildings Ordinance* for contravening the town plans

L. W. C. Lai et al. (eds.), *Principles of Land Administration at Work*, https://doi.org/10.1007/978-981-95-2972-8

Appendix D: Redevelopment of bus depots upon lease modifications: a valuation analysis by way of a direct accommodation value (AV) comparison method[1]

Lai and Kwong (2015) found that there was no valuation or documentary evidence showing that there was any government concession to franchised bus companies China Motor Bus (CMB) and Kowloon Motor Bus (KMB) in terms of lease restrictions or land premia in land allocation.

This short technical note shows that there is evidence that there iscon-cession in the assessment of premia for lease modification for change in use of land approved by the Town Planning Board, whether by way of modification letter or surrender and exchange, of the former bus depot's land for industrial or non-industrial use based on a valuation study of three sites. This finding completes Stage II of the research project undertaken by the first author. The results are discussed in terms of the landscape of the franchised bus industry of Hong Kong and broader economic theorisation of the role of the state.

[1] This section is based on Lai et al. (2015).

L. W. C. Lai et al. (eds.), *Principles of Land Administration at Work*, https://doi.org/10.1007/978-981-95-2972-8

Assessment of the Before and After Values of Four Bus Depot Sites

This exercise involved four bus depots: Inland Lot No.8849 (IL8849) and Inland Lot No.7550 (IL7550) in North Point owned by CMB; and Kwun Tong Inland Lot No.733 (KTIL733) and Kwai Chung Town Lot No.215 (KCTL 215) owned by KMB.

IL8849 was re-granted in exchange for the surrender of IL 5532 and IL7178, while KTIL733 was re-granted upon the surrender of KTIL 192. The leases of the other two land parcels were modified with letters of modification.

To ascertain if the actual modification premia for these four depots, as shown on the Conditions of Exchange or Modification Letters, were reasonable, the authors assessed their "before values" and "after values".

For IL8899, IL7550, and KCTL215, a direct accommodation value (AV) comparison method was adopted to ascertain their before values and after values. A total of 13 sales comparables comprising five office/non-industrial sites, five industrial sites, and three residential sites were obtained from public records, which can be found at the Land Registry. Amongst the 13 sites, 10 were situated on Hong Kong Island and Kowloon. They changed hands on the private land market between 1993 and 1997. The remaining three sites were sold via public auction by the government to developers during the same period.

As for a premium assessment of KTIL 733, owing to a lack of site comparables, a residual approach was employed to ascertain its market value.

The before and after values of the three depot sites, assessed by the said means, were used as benchmarks to evaluate if their actual premia were reasonable. The findings are summarised in Table A.1.

Conclusion and Discussion

As the differences between our assessed premia and actual premia were less than 10% or so, our conclusion is that there the premia charged by government for modifying the lease to allow redevelopment of the former depot sites did reflect the market price level. In otherwise, there is no evidence of concession in favour of the landowners.

The franchised bus industry in Hong Kong is a rare successful example in the world in which in the operators are private business firms receiving no direct government subsidy (Lai et al. 2011) and enjoying economies of

Table A.1 A comparison of the assessed and actual premia

Lot number (Bus company)	*IL8849 (CMB)*	*IL 7550 (CMB)*	*KTIL733 (KMB)*	*KCTL215 (KMB)*
(1)Actual Premium	$887,000,000 (per Conditions of Exchange dated 22/6/1995) (Surrendered lots: IL5532 and IL7178)	$430,350,000 (per Modification Letter dated 13/3/1997)	$464,000,000 (per Conditions of Exchange executed on 19/11/1996) (Surrendered lot: KTIL 192)	$186,550,000 (per Modification Letter dated 23/4/1996)
(2)Assessed before value	$3,025,569,000 (as at 22/6/1995)	$382,500,000 (as at 13/3/1997)	$1,141,240,000 (as at 19/11/1996)	$1,376,769,000 (as at 23/4/1996)
(3)Assessed after value	$3,936,480,000 (as at 22/6/1995)	$808,500,500 (as at 13/3/1997)	$682,270,000 (as at 19/11/1996)	$1,556,207,490 (as at 23/4/1996)
(4)Assessed premium (3)-(2)	$910,911,000(as at 22/6/1995)	$426,000,000(as at 13/3/1997)	$458,970,000(as at 19/11/1996)	$179,438,490(as at 23/4/1996)
(5)Difference between the actual premium and the assessed premium (1)-(4)	–$23,911,000(as at 22/6/1995)[–2.7%]	$4,350,000(as at 13/3/1997)[+10.2%]	$5,030,000(as at 19/11/1996)[+1.1%]	$7,111,510(as at 23/4/1996)[+3.8%]
Is the actual premium fair and reasonable?	Yes	Yes	Yes	Yes

scale (Lai et al. 2012). Though their operations are protected legally by franchise licences, they have been highly innovative in a Schumpeterian sense (Lorne and Lai 2011; Lai and Lorne 2012). The findings of this technical note complete a study on whether there was any indirect state-subsidy to the operators other than provision of free and well-planned bus terminals (Lai et al. 2011) in the form of concessions in premia of lease-hold land for depot uses. Lai et al. (2013) and Lai and Kwong (2015) confirmed that there was none at the stage bus depots were acquired from the government. This note shows valuation evidence that there was no subsidy either when the leases of these depots were redeveloped.

In terms of wider Coasian economics reasoning, there is adequate empirical evidence based on the aforesaid research that the regulatory rules of the state can enlarge a market, which Lai and Lorne (2015) have generalised into a "Fourth Coase Theorem". State franchising of public transport in Hong Kong is not the same as state provision of transport services but akin to Crown franchising rights to lighthouse merchants to build and manage private lighthouses in England and Wales (Coase 1974; Lai et al. 2008a, b).

Authors Alterman Amad

Andreas
Archer
Arijs
Arruñada
Barber
Bobkova
Bocking
Buitelaar
Burrough
Castro
Campbell
Chau
Cheung
Ching
Coase
Cooper
Corson
Cosgrove

D'Arcy
Dale
Davies
Dawe
Dennett
De Soto
Deuskar
De Vries
Doebele
Dorrian
Edwards
Ehlers
Ellickson
Empson
Enemark
Fennell
Franks
Geddes
Gillispie
Gombrich
Gupta
Hall
Hayek
Ho
Home
Jourdain
Kalbro
Kwong
Lai
Leung
Lo
Mezey
Mnookin
Monmonier
Mott
Merry
Nagel
Nissim
O'Connell

Maraist
Mitchell
Monmonier
Mott
Muñoz-Gielen
Mwasumbi
Palka
Peel
Plessis
Poon
Pousin
Pryor
Rajabifard
Roberts
Sait
Schubert
Shogren
Tan
Tang
Tau
Wallace
Wickstead
Williamson
Wolf
Wong
Yeh
Zevenbergen
Zhang

Court Cases Cavendish Property Development, Ltd. v. Attorney General [1987]

Fully Profit (Asia) Ltd v The Secretary for Justice for and on behalf of the Director of Lands (FACV No.17 of 2012)

Hang Wah Chong Investment Co, Ltd. v Attorney-General [1981] HKLR 336

Mexx Consolidated (Far East) v. Attorney General (High Court Miscellaneous Proceedings No.2421 of 1986) HKLR 1210–1220

Sky Heart Limited v. Lee Hysan Company Limited

Sime Darby Motor Services Limited v Director of Lands [2024] HKCA 207

Simmonds Aerocessories (Western) Limited v. Pontypridd Area Assessment Committee and Another [1944]

Guidelines Town Planning Board (1990) *Town Planning Board Guidelines for Application for Office Use in Industrial Buildings within Industrial Zone under Section 16 of the Town Planning Ordinance* (TPB PG-No.6 of December 1990)

Town Planning Board (1997) *Town Planning Board Guidelines for Application for Office and Showroom Uses in Industrial Building within Industrial Zone under Section 16 of the Town Planning Ordinance* (TPB PG-NO.1A of September 1997)

Town Planning Ordinance, Chapter 131, Laws of Hong Kong

Websites Lands Department Website:
https://www.landsd.gov.hk/en/index.html

Geoinfo Map Website: https://www.map.gov.hk/gm/map/

References

Alterman, Rachelle. 2012. Land Use Regulations and Property Values: The 'Windfalls Capture' Idea Revisited. 2012. Chap. 33 in *Oxford Handbook on Urban Economics and Planning*, ed. Nancy Brooks, Kieran Donaghy, and Gerrit-Jan Knapp, 755–786. Oxford University Press.

Amad, Paula. 2012. From God's-Eye to Camera-Eye: Aerial Photography's Post-Humanist and Neo-Humanist Visions of the World. *History of Photography* 36 (1): 66–86.

Archer, Raymon Walter. 1981. *Bibliography on Land Pooling/Readjustment/ Redistribution for Planned Urban Development in Asia and West Germany*.

Archer, Raymon Walter. 2000. Urban Redevelopment with Landowner Participation with the Land Pooling/Readjustment Technique. In *Planning for a Better Urban Living Environment in Asia*, ed. G. A. Yeh and M. K. Ng, 252–277. Aldershot: Ashgate.

Arijs, Hilke. 2014. Images of Value: Why Assessing the Value of Image Collections is Worthwhile. In *CoMa 2013: Safeguarding Image Collections*, ed. Arijs Hilke, 21–45. New Castle upon Tyne: Cambridge Scholar Publishing.

Arruñada, Benito. 2018. Evolving Practice in Land Demarcation. *Land Use Policy* 77:661–675.

Bobkova, Evgeniya, Lars Marcus, Meta Berghauser Pont, Ioanna Stavroulaki, and David Bolin. 2019. Structure of Plot Systems and Economic Activity in Cities: Linking Plot Types to Retail and Food Services in London, Amsterdam and Stockholm. *Urban Science* 3 (66):

L. W. C. Lai et al. (eds.), *Principles of Land Administration at Work*, https://doi.org/10.1007/978-981-95-2972-8

Bocking, Stephen. 2009. A Disciplined Geography: Aviation, Science, and the Cold War in Northern Canada, 1945–1960. *Technology and Culture* 50 (2): 265–290.

Bowden, Leonard W., and William G. Brooner. 1970. Aerial Photography: A Diversified Tool. *Geoforum* 1 (2): 19–32.

Buildings Department. 1999. *Building Development & Control in Hong Kong.* HKSAR Government Printer.

Buitelaar, Edwin. 2021. Planning is Zoning: A Response to Lawrence W.C. Lai. *Planning Practice & Research*1–3.

Burrough, P. A. 1986. *Principles of Geographical Information Systems for Land Resources Assessment.* Oxford: Oxford University Pres.

Campbell, J. B. 1987. *Introduction to Remote Sensing.* New York, London: Guilford Press.

Castro, Teresa. 2009. Cinema's Mapping Impulse: Questioning Visual Culture. *Cartographic Journal* 46 (1): 9–15.

Chau, K. W., Lawrence W. C. Lai, and Mark H. Chua. 2022. Post-Colonial Conservation of Colonial Built Heritage in Hong Kong: A Statistical Analysis of Historic Building Grading. *Environment and Planning B: Urban Analytics and City Science* 49 (2): 671–686.

Cheung, Steven N. S. 1982. *Will China Go Capitalist?* London: Institute of Economic Affairs.

Ching, Ken S. T., and Circle K. Y. Yuen. 2024. An Observation Post (OP) on a Private Land Parcel on Red Hill. *Survey and Built Environment* 33 (2): 13–28.

Coase, Ronald H. 1937. The Nature of the Firm. *Economics* 4 (16): 386–405.

Coase, Ronald H. 1960. The Problem of Social Costs. *Journal of Law and Economics* 3:1–44.

Coase, R. H. 1974. The Lighthouse in Economics. *Journal of Law and Economics* 17 (2): 357–376.

Coase, Ronald H. 1988. *The Firm, the Market and the Law.* Chicago: Chicago University Press.

Committee for World Food Security (CFS) and the Food and Agriculture Organization (FAO). *Voluntary Guidelines on the Responsible Governance of Tenure of Land, Fisheries And Forests in the Context of National Food Security, Food and Agriculture Organization of the United Nations, Rome, Section 2 (General Matters)*, 3–10.

Cooper, J. T. The Large-Scale Mapping of Hong Kong by Air-Survey. In *Report of Proceedings of the Conference of Commonwealth Survey Officers 1967*, 473, 1968–479. London: Her Majesty's Stationery.

Corson, M. W., and E. J. Palka. 2004. Geotechnology, the US Military and War. Chap. 18 in *Geography and Technology*, ed. S. D. Brunn, S. L. Cutter, and J. W. Harrington Jr., 401–430. Springer Nature.

Cosgrove, Denis. 1994. Contested Global Visions: One-World, Whole-Earth, and the Apollo Space Photographs. *Annals of the Association of American Geographers* 84 (2): 270–294.

Council for Sustainable Development (CSD). 2009. *Building Design to Foster a Quality and Sustainable Built Environment, Invitation for Response Document.* CSD. http://www.susdev.org.hk/en/irdoc/index.aspx.

D'Arcy, Michelle, Marina Nistotskaya, and Ola Olsson. 2021. *Land Property Rights, Cadasters and Economic Growth: A Cross-Country Panel 1000-2015 CE.* Working Paper in Economics No.800. Department of Economics, University of Gothenburg, March.

Dale, P. F. 1979. Photogrammetry and Cadastral Surveys within the Commonwealth. *The Photogrammetric Record* 9 (53): 621–631.

Davies, Stephen N. G. 2024. Counter-Current: The Move from Private to Public in the Provision of British Charts and Pilots in the China Seas. *Surveying & Built Environment* 33 (2): 5–39.

Davies, Stephen N. G., Y. K. Tan, and W. C. Lai Lawrence. 2022. Japanese Occupation Period Military Structures near Hong Kong's Northeastern Border: An Initial Survey. *Surveying & Built Environment* 31 (2): 64–147.

Davies, Stephen N. G., Lawrence W. C. Lai, Y. K. Tan, and H. C. Chiu. 2024. Discovery Flows From Mapping for Conservation Planning: The Case of the Unofficial Finding and Mapping of World War II British Hong Kong Defence Structures. *Town Planning Review*. in print.

Dawe, H. G. 1969. Aerial Survey: Colony of Hong Kong. *Photogrammetric Record* 6 (34): 335–347.

De Soto, Hernando. 2001. *The Mystery of Capital.* London: Black Swan Book.

Dennett, D. C. 1998. *The Intentional Stance (6th Printing), Cambridge.* Massachusetts: The MIT Press.

Deuskar, C. 2013. *George Washington and Land Readjustment.* July 31. https://blogs.worldbank.org/sustainablecities/george-washington-and-land-readjustment.

Doebele, William A. 2007. In Foreword. In *Analyzing Land Readjustment: Economics, Law and Collective Action*, ed. Yu-hung Hong and Barrie Needham, vii–xiii. Lincoln Institute of Land Policy.

Dorrian, Mark, and Frédéric Pousin, eds. 2013. *Seeing from Above: The Aerial View in Visual Culture.* IB Tauris.

Edwards, Bruce. 2015. The Insatiable Demand for Sand. *Finance & Development (IMF)* 52 (4): 46–47.

Ehlers, J. H. 1928. *Reconstruction and Development of the Tokyo-Yokohama District.* Washington: Department of Commerce.

Ellickson, Robert C. 2012. The Law and Economics of Street Layouts: How a Grid Pattern Benefits a Downtown. *Alabama Law Review* 64:463–509.

Empson, Hal. 1992. *Mapping Hong Kong: a Historical Atlas.* Hong Kong: Government Information Service.

ESRI. 2024. *Overview of georeferencing in ArcGIS Pro 3.2.* ESRI ArcGIS On-line Help. https://pro.arcgis.com/en/pro-app/latest/help/data/imagery/overview-of-georeferencing.htm.

Fennell, Lee Anne. 2019. Property Beyond Exclusion. *William & Mary Law Review* 61:521–572.

Franks, C. A. M. 1999. Characteristics of Some Rainfall-Induced Landslides on Natural Slopes, Lantau Island, Hong Kong. *Quarterly Journal of Engineering Geology and Hydrogeology* 32 (3): 247–259.

Geddes, Patrick. 1908. Boundaries and Frontiers. *Westminster Review* 169 (3): 257–260.

Gillispie, C. C. 2004. *Science and Polity in France: The Revolutionary and Napoleonic Years.* Princeton UP: Princeton.

Gombrich, Ernst H. 1980. Standards of truth: The Arrested Image and the Moving Eye. *Critical Inquiry* 7 (2, Winter): 237–273.

Gupta, N., and R. Devillers. 2017. Geographic Visualization in Archaeology. *Journal of Archaeological Method and Theory* 24:852–885.

Hackeloeer, Andreas, Klaas Klasing, Jukka M. Krisp, and Liqiu Meng. 2014. Georeferencing: A Review of Methods and Applications. *Annals of GIS* 20 (1): 61–69. https://doi.org/10.1080/19475683.2013.868826.

Hall, Robin. 1978. Teaching Humanistic Geography. *The Australian Geographer* 14 (1): 7–14.

Hayek, Friedrich A. 1960. *The Road to Serfdom.* Chicago: University of Chicago Press.

Ho, Hoi-Yan, Jonathan King, and Mark Wallace. 2006. *A Basic Guide to Air Photo Interpretation in Hong Kong.* Applied Geoscience Centre, Department of Earth Sciences, University of Hong Kong.

Home, Robert. 1997. *Of Planting and Planning: The Making of British Colonial Cities.* London: E and Spon.

Home, Robert. 2003. 'An Irreversible Conquest'? Colonial and Postcolonial Land Law in Israel/Palestine. *Social and Legal Studies* 12 (3): 291–310.

Home, Robert. 2007. Land Readjustment as a Method of Development Land Assembly: A Comparative Overview. *Town Planning Review* 78 (4): 459–483.

Home, Robert. 2018. Why Land Readjustment in the British Former Colonies, But Not in the United Kingdom? In *Land Readjustment: Solving Urban Problems Through Innovative Approach*, ed. Felipe Francisco De Souza, Takeo Ochi, and Akio Hosono, 189–203. Japan International Cooperation Agency (JICA): Tokyo.

Hong Kong Government. 1963. *Accountant General Annual Report.* Hong Kong: Government Printer.

Hong Kong Government. various years. *Hong Kong Annual Report (1990)*. Hong Kong: Government Printer.

Hong Kong Institute of Surveyors. 1999. *Code of Measuring Practice*. Hong Kong: HKIS.

Hong Kong Special Administrative Region Government. 1997. *Building (Planning) Regulations*. HKSAR Government Printer.

Hong Kong Special Administrative Region Government. 2000, various years. *Hong Kong Annual Report (2000)*. Hong Kong: Government Logistics Department.

Hong Kong Special Administrative Region Government. 2018. *Chronology of Events*. 7th ed. Hong Kong: Rating & Valuation Department.

Hong Kong Special Administrative Region Government. 2024. *Your Rates and Government Rent*. Hong Kong: Rating and Valuation Department. (Pamphlet).

Intergovernmental Committee for Surveying and Mapping (ICSM). 2015. *Cadastre 2034: Powering Land and Real Property (Cadastral Reform and Innovation for Australia – A National Strategy)*. Canberra ACT: Australia.

Jourdain, William Robert. 1925. *Land Legislation and Settlement in New Zealand*. WAG Skinner, Government Printer.

Kalbro, Thomas. 2019. Economics of Property Formation-Adjustment of Property Boundaries with Examples from Swedish Legislation. *Nordic Journal of Surveying and Real Estate Research* 2 (1): 82–95.

Kwong, Valerius W. C.. 2008. *Voluntary and Imposed Racial Segregation Zoning: A Coasian-Olson Hong Kong Comparative Empirical Analysis*. Ph.D Thesis, Department of Real Estate & Construction, University of Hong Kong.

Kwong, Jason W. Y. 2020. Historical Research on Density Zoning: A Development Control Policy Through Administrative Means. *Surveying & Built Environment* 29 (1): 26–38.

Kwong, Jason W. Y., Lawrence W. C. Lai, K. W. Chau, N. H. Vincent, and Chan. 2021. A Race Between Urban Growth and Regulation: An Empirical Case Study on the Layout Plan. *Land Use Policy* 101:105184.

Lai, Lawrence W. C. 1998a. The Leasehold System as a Means of Planning by Contract: The Case of Hong Kong. *Town Planning Review* 69 (3): 249–275.

Lai, Lawrence W. C. 1998b. The Use of Aerial Photographs in Planning Enforcement Against Unauthorized Development. In *Lai Zoning and Property Rights: A Hong Kong Case Study*, ed. W. C. In Lawrence, 2nd ed., 157–174. Hong Kong: Hong Kong University Press.

Lai, Lawrence W. C. 1999. *Town Planning in Hong Kong: A Review of Planning Appeal Decisions*. Hong Kong: Hong Kong University Press.

Lai, Lawrence W. C. 2000a. Housing 'Indigenous Villagers' in a Modern Society: An Examination of the Hong Kong 'Small House' Policy. *Third World Planning Review* 22 (2): 207–230.

Lai, Lawrence W. C. 2000b. Not Small (on the Small House Policy). *Letters to the Editor, South China Morning Post*, July 2, p. 11.

Lai, Lawrence W. C. 2011. *The Ideas of Ronald H. Coase: Market Failure and Planning by Contract for Sustainable Development.* 1st ed. Abingdon, Oxon: Routledge Studies in the History of Economics.

Lai, Lawrence W. C. 2017. Solving the 'Problem' of the Small House Policy. *Hong Kong Economic Journal*B07.

Lai, Lawrence W. C. 2021. A Dialogue on Town Planning and Boundary Delineation. *Planning Practice & Research* 36 (5): 483–490.

Lai, Lawrence W. C. 2023a. "No Property is an Island": The Private Lot as the Basic Unit of Land Use Planning & Management of a Wider World. *COSMOS + TAXIS* 11 (1–2): 90–96.

Lai, Lawrence W. C. 2023b. A Neo-Institutional Economic Centennial Literature Review (1919–2019) of Research Publications on Land Readjustment. *Surveying & Built Environment* 32 (1): 6–84.

Lai Lawrence W. C., and Kwong J. W. Y. 2015. *Hong Kong Land Policy for Bus Depot Allocation: A Valuation Analysis, Surveying and Built Environment* 23 (1): 23–55.

Lai, Lawrence W. C., and Stephen N. G. Davies. 2017. A Coasian Boundary Inquiry on Zoning and Property Rights: Lot and Zone Boundaries and Transaction Costs. *Progress in Planning* 118:1–28.

Lai, Lawrence W. C., and Stephen N. G. Davies. 2020. 'Surveying Was a Kind of Writing on the Land': The Economics of Land Division as Town Planning. *Planning Theory* 19 (4): 421–444.

Lai, Lawrence W. C., and Stephen N. G. Davies. 2022. Is Non-Zoning of Land Impossible? Eight Fundamental Propositions of Zoning. *Journal of Environmental Policy & Planning*1–16. https://doi.org/10.1080/1523908X.2022.2098096.

Lai, Lawrence W. C., and Daniel Chai Wing Ho. 2000. *Planning Buildings for a High-Rise Environment: A Review of Building Appeal Decisions.* Hong Kong: Hong Kong University Press.

Lai, Lawrence W. C., and Winky K. O. Ho. 2001. Small is Beautiful: A Probit Analysis of Planning Applications for Small Houses in Hong Kong. *Environment and Planning B: Planning and Design* 28 (4): 611–622.

Lai Lawrence, W. C., K. W. Chau Lai, Alwin Chan, and Lennon H. T. Choy. 2018. Two Dialogues on Land Readjustment in Hong Kong. *Surveying & Built Environment* 27 (1): 5–9.

Lai, Lawrence W. C., and Frank T. Lorne. 2014. Ambiguous Property Rights: A Taxonomic and an Exploratory Account of Post-Colonial Rural Housing in Chinese Hong Kong. *Urban Studies* 51 (10): 2052–2067.

Lai, Lawrence W. C., S. K. Wong, Eric C. K. Ho, and K. W. Chau. 2008. Time is of the Essence? An Empirical Application of the Corollary of the Coase Theorem. *Review of Urban & Regional Development Studies* 20 (1): 34–51.

Lai, Lawrence W. C., Stephen N. G. Davies, Y. K. Tan, and P. Yung. 2009. The Gin Drinker's Line: Reconstruction of a British Colonial Defence Line in Hong Kong Using Aerial Photo Information. *Property Management* 27 (1): 16–41.

Lai, Lawrence W. C., Valerius W. C. Kwong, and Jason W. Y. Kwong. 2011. Segregation Legal and Natural: An Empirical Study of the Legally Protected and Free Market Housing Ownership on the Peak. *Habitat International* 35 (3): 501–507.

Lai, Lawrence W. C., Mark H. Chua, and Frank T. Lorne. 2014. The Coase Theorem and Squatting on Crown Land and Water: A Hong Kong Comparative Study of the Differences Between the State Allocation of Property Rights for Two Kinds of Squatters. *Habitat International* 44:247–257.

Lai, Lawrence W. C., K. W. Chau, and Frank T. Lorne. 2016a. The Rise and Fall of the Sand Monopoly in Colonial Hong Kong. *Ecological Economics* 128:106–116.

Lai, Lawrence W. C., Stephen N. G. Davies, and F. T. Lorne. 2016b. Creation of Property Rights in Planning by Contract and Edict: Beyond "Coasian Bargaining" in Private Planning. *Planning Theory* 15 (4): 418–434.

Lai, Lawrence W. C., Daniel C. W. Ho, Kwong Wing Chau, and Mark H. Chua. 2016c. Repeated Planning Applications by Developers Under Statutory Zoning: A Hong Kong Case Study of Delays and Design Improvements in Private Residential Development. *Land Use Policy* 57:709–718.

Lai, Lawrence W. C., Daniel C. W. Ho, and H. F. Leung. 2017. *Change in Use of Land: A Practical Guide to Development in Hong Kong, Hong Kong*. 3rd ed. Hong Kong University Press.

Lai Lawrence W. C., Chau K. W., and Cheung P. C. W. 2012. Scale Economies of the Franchised Buses and Ferries of Hong Kong, 1948 to 1998. *Review of Urban and Regional Development Studies* 24 (3): 121–140.

Lai Lawrence W. C., Chau K. W., Kwong J. W. Y., Ching S.T., Cheung P. C. W., and Lorne F. T. 2013. Acquisition and Redevelopment of Bus Garages: A Hong Kong Land Policy and Planning Case Study. *Habitat International* 39: 75–84.

Lai, Lawrence W. C., K. W. Chau, C. W. Polycarp Alvin, and Cheung. 2018a. Urban Renewal and Redevelopment: Social Justice and Property Rights with Reference to Hong Kong's Constitutional Capitalism. *Cities* 74:240–248.

Lai, Lawrence W. C., Stephen N. G. Davies, K. W. Chau, Ken S. T. Ching, Mark H. Chua, H. F. Leung, and Frank T. Lorne. 2018b. The Determination of the "True" Property Boundary in Planned Development: A Coasian Analysis. *Annals of Regional Science* 61:579–599.

Lai, Lawrence W. C., K. W. Chau, and Lennon H. T. Choy. 2018c. Stock and Flow of Land: Freeing Land from Rigidities for Urban Development in Hong Kong. *Editorial, Surveying & Built Environment* 27 (1): 5–9.

Lai Lawrence W. C, Davies S. N. G, and Lorne F. T. 2008a, The Political Economy of Coase's Lighthouse in History (Part I): A Review on the Theories and Models of the Provision of a Public Good. *Town Planning Review* 79 (4): 395–425.

Lai Lawrence W. C., Davies S. N. G., and Lorne F. T. 2008b. The Political Economy of Coase's Lighthouse in History (Part II): Lighthouse Development along the Coast of China. *Town Planning Review* 79 (5) 555–579.

Lai Lawrence W. C., Liu K. T., Cheung P. A. C. W., Wong C. T. S., and Kwong J. W. Y. 2015. Redevelopment of Bus Depots upon Lease Modifications: A Valuation Analysis. *Surveying and Built Environment* (24): 37–40.

Lai Lawrence W. C., and Lorne F. T. 2012. Schumpeterian Innovations, the Coase Theorem, and Sustainable Development: A Hong Kong Case Study of Bus Innovations. In David Emanuel Andersson (Ed.), *The Spatial Market Process, Advances in Austrian Economics* 16: 141–179.

Lai Lawrence W. C., and Lorne F. 2015. The Fourth Coase Theorem: State Planning Rules and Spontaneity in Action. *Planning Theory, published on-line 9 December 2013* (14) 1: 44–69.

Lai, Lawrence W. C., Stephen N. G. Davies, Edwin H. W. Chen, Mark Hansley Chua, and C. L. Lin. 2020. The Production and Consumption of Land Use Planning: A Neo-Institutional Economic Perspective and Three Taiwan Case Studies of Planning Layering. *Land Use Policy.*

Lai, Lawrence W. C., Stephen N. G. Davies, Frank T. Lorne, K. W. Chau, and Lennon H. T. Choy. 2020b. A Neo-institutional Economic Analysis of Revising Informal and Formal Proprietary Boundaries. *Journal of Environmental Policy & Planning*1–18.

Lai, Lawrence W. C., Y. K. Tan, and Stephen N. G. Davies. 2021. *Pillboxes on Hong Kong Island in the Era of World War II.* Hong Kong: Hong Kong Institute of Surveyors.

Lai, Lawrence W. C., Stephen N. G. Davies, Lennon H. T. Choy, and K. W. Chau. 2022a. Land Planning, Property Rights & Management of Built Heritage: Some Hong Kong Observations of Colonial Military Buildings. *LAND*11:1516.

Lai, Lawrence W. C., Stephen N. G. Davies, K. W. Chau, Lennon H. T. Choy, Mark Hansley Chua, and Terry K. W. Lam. 2022b. A Centennial Literature Review (1919–2019) of Research Publications on Land Readjustment from a Neo-Institutional Economic Perspective. *Land Use Policy* 120:106236.

Lo, C. P. 1979. Surveys of Squatter Settlements with Sequential Aerial Photography – A Case Study in Hong Kong. *Photogrammetria* 35 (2): 45–63.

Lorne, F. T., and Lai Lawrence, W. C. 2011. Schumpeterian Innovation for Regulated Natural Monopoly as a Corporate Strategy. *International Journal of Information Systems for Logistics and Management* (7) 1: 1–7.

Maraist, Patrick W. 1995. A Statutory Beacon in the Land Use Ripeness Maze: The Florida Private Property Rights Protection Act. *Florida Law Review* 47:411–458.

Merry, M. 1997. *Tenancy Law in Hong Kong*. 3rd ed. Hong Kong: Butterworths.

Mezey, N. 2004. Erasure and Recognition: The Census, Race and the National Imagination. *Northwestern University Law Review* 97 (4): 1701–1768.

Mitchell, David, Siraj Sait, Jean du Plessis & Agnes Mwasumbi. 2019. *Core Values and Principles of Responsible Land Administration*. Responsible Land Administration Teaching Essentials," a project initiated and funded by the Global Land Tool Network (GLTN) and UN-Habitat.

Mnookin, Jennifer L. 1998. The Image of Truth: Photographic Evidence and the Power of Analogy. *Yale Journal of Law and the Humanities* 10 (1): 1–74.

Monmonier, Mark. 2018. *How to Lie with Maps*. 3rd ed. Chicago: University of Chicago Press.

Morabito, Vince. 1998. The Constitutional Restriction on Taxes Imposed on Crown Property. *Journal of Australian Taxation* 1:41–56.

Mott, P. G. 1963. Aerial Methods of Surveying for Civil Engineering. (Includes Plates). *Proceedings of the Institution of Civil Engineers* 26 (4): 497–512.

Muñoz-Gielen, Demetrio. 2016. Proposal of Land Readjustment for the Netherlands: An Analysis of Its Effectiveness from an International Perspective. *Cities* 53:78–86.

Nagel, T. 1986. *The View from Nowhere*. Oxford: Oxford University Press.

Nissim, Roger. 1997. *Land Administration and Practice in Hong Kong*. Hong Kong: Hong Kong University Press.

O'Connell, Lauren M. 1998. Viollet-le-Duc on Drawing, Photography, and the 'Space Outside the Frame'. *History of Photography* 22 (2): 139–146.

Poon, Thomas N. T., and Edwin H. W. Chan, eds. 1998. *Real Estate Development in Hong Kong*. Hong Kong: Pace Publishing Ltd.

Pryor, Edward G. 1975. The Acquisition of Land for Urban Development by Exchange in Hong Kong and Taiwan. *Town Planning Quarterly, Auckland* 41:27–29.

Roberts, Philip James. 1975. *Valuation of Development Land in Hong Kong*. Hong Kong: Hong Kong University Press.

Schubert, Dirk. 2017. Review of Manuale zum Städtebau. Die Systematisierung des Wissens von der Stadt 1870–1950: edited by Vittorio Magnago Lampugnani, Katrin Albrecht, Helene Bihlmaier and Lukas Zurfluh, Berlin, Dom Publishers, 2020. *Planning Perspective* 35 (2): 392–394.

Shogren, Jason F., Gregory M. Parkhurst, and Chad Settle. 2003. Integrating Economics and Ecology to Protect Nature on Private Lands: Models, Methods, and Mindsets. *Environmental Science and Policy* 6 (3): 233–242.

Survey and Mapping Office. 1995. *Explanatory Notes on Geodetic Datums in Hong Kong Hong.* Kong: Lands Department.

Tan, Y. K., Stephen N. G. Davies, and Lawrence W. C. Lai. 2022. *Pillboxes Along the Gin Drinker's Line, 80 Years After World War II.* Hong Kong: Hong Kong Institute of Surveyors.

Tang, Conrad H. W., and H. D. Zhang. 2012. Direct Georeferencing and Orthophoto Correlation with Demarcation District. *Surveying & Built Environment* 22:73–86.

Tau, Yu Ming. 2015. *HKIS CPD PowerPoints (Cadastral Surveying)*, May 8.

United Nations. 2016. *New Urban Agenda, Habitat III Secretariat.*

Wickstead, Helen, and Martyn Barber. 2012. A Spectacular History of Survey by Flying Machine! *Cambridge Archaeological Journal* 22 (1): 71–88.

Williamson, Ian, Stig Enemark, Jude Wallace, and Abbas Rajabifard. 2010. *Land Administration for Sustainable Development.* Redlands, CA: ESRI Press Academic.

Wolf, P. R. 2000. *Elements of Photogrammetry; with Application in GIS.* 3rd ed. New York: McGraw Hill.

Wong, W. S., and Edwin H. W. Chan, eds. 1997. *Professional Practice for Architects in Hong Kong (Chapter 3).* Hong Kong: Pace Publishing Ltd.

Yeh, A. K. O. 1994. Land Leasing and Urban Planning: Lessons from Hong Kong. *Regional Development Dialogue* 15:3–21.

Youngman, Joan M. 1996. Tax on Land and Buildings. In *Tax Law Design and Drafting*, vol. 1, 264–291. International Monetary Fund.

Zevenbergen, Jaap, Walter de Vries, Rohan Mark Bennett, eds. 2015. *Advances in Responsible Land Administration.* Routledge, 2016.

Author Index[1]

[1] Note: Page numbers followed by 'n' refer to notes.

L. W. C. Lai et al. (eds.), *Principles of Land Administration at Work*, https://doi.org/10.1007/978-981-95-2972-8

Subject Index[1]

A

B

[1] Note: Page numbers followed by 'n' refer to notes.

L. W. C. Lai et al. (eds.), *Principles of Land Administration at Work*, https://doi.org/10.1007/978-981-95-2972-8

MIX
Papier | Fördert gute Waldnutzung
FSC® C083411

Kolibri 360 GmbH
Ferdinand-Jühlke-Straße 7
99095 Erfurt, Deutschland
produktsicherheit@kolibri360.de